Be Jane's GUIDE to
HOME EMPOWERMENT

Be Jane's GUIDE to
HOME EMPOWERMENT

Projects to Change the Way You Live

Heidi Baker and **Eden Jarrin**

Clarkson Potter/Publishers
NEW YORK

3 0645 10156105

Copyright © 2006 by Heidi Baker and Eden Jarrin, Be Jane, Inc.
www.bejane.com

Illustrations on pages 56, 57, 58, 59, 61, 62, 66, 71, 84, 95, 102, 121, 125, 126, 150, 160, 171 (right), 172 (right), 173, 174, 177, 183, 184, 204, 205, 206, 207, 218 (right), 221 (right), 222, 232, and 233 and Jane Tip illustration by Patrick Welsh, copyright © 2006 by Be Jane, Inc.
All other illustrations by Manfred Geier, copyright © 2006 by Be Jane, Inc.

Photographs on pages 14, 27, 32, 38, and 236 by Kevin Break, copyright © 2006 by Be Jane, Inc.
All other photographs copyright Michael Weschler.

Photographs of Janes profiled courtesy of the profilees.

All rights reserved.
Published in the United States by Clarkson Potter/Publishers, an imprint of the Crown Publishing Group, a division of Random House, Inc., New York.
www.crownpublishing.com
www.clarksonpotter.com

Clarkson N. Potter is a trademark and **Potter** and colophon are registered trademarks of Random House, Inc.

Library of Congress Cataloging-in-Publication Data
Baker, Heidi.
 Be Jane's guide to home empowerment : projects to change the way you live / Heidi Baker and Eden Jarrin
 1. Dwellings—Maintenance and repair—Amateurs' manuals. 2. Dwellings—Remodeling—Amateurs' manuals. 3. Do-it-yourself work. I. Jarrin, Eden. III. Title.
TH4817.3.B34 2006
643'.7—dc22   2006009522

ISBN 978-0-307-33990-4

Printed in the United States of America

Design by Chalkley Calderwood Pratt

10 9 8 7 6 5 4 3 2 1

First Edition

Acknowledgments

We would like to thank the many people involved in making this book possible. From those who had a hand in the actual production to the wonderful women of the Be Jane community who blessed us with their empowering stories, advice, and inspiration and hundreds of valuable tips and tricks they learned along the way.

We also want to thank them for convincing us that this book was something we should create. On that note, we can't wait to hear all of the stories from your new adventures!

Even though neither of us has children yet, writing this book has been the closest thing we've known to giving birth. The book that you hold in your hand now is a labor of love created for all those women out there who never thought they could take on even half of the projects described within. Regardless of the numerous late nights and long weekends, we were able to create something we are proud of and that we hope you will enjoy.

We would also like to thank a few individuals without whom this book might not have been possible.

Our many late night hours were certainly less stressful knowing that we had the loving support of our literary agent, Matthew Guma. Thank you for not allowing us to accept

> "My house wouldn't be a home without you."
>
> Michelle S.
> Washington D.C.
> Age 51

less than what *you* knew we deserved. To our editors at Clarkson Potter, Elissa Altman and Aliza Fogelson, we want to thank you for how much your input added throughout the process and how your guidance allowed us to truly deliver on the promise. To our creative director, Marysarah Quinn, it was through your creative hands that we were able to bring the concept of this book into reality. To our photographer, Michael Weschler, bubble baths and cheese fondue will forever have a different meaning. Thank you for your patience and beautiful pictures. To our illustrator, Patrick Welsh, we can't thank you enough for your creativity and admirable work ethic, which show through in every illustration you created for us. Thanks also to Manfred Geier for his illustrations. A special thank-you to Ryobi, Ridgid, Husky, and everyone at T.T.I. and Imre Communications for providing products for our photo shoots and project testing.

Most important, to our husbands, Phil Breman and Ed Jarrin: Phil, thank you for your endless research and for rereading projects over and over again. The love and attention you paid to each detail show on every page. We love you for it and for your belief in our vision since the start. Eddie, your support has been unwavering since the beginning. Thank you for allowing us to use your home numerous times for photo shoots and brainstorming, as well as for believing we could accomplish this amazing feat.

We'd also like to thank two wonderful Janes who helped us find our voice with their astounding inspiration and creativity: Brooke Coe and Alyssa Waddell.

"Be Jane is a lifesaver!"

Lisa S.
Bellevue,
Washington
Age 26

We must not forget to thank all of the women who applied to be in our Jane Profiles. Each and every one was gracious in giving her time for interviews as well as pictures, offering wonderful stories and experiences to include in this book. Your stories help bring the pages alive and will empower thousands of women all over the world to take on projects they never believed possible. You are the women we all look up to.

And, last but certainly not least, we would like to thank our entire staff at Be Jane. All of you work so tirelessly to help us accomplish our vision of empowering women to take on home improvement by first enriching their lives through Home Empowerment. And for that, we are truly grateful to all of you.

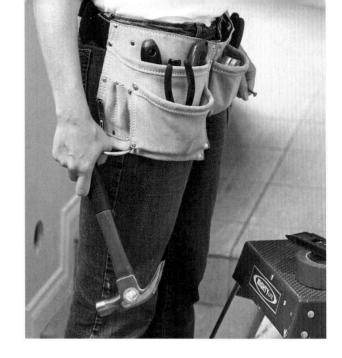

Contents

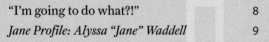

Introduction

10 Part I The Basics 12

Tools

Safety Basics 26

Painting Basics 33

Introduction

Welcome

Why even consider purchasing a book like this? Maybe you've never done home improvement before and are just curious. If you have, how is this book any different from all of the rest that are already out there?

Most home improvement books focus exclusively on the "how to"—how to fix your toilet, how to paint your house, how to install a faucet. Well, we decided that although it's nice to know how to install a faucet or tile your counter, why would you *want* to? One doesn't simply wake up one morning and decide that today is the day to learn home improvement. The realization has to come to you. Usually, it comes through years of living in a home that is *less than*.

Right now, you might be living in a house that just doesn't make you happy. The good news is you can change that, and when you change your home, you change your life. This is what we like to call the *why-to*.

Most other home improvement books begin by congratulating you on "taking the first step toward being a do-it-yourselfer." They completely ignore the fact that maybe you've never done this before. And that maybe you're a bit frightened or intimidated by this new adventure.

Look, getting started doing home improvement projects was one of the most difficult things either of us has ever done. Just the

> "Here's to doing it ourselves!"
>
> Sharon E.
> Washington, D.C.
> Age 50

> "I always hesitate in asking a man for help, for fear of sounding stupid."
>
> Jan L.
> Merced, California
> Age 52

thought of some of the projects we were planning to take on was enough to make us reconsider. But neither of us had the means to hire someone, so there was our answer to "why-to": There was no one else to do it. We either had to change our homes ourselves, or live in our homes the way they were.

To be brutally honest, there were many days when each of us wished we had been able to call it quits. To be able to just call up some professional to come in and save the day would have solved our immediate problems, but it would have also confirmed what we and everyone else had said about our own inabilities.

So if it is so daunting, why would anyone in her right mind even consider taking on these projects? For us, and the many women we've heard from out there, the answer is simple: Home improvement will provide you with a sense of self-empowerment unlike anything else you'll ever do.

In the same way that looking great does wonders for your self-esteem, so too can living in surroundings you love make you feel great. Start by thinking of the things you could do in your home that would forever change how you feel about your life. Then try your first project. Once you get started, it won't be long before you feel that sense of empowerment begin to fill you at your core. And about the fear and exhaustion factor: While neither of us has had a child, we see completing a project as something like having a baby. When you finish a project, the feeling of empowerment that comes with knowing "*I* did that!" will overshadow the hardships you went through to create it. Once you start to complete your projects, your house will fill you with a sense of pride. You will begin to look around and see the results of your efforts, knowing that you accomplished the seemingly impossible. And that you did it yourself.

We launched the Be Jane community because we had both come off an intense, emotional roller-coaster ride of an experience working on our homes. As we changed our homes, they in turn changed us. The fears we had about our own inabilities surrounding home improvement projects were obliterated one by one. As each fear was conquered, we learned to question and eventually disbelieve other fears we had in our lives outside of our homes—both in our personal lives and at work.

Many of our members have experienced this sensation as well, and refer to it as a kind of awakening. They find, as we have, that this newfound sense of self-confidence and pride

"I feel much more secure in this world. I have less fear that I can't do something. I don't feel that I need someone else to do something."

Leslie Y.
Goshen, Indiana
Age 35

_____

"Don't be intimidated. It's not as hard as you think."

Laurel R.
Jacksonville,
Florida
Age 49

carries well beyond the realm of home improvement; it positively affects every part of our lives.

We refer to the thousands of women who have contacted us as *Janes*—or, more formally, as *Janes of All Trades*. They are women just like us who were willing to take a chance, step outside their comfort zone, and accomplish what they once saw as impossible. We had no idea there were so many amazing women out there who did home improvement, and we are honored that they have shared their stories with us. We felt so strongly about them that we asked them to allow us to share their stories with you. You will find them woven into each section.

So the answer to our original question is simple: What makes this book different? It isn't about home improvement. It's about home *empowerment*.

What's the difference? Home improvement will help you solve home-related problems and issues such as maintenance and repair, while home *empowerment* is about changing how you live by changing the place you live in.

Reading this book is *your* first step toward becoming a Jane. And, instead of saying congratulations, we'd like to say welcome.

Welcome to a new way of looking at home improvement. Welcome to Home Empowerment.

Welcome to Be Jane.

How Jane Came to Be

You might be wondering what made two ordinary females decide to pick up a jigsaw and nail gun in the first place. A handful of years ago, we each bought a home and wondered what we had gotten ourselves into. We hadn't met yet, but our lives were on a parallel track. We were both in "new" houses that weren't exactly new, but neither of us could afford to bring in a team of contractors; we each quickly realized the only option we had was to do it ourselves.

Although we laughed about it later, we were appalled by the resistance we met at the mere idea that we might tackle a few home improvement projects. The negative comments seemed to come from everywhere—our friends, our family, even the people at the home improvement centers who were supposedly there to help us. We'd hear things like "Oh, sweetie, you can't do that. You need to hire someone." Or "Really, *you* do stuff like that? You just don't *look* like that kind of girl." We'll never forget the sarcastic chuckles and smirks we'd get after explaining what we were attempting to do: "I'd love to see a picture of *that* when you're finished!"

Neither of us can tell you that those comments didn't get to us. More often than not, they made us doubt our own abilities and wonder if we really *were* kidding ourselves. At the time, if either of us had actually had the money to go out and hire a professional to do the work, we probably wouldn't be where we are today. But when you are living in a home that makes you unhappy and the only person you can afford to bring in to change it is you, you have no choice but to step up to the plate. So we did.

We worked on our homes to the point that we were proud to have guests over to see our handiwork, even if it was only in one room at a time. Needless to say, they were shocked and amazed to see how our houses had changed. We loved it each and every time someone exclaimed, "You did that?!" (We still do, by the way.) But while amazing our guests was definitely enjoyable, what came next surprised each of us more than we could have imagined. We expected questions and comments from the husbands and boyfriends, but what we never saw coming was our sisters, mothers, and girlfriends asking how we did this or that, and asking if we'd come over and help *them*. We could see the transition happening right before our eyes. The women in our lives thought if we could do it, then so could they.

Home improvement permanently changed each of us in ways too numerous to count but easy to recognize. It was even visible in those

> "I never thought I could do some of the things I've done."
> Marie G.
> Huntington, New York
> Age 61

> "Don't be afraid to try something new. You'll get such a sense of accomplishment once you've done it."
> Lydia C.
> Escondido, California
> Age 25

friends and family members whom we'd taken under our wing. It was a newfound sense of pride and confidence that went far beyond the home. Tearing down a wall or putting in a new light tore down obstacles in all of our lives that had been there for years. Suddenly, whenever a new obstacle cropped up, it became less of a barricade and more a simple hurdle just waiting to be jumped.

The two of us met by sheer fate. All it took was a simple realization that we had each taken it upon ourself to fix up our home. We were sisters from that moment on. We talked about everything each of us had been through and laughed at how we'd gotten the same responses to the mention of taking on a home improvement project. We talked about how neither of us could find a place to ask what was quite often seen as a "stupid question." But when we began to talk about how we had each influenced other women to take on home improvement themselves—that was when we knew we had to do more. We knew that there had to be hundreds if not thousands of other women who had been through

"Being a military wife, you have to Be Jane. Deployments keep him away months at a time, and the toilet isn't going to fix itself!"

Annette F.
Fayetteville, North Carolina
Age 28

———————

"I am a single mom of three. I have had to learn how to do lots of things. But I'm thankful for my mom, who is a Jane all on her own."

Kimberly N.
Kinder, Louisiana
Age 47

similar experiences and felt they were the only ones out there. We also wanted to inspire women who knew that they could take on home improvement projects but didn't know where to turn.

Even more important, we wanted to create a place where we could show all women that they can turn the house they live in into the home they love.

This prompted the two of us to start a community of like-minded women who help one another out. One of the wonderful things about having a community to turn to is having a network of friends who are there to help answer any questions you might have in a way that is inspiring, thought-provoking, and empowering. This is especially important because in our experience, the one thing we know for sure is that there is a solution to every problem and an answer to every question. Part of being a Jane is not so much knowing the answers and solutions but having the courage to ask and to try.

We now consider you a member of the Jane community, and as such we never want you to feel like you're alone during the process. If you haven't already, be sure to visit us online at www.BeJane.com, where you can join other women who may have answers to your questions or can steer you in the right direction. Throughout this book, you'll be introduced to many of these women through our Jane profiles. Remember, these are *real* women, just like you, who once believed they weren't strong enough, capable enough, or confident enough to conquer this realm. We hope their stories will entertain and inspire you as you pursue your own path.

We promise you, if you change your home, you'll change your life forever.

Jane Profile

My children know that Mom uses the power tools in the family.

Mary "Jane" Caputo-Kamerer

Age: 43

From: Charlotte, North Carolina

Favorite tool: I like my drill. However, I'd have to say that my power sander has alleviated lots of hand sanding from my furniture refinishing.

Projects accomplished: I like to take old but well-made furniture from secondhand stores and refinish it into like-new pieces. I have also installed lighting fixtures, replaced toilet parts, tiled a bar counter in a living room, faux-finished walls and ceilings, installed a new kitchen faucet, regrouted my in-laws' shower stall, cut and installed Peg-Board in a garage, and helped an old boyfriend install drywall in his fixer-upper house. My latest project: I designed the majority of our new home.

Inspiration for starting home improvement: Growing up in an Italian family, the girls were expected to learn to cook. I knew that the best teacher was my mom. So when I had the opportunity in junior high to take something other than cooking/home economics, I took wood shop. My father, who liked to tinker at his cellar workbench, told me that if I got basic instruction at school, he would help me make some things. Together, we made my first project, a set of picture frames. When my parents had their own home and six children, they became do-it-yourselfers to save money. With my mom's ideas, assistance, and encouragement, they built large play equipment for us children, window valances, and porch additions, painted the walls, and installed extra toilets. Their pride in their accomplishments played a major role in my interest in doing the same.

Fears about home improvement: Initially, I was very afraid of cutting the power cord to the power tool, or even worse, severing a finger.

With any project I did early on, I was always afraid that I'd get started and then end up with an "Oh my gosh, how am I going to fix this?" situation.

How has doing home improvement affected your life? I grew up in the feminist era, so I feel like I'm a good mom if I teach my kids, particularly my daughter, how to do home improvement. It's different living in the South and being a woman who does home improvement. Many people find a woman who wants to talk power tools, or who understands this type of stuff, an interesting concept.

How has doing home improvement affected others in your life? My children know that Mom uses the power tools in the family, and they come to me when something needs to be repaired. Dad is a doctor and doesn't use power tools, since hurting himself might mean his surgery days are over. I'm proud that my daughter has an interest in creative projects. For her, our doing a project together is quality time. My love of home improvement has definitely rubbed off on her. She's not afraid to try to do something herself.

Advice for others just getting started in home improvement: Don't be afraid to paint. Painting is easy to cover.

And overall, don't be afraid. Just about everything is fixable. Mainly, don't be afraid to start. A journey of a thousand miles begins with one step.

"I'm going to do what?!"

The idea of starting a project you've never done before is enough to make anyone worry. In fact, if you've ever taken on a home improvement project, you're probably familiar with that voice in the back of your head yelling, "I'm going to do what?!" Or it might be "What if I completely screw this up?" or "I can't take on a project like that. I'm not a contractor!"

It's exactly these kinds of thoughts that have been keeping you from living the life you want to live. We're not saying these concerns aren't real and shouldn't be taken seriously, but we want you to realize that if you've never done anything like this, you're dealing with nothing more than fear of the unknown. We all remember as children being afraid of the monster in our closet or under our bed. But eventually we managed to summon our courage, walk across the room, and *turn on the light*!

Keeping that in mind, suppose for a moment that all of your preconceived notions

"I had no fears at first. Ignorance is bliss."
Catherine R.
Madison, Wisconsin
Age 39

"If it looks scary, it's worth trying."
Yvonka H.
Boyton Beach, Florida
Age 43

about not being able to do home improvement are really figments of your imagination. Now stay with us for a moment longer and think about what you would do if you could change your home—if you were able to do it yourself. Would you make your home into a place that reflected more of you? Would you create your own personal oasis? Would you finally feel the sense of pride and comfort you've longed for in your home? If even one of these things rings true to you, then it's time you put aside your fears and start taking some action.

So go ahead, turn on the light!

Jane Profile

Even if you mess up, it can be fixed. If not, then call it art!

Alyssa "Jane" Waddell

Age: 30

From: White Pines, Tennessee

Favorite tool: Compound miter saw—it makes cutting flooring, baseboards, crown molding, et cetera, so much easier than a regular miter saw. Plus, any tool that makes a man cringe when he sees you using it is well worth any nicks you might endure!

Projects accomplished: Laying laminate flooring, laying linoleum tiles, refinishing kitchen cabinets, installing a ceiling fan, installing dimmer switches, installing light fixtures, updating door handles, building shelves from scratch, building a window seat from scratch, installing baseboards, roofing houses with shingles, framing, hanging floating shelves, putting up stained-glass film, building a porch with stairs, installing blinds, installing curtains, painting, painting, and more painting.

Inspiration for starting home improvement: I like beautiful things. I want to be surrounded by a peaceful, aesthetically pleasing environment, so I took it upon myself to create it. Also, my parents are excellent role models in the home improvement field. My dad, Al, is a general contractor, and my mother, Carol, is a designer. Maybe a part of me wanted to show them I'm proud of my genes and the abilities I inherited from them. (I fought against all things related to my dad's home improvement business as a teenager.) As it turns out, I am my parents' daughter after all.

Fears about home improvement: Electrocution. Nail through the thumb, nail through the hand, nail through the foot—pretty much nails anywhere in my body. Sawing off a finger, sawing off my hand, sawing off my foot—pretty much removing any part of my body. But I'm not totally self-centered; I'm afraid of hurting other people too (see fears previously listed, but insert "someone else's"). Most of all, I'm afraid my work won't live up to my own high standards. Other than those few "minor" things, I'm pretty fearless.

How has doing home improvement affected you and others in your life? My favorite part is that I have more to talk about with my dad. My fiancé, Rudy, and I have much more to do together because he too is a do-it-yourselfer. As for my girlfriends, they look at me with more admiration and are also motivated to tackle home improvement projects themselves.

Advice for others just getting started in home improvement: If a scrawny girlie-girl with spaghetti arms can drive a roofing nail in with two hits, then anyone can do this stuff. It sounds like such a cliché, but it's so true: Just believe in yourself and do it. Even if you mess up, it can be fixed. If not, then call it art! And when a project *does* come out perfect . . . that is an adrenaline rush that nothing can compete with. Be fearless. Be Jane.

PART I

The Basics

If you've never done home improvement before, you may feel like you're jumping into a pool of cold water. So, before you jump, we want to make sure you are a bit better prepared.

This section assumes you have no existing knowledge of home improvement, basic skills sets, tools, or knowledge of how your house works. Even if you do have some of this knowledge, you may want to read through the basics to give yourself a little refresher course.

We begin by reviewing what every Jane should have in her toolbox—explaining what each tool is and what it is used for. We chose these specific tools because they are common, and the vast majority of them will be used in the projects that follow.

We hope that you'll find, as we have, that beyond a few basic points, safety concerns, and skill sets, home improvement really isn't all that difficult. It may be challenging at times, but the basic principles don't change. The best part of all is that once you learn it, try it out, and continue working at it, it becomes a passion that will challenge you to be the best you can be.

Tools

If you're new to home improvement, anything more than a hammer and screwdriver might seem like another language. Well, you're definitely not alone. Each day we receive hundreds of comments from women all across the country who feel the same way. The most common concern when starting out is not only knowing which tools are which or what they're used for but also knowing which tools are the *must*-haves for an everyday toolbox.

The good news is that understanding tools and what they do isn't rocket science by any means. In this section, we lay out the tools that you'll be using for the projects featured later on. We begin by showing you what each tool is, what its typical uses are, and why it's important to actually own one.

At first glance, learning about tools may seem intimidating. But always remember: If you have the right tool for the job, the job becomes much, much easier. A tool is a device that enhances or improves the execution of a given task. Tools were invented to make things easier. So even though they might look or sound a bit scary at first, you'll quickly discover that every tool serves the same purpose: to help you.

HAND TOOLS

Logically, every tool made for doing home improvement could be considered a hand tool because we use them with our hands. But there *are* differences between hand tools and power tools.

"Most projects are easy if you have the right tools."

Suzanne W.
Marietta, Georgia
Age 51

"My motto is 'There's nothing like a woman with a tool in her hand.'"

Cris W.
Inver Grove
Heights,
Minnesota
Age 46

The term *hand tools* covers any tool you can hold in the palm of your hand that is neither electric nor pneumatic (pneumatic tools are powered by compressed air).

Here are the essential elements for every tool kit:

Tape Measure

A tape measure is one of those basics (like the perfect black skirt you can wear with anything) that every Jane should have. When shopping for one, ask yourself the following questions:

■ **HOW LONG SHOULD IT BE?** Size definitely matters here. The smallest size you should consider buying is 25 feet. Measuring something that is longer than your tape measure is not only frustrating but can also be the source of incorrect measurements!

■ **DOES THE TYPE OF BLADE MAKE ANY DIFFERENCE?** The blade is the actual tape measure itself. The wider the blade, the farther it will extend without "breaking." (This is the point at which the tape measure

falls limp.) To check, simply pull the tape straight out. You should be able to pull it out 5 to 10 feet before it falls. This feature may not seem important, but it is very useful when you're doing projects alone.

■ **WHAT TYPE OF MARKINGS DOES IT HAVE?**
Make sure the tape has markers at intervals of no less than ⅛ inch. Some tape measures have a protective coating over the first 12 inches of the blade. This may not seem relevant until you've used your tape over and over and the first 12 inches become worn and illegible.

> "I have always tried to do things by myself, and I love the feeling of accomplishment it brings."
>
> Christina A.
> San Diego,
> California
> Age 33

Hammers

Adding a hammer to your toolbox is a given. The question is, "Which hammer is the right one for me?" If you've shopped for a hammer before, you probably just tried it out by feeling the grip and testing the weight. In the end, you probably bought the one that resembled something your dad used or the one that looked the coolest. (You know you've done it; we certainly have.) Through our own experiences and the comments of other Janes, we've come up with these important points to consider when buying an everyday hammer:

1. **Weight.** The weight decides what kinds of projects the hammer should be used on. The heavier the head of the hammer, the more force you'll be able to exert on whatever it is you are hammering. The ideal weight for an everyday hammer is **20 ounces,** but that can get heavy quickly (and cause you to get clumsy). For ease of use and less chance you'll accidentally hammer a thumb, you probably want a **16-ounce hammer** instead. This will give you enough weight to do both light projects, like hanging a picture, to some heavy-duty projects, like nailing shingles in your roof.

2. **Handle.** The handle of a hammer is available in many materials: wood, metal, rubber, and fiberglass. When choosing, ask yourself, "Does it fit my grip?" and, "Does it protect me from vibrations while I'm using it?" To minimize vibration, the best choice is probably a synthetic neck with a rubberized grip or all wood. After all, who wants to end up with tennis elbow from hammering?

3. **The Claw.** This is the split hoof on the end of your hammer. It is either curved or flat; the curved variety is used to remove nails, while the flat is often used as a crowbar or pry bar. For your everyday toolbox, a curved claw is best.

Screwdrivers

The possibilities are many when shopping for screwdrivers. Most of us are familiar with the typical flathead and Phillips head screwdrivers that come in varying sizes. You can purchase a full set of these fairly inexpensively. One common problem when working on a project is finding yourself in need of several types and sizes of screwdriver. It's just not convenient to carry an entire set of screwdrivers with you. One great tool that solves this problem is what's known as a **multi-bit ratchet screwdriver.** This neat little tool allows you to have all of your screwdrivers in *one*! It's a screwdriver with interchangeable heads (flat, Phillips, hex, and sometimes even an Allen wrench). Add this to your tool belt and never go searching for another screwdriver again!

Wrenches

Wrenches come in a wide variety of configurations for many uses. Basically, a wrench is any tool with fixed or movable jaws used to seize, turn, or twist objects such as nuts and bolts.

Here's a list of common wrenches and their uses:

1. Box wrench (open-end and combination). These are the most common wrenches, used for tightening and loosening everyday things like nuts and bolts.

2. Adjustable wrench (crescent wrench). Make sure to purchase one at least 9 inches long. The longer the handle of your wrench, the more leverage you'll have and the less strength it will take to move a nut or bolt.

3. Socket wrench. These wrenches actually have a depression, or socket, in which to insert the nut or bolt, allowing for better traction. These wrenches aren't adjustable, so you will need the exact size wrench for a given nut or bolt.

"I don't own many tools, but I have upgraded from my butter knife."

Angela B.
Madison,
Michigan
Age 32

"I have a cordless drill, a regular drill, a hand saw, several screwdrivers, and more—I'm ready for anything!"

Linda C.
Portland, Oregon
Age 46

4. Allen wrench (keys or hex). These are made for use on fasteners with a hexagonal socket head or depression. (If you've ever put together a piece of furniture from Ikea, you've probably used an Allen wrench.)

5. Pipe wrench. This is an adjustable wrench with one fixed jaw and one movable jaw, used to turn pipes. One benefit of learning how to use a pipe wrench properly is that you may no longer have to deal with the plumber who's normally attached to it!

Pliers

Pliers come in many configurations to do lots of different jobs. They are typically used for gripping things but can cut as well. Here are a few typical sorts:

1. Tongue-and-groove pliers. Also known as *groove-joint pliers,* these can be opened and closed to adapt to many sizes. They are great for tightening and loosening and for extracting nails. This versatile tool can go from holding something paper thin to holding an object $4\frac{1}{2}$ inches thick. If only jeans expanded so easily!

2. Slip-joint pliers. These are probably the most versatile pliers of them all. They grab round as well as flat objects and adjust to many sizes. Often these pliers are made with serrated surfaces (sawlike edges) on their flat or curved jaws, which add to their multipurpose abilities.

3. Needlenose pliers. These get their name from their long thin tips. They have a wide variety of uses but are especially good for bending wire; many come with a built-in wire cutter. They are also convenient to have around the house for fixing small things (like jewelry).

4. Locking pliers. These are commonly known as vice grips, and they work as a clamp. They also cut, lock, grip, and adjust—this tool does it all!

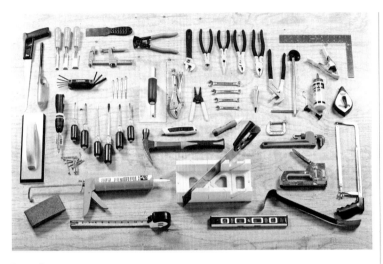

Level

A **level** and a **plumb bob** (also called a *plummet*) are essentials. These two tools let you know if the area you are working on is flat (level) or straight up and down (plumb).

You will want to invest in a good-quality level with clean, smooth edges. You may also want to consider purchasing two: a **carpenter's level,** which is at least 3 to 4 feet long, and a **torpedo level,** which is usually 12 to 16 inches long. To use a level, you simply hold it against whatever it is you're checking and look to see if the air bubble in the liquid container on the level is centered between the two lines. If it is, you're level!

The **plumb bob** has been used since the building of the pyramids. Of course, back then it was just a rock on a string, and now the tool is slightly higher tech. It works in much the same way as a level but determines vertical accuracy instead of horizontal.

Chalk Line

How much do you hate having to draw long, straight lines with a ruler? If you have to draw a line on anything that is at least 3 feet long, it's just *too* long to be done accurately with a standard ruler! What you need is a **chalk line.**

This unique tool is nothing more than a metal reel that contains coiled string and

colored chalk (blue, orange, yellow, or red). To use it, begin by marking the starting and ending points of your line. Next, hold the string up on one end (the line usually has a metal piece that helps you do this by yourself), unreel it to the other end, pull it taut, and then just snap the line. Now you have a perfectly straight line ready to guide you. Reel in the string and you're done!

Hand Saws

Hand saws might seem like something your grandfather used, but they're still an important element of the everyday toolbox. Here are some of the most useful:

1. Coping saw. This tool is perfect when you have to make angled or molding cuts. It has a thin, easily maneuverable blade that allows you to make detailed cuts such as curves and circles in thick and thin materials.

2. Hacksaw. A good hacksaw can be used to cut through certain metals, plastics, and sometimes even glass. Hacksaws are available at lengths of 8 inches, 10 inches and, most commonly, 12 inches. The blade is attached by a screw and a wing nut on either end; the resulting tension yields a clean cutting experience.

3. Back saw. A back saw comes in handy when using a **miter box** (see page 17). It is rectangular in shape, has a stiff back, and features fine teeth that make it one of the more accurate cutting tools. The back saw is typically used to make crosscuts, or angled cuts. For a good example of this type of cut, look at the corners of any baseboard or crown molding—those angled cuts could have been made by a back saw.

Stud Finder

A **stud** isn't just a male horse or Brad Pitt. Studs are the wood beams that make up the inside framing of your walls. They are located *behind* the **drywall** (otherwise known as

wallboard and **Sheetrock**). Unless you were born with X-ray vision, how can you know what's behind your walls? That's where a **stud finder** comes in.

This handheld battery-operated device tells you exactly where the studs are located within your walls. You want to know this because the studs are the strongest points of a wall. If you need to hang something heavy such as a mirror, or if you need to attach something to the wall and don't want it coming out of the drywall the second after you put it up, you need a stud finder.

Some models have sophisticated displays that not only tell you where a stud is but also detect electrical wires, plumbing, and the dimensions of the stud.

Squares

Huey Lewis was right—it *is* hip to be square. If you take a good look around your home, you will see it is made up primarily of 90-degree angles. To keep things square, you need these tools:

1. A **framing square** helps you measure cuts at a precise 90-degree angle. Framing squares are also great for figuring other angles and for taking general measurements, since most have ruler markings on the face.

2. A **layout square** is a right-angle-shaped tool that helps you check for 90 degrees and beyond. It also makes an excellent cutting guide when trying to determine irregular angle sizes.

3. A **combination square** helps you check for 45-degree angles. Because the measuring blade slides and locks, you can measure these much more accurately.

Miter Box

This is one of our favorite tools. Those corners you see on your crown and base molding and around your windows and doors are mitered cuts, which means they are two 45-degree

Jane Tip

Manual caulking guns are great and very inexpensive, but if you have a big caulking job you may want to consider purchasing a power caulking gun. For about $50, this tool makes any caulking application a snap.

Jane Tip

When shopping for a wire stripper, make sure to ask for a **combination stripper** (also known as an **adjustable stripper**) that comes with a self-opening spring. This will keep you from having to pry the stripper open when you need it.

angles put together to form a 90-degree angle. Using a miter box in combination with a back saw (see page 16), you can make these same accurately angled cuts.

A miter box is a U-shaped box made of plastic with a bottom and two sides. Both sides have three sets of markers that direct the motion of the back saw to ensure an accurate cut. Simply place the piece to be cut into the miter box, align your saw with the appropriate marker, and saw away!

Caulking Gun

A **caulking gun** helps accurately position caulk neatly and easily. You can place caulk without a caulking gun, but it's harder to force the caulk into cracks and crevices. To use the gun, purchase a tube of caulk, cut the tip, and puncture the foil inner seal (we typically use the end of a wire hanger). Load the tube of caulk into the gun and pull on the trigger. Drag a bead (or line) of caulk along whatever you're caulking, making sure to have a paper towel around to catch any extra that comes out. You'll eventually learn to decrease the pressure so you can stop the flow of caulk with greater control.

Voltage Tester

If you're thinking at all about working on electricity, then you need to be able to check if the power is off before getting started. The traditional way to do this is with a device called a **voltage tester,** also known as an **electrical tester.** One unit in particular looks like a pen with a plug on the end that you place in a socket or outlet to sense current. If the power is on, the light inside illuminates or the unit makes a noise. Some of these devices are so sensitive you can just wave them in the general area of the current for them to function.

Jane Profile

If guys can do it, so can girls.

Jane (for real!) Sherman

Age: 32

From: Wading River, New York

Favorite tool: I would have to say my favorite tool is a cordless drill with screwdriver and socket set attachments. I like to build furniture, and I can do it in a third of the time with this tool.

Projects accomplished: I have done a lot of projects, but my pride and joy is my baby's nursery. I painted a blue sky ceiling with accents to match the bedding.

Inspiration for starting home improvement: We moved into a new house, and it was stark white. I slowly but surely had to change it. Unfortunately, my husband didn't know which end of the hammer to use, but luckily I had a dad who did it all. My dad knew how to fix everything, and if he didn't, you never knew it. He would always just figure out how.

Fears about home improvement: I was afraid of damaging the house, but I learned quickly that it was either me or my husband, so I just braved on. I learned that most jobs were easy enough. Besides, I knew that if guys can do it, so can girls. I knew that as long as I could read, I could learn anything.

How has doing home improvement affected your life? I always knew you could do it yourself, but I thought you had to marry a do-it-yourselfer and help him. Obviously, I didn't. So I do it myself now, and *he* helps *me*. It's given me such a sense of accomplishment because if I'm not happy with something, I know I can change it without having to pay someone.

How has doing home improvement affected others in your life? People are always impressed when I tell them I've tackled a task, and I love to help them with their home improvement projects as well. Also, I think I've inspired a few of my friends and sisters to do things on their own. Their husbands didn't want to do these things, so I've helped them do it themselves. One friend was thrilled after we did her daughter's room. We repainted the bedroom set she had when she was a little girl, gave it a new life, and now it's in her daughter's room!

Advice for others just getting started in home improvement: Do your homework. Be brave, be bold, be organized. Be Jane, because anything boys can do girls can do better! Be creative, have fun, and find your inner Jane; she's there just waiting to strap on a tool belt if you let her.

Wire Strippers

Now that you know how to check for live wires, you need to know how to strip the plastic casing that goes around them. For that you need a **wire stripper.** Trust us, you don't want to use scissors to score and remove the casing. You might nick the wire, which could cause a failed connection or even a short.

Clamps

If you need to keep two things pressed together for a while and you have only one set of hands, then the tool you need is a **clamp.** Clamps come in many types for many applications. Here are three common types:

1. **C-clamp.** If you guessed that this clamp is in the shape of a *C*, then give yourself a star! This versatile metal clamp is used to hold together two things being glued or to hold down an object you are hammering or sawing.

2. **Bar clamp.** This clamp has two surfaces attached to a bar that when brought together, become a clamp. It is a good tool for holding any two pieces to each other. Bonus feature: You can tighten the clamp with one hand while holding the pieces together with the other.

3. **Spring clamp.** This clamp is just like a large clothespin.

Pry Bar

Now that you've learned how to put things together, let's show you how to tear them apart. The best thing for aesthetic demolition that won't leave marks behind is a **pry bar.** You've probably heard of a **crowbar,** but it typically causes more damage than the pry bar, which is flat. The pry bar also has one or two places to help remove any nails left behind, as well as claws (like those on a hammer) to help you get into tight spots. It's one of those tools that you buy thinking, When will I *ever* use this? and end up saying, "How did I *ever* live without one?!"

Flashlights

A good-quality **flashlight** is essential. Your best bet is one that is durable and sturdy and can take a drop or two without breaking.

One light you might not have thought of is a **headlamp.** This is the light that hikers and campers wear if they're out at night. Headlamps usually come with an elastic band for your head and are great because they free up your hands for working.

Chisel

A **chisel** is a must-have tool. There are many types of chisel, each with a blade made to work with materials such as brick, wood, and even metal. Chisels are used to cut or chip away excess, but as many great sculptors have shown us, they are used to shape as well.

Putty Knife

The **putty knife,** a great multipurpose tool, is typically a flat piece of metal (the blade) that can be used to smooth surfaces or to remove finishes such as paint or wallpaper. Putty knives come as either *flexible* or *rigid,* even though each can be used universally. Usually the flexible putty knives are for applying materials like spackle or putty on flat or slightly round surfaces, and the rigid putty knives are for removing paint and old wallpaper, or wherever you need good scraping action.

Utility Knife

Do not overlook the ever-useful **utility knife,** sometimes known as a **box cutter.** Utility knife blades are extremely sharp, making them useful for cutting straight lines against a flat metal edge or even for incising curved lines into softer materials following a template. You can cut plastic, shave wood, score (or cut) drywall, open packages, and much more with this one tool.

Plunger

Another must-have is a **plunger.** You've probably got at least one in your home, but consider picking up a plunger that has what's known as a *flange extension.* This plunger looks just like your everyday plunger except the end is not open but rather shaped like a pair of puckered lips. This funny-looking addition allows you to get better suction when plunging a drain or a toilet. It also lessens the chance of water splashing up at you. After all, the worst part of plunging a toilet is getting doused with a shot of toilet water. Remember: flange extension!

Staple Gun

For a more immediately gratifying way of putting two things together than glue, you need a **staple gun.** This tool is more powerful than an office stapler and uses heavy-duty staples to keep things in place. Some models even shoot rounded staples (for cords) as well as small nails.

Sanding Block

If you need to hand-sand something that is flat, get a **sanding block.** You attach a piece of sandpaper to the ends of the block and sand without touching the sandpaper itself. A sanding block allows you to use any kind of sandpaper you need. Changing out used pieces is a breeze.

NOT EXACTLY HAND TOOLS, BUT . . .

Extension Cords

Be sure to have an **indoor/outdoor extension cord** of at least 25 feet in length. Usually bright orange in color, these heavy-duty cords provide you power where you need it. One of the dangers in working with power tools is losing power midway through a job. Prevent this problem by giving yourself enough slack in the cord to account for any movement of the tool.

Jane Tip:

It's important to know that while heavy-duty staple guns will help you do heavy-duty projects, typically they require more strength to use than electric versions. Applying a lot of arm power can be difficult when working overhead or in tight spaces, so if you have a heavy-duty project but don't have the strength to use a regular staple gun—or if you just like the feeling of power—consider an **electric** or **pneumatic** staple gun. Squeeze the trigger, and a staple shoots into place.

Butane Lighter

A **butane lighter** is always good to have on hand, not only for relighting pilot lights but for lighting candles in the dining room you just repainted! Butane lighters are the best because most are childproof and have enough fuel to last for years.

POWER TOOLS

Power tools level the playing field of home improvement. With power behind you, it doesn't make a difference if you are 4 foot 10 inches and can't even lift a full water pitcher; you can still cut a piece of lumber or drill a hole as fast as a 6-foot-3-inch bodybuilder.

Before we get into the types of power tools needed for the projects featured in this book, let's establish the difference between electric and pneumatic power tools. The first category is as simple as it sounds; **electric power tools** are powered by electricity. **Pneumatic power tools,** in contrast, use compressed air to create force (although you still have to plug in the compressor). A familiar example is a pneumatic nail gun, which uses the air compressor to build enough pressure to drive the nail into whatever surface you're working with.

All of these tools are easy to work and will make any job easier. Using most power tools is

Jane Profile

Be patient,
especially if
you're doing it
alone.

Catherine "Jane" Reynolds

Age: 37

From: Austin, Texas

Favorite tool: That's a tough call: I love my cordless power drill, but I also love my grandfather's old, beat-up wooden hammer.

Projects accomplished: I have remodeled three houses, and I just bought and am working on a fourth. I've worked on everything from surface structures to wall removals and basic plumbing, and I've even done electrical work. Nothing is off-limits to learning and trying and trying again.

Inspiration for starting home improvement: I started tackling home projects after I purchased my first house. It was a neighborhood reject that was a fixer-upper, to say the least, but it was the only one I could afford in that particular neighborhood. I had no fears at first; ignorance is bliss. I thought, If they can do it, so can I. The person who inspired me the most with both the "just-do-it" attitude and the "do-it-well" attitude was Martha Stewart.

Fears about home improvement: Not being able to make the project look professional or being able to truly do it well. Not being able to put a nice, polished touch on it. I was always afraid, and still am, of not being able to accomplish what my vision is. The funniest thing of all is if I look back at all of my past projects I can see that I have been able to accomplish most projects better than I expected. They have all come out very well. It amazes me that I'm still afraid.

How has doing home improvement affected your life? How hasn't it?! It has been very satisfying to accomplish what a lot of people my age haven't. It's made me feel I can do other things as well and has allowed me to create a great balance between my working and my nonworking time. It's been nice to have the confidence to know that I can tackle more than screwing in a lightbulb.

How has doing home improvement affected others in your life? It's been a mixed response. Some people have sat back and watched, and others have been inspired to give it a try themselves. The ones who've taken on projects themselves say they feel pretty confident and want to try it because of all they've seen me do.

Advice for others just getting started in home improvement: Be patient, especially if you're doing it alone. It seems to take a lot longer than you'd think. A lot of times things don't fit together right away. Be ready to have your house in boxes and kind of disheveled. You just don't finish it overnight if it is a do-it-yourself project. Be prepared to keep learning as things go wrong. Keep going and keep trying, and things will come together.

Jane Profile

You will be able to look at your finished project and say, "That's right, I did it!"

Heidi "Jane" Baker

Age: 37

From: Detroit, Michigan

Favorite tool: It's a tie between a compound miter saw and a finishing nailer. I just love the speed I can cut with when I use my compound miter saw, but my finishing nailer offers amazing instant gratification.

Projects accomplished: I've done a great deal of updating to my home and many of my friends' homes. I've laid stone floors and countertops, redone kitchen cabinets, installed baseboard and crown molding, replaced electrical outlets, installed dimmer switches and light fixtures, put in new bathroom vanities (sink, faucet, cabinet, and all), and created door archways. I would have to say, though, that my favorite project of all was building my very own walk-in closet—after all, I am a girl! I had fun building it, and more fun using it!

Inspiration for starting home improvement: I bought my first house when I was thirty, and while I had enough money to get in the house, I didn't have enough to pay someone to fix it up for me. I was house rich and cash poor, and my house looked like a 1960s comeback show. I didn't feel like I was living in my own home. So, one room at a time—heck, one project at a time—I made the house mine!

Fears about home improvement: When I first got started I was afraid I would screw it up, the *it* being anything and everything I tried to work on. I was especially afraid of working around electricity. Even though I'd love to tell you my fear of home improvement went away completely, I can't. I still get nervous whenever I start a home improvement project. Regardless of my numerous successes, I still start thinking, "What if I fail?" Luckily, I know that's just a game I play with myself, and usually I quickly realize I'm the only one standing in my way. I've learned to answer my own question with "If I do, so what?" and get started.

How has doing home improvement affected your life? Before I began working on my home, I would never have believed that I could write a book or be on a national television show. I'm just your average everyday normal girl. Now I take on things I never thought I could do. It's the most empowering feeling I've ever known, and I am forever changed because of it.

How has doing home improvement affected others in your life? To my surprise, my girlfriends started taking on projects that they never would have dreamed of doing. When my friend's father asked her why she thought she could do a project she was taking on, she replied, "Heidi put in crown molding. I think I can sand down and repaint my baseboards!" When I realized the impact I had on those close to me, I chose to make an even bigger one by cofounding Be Jane. Now I get e-mails from women all over the world thanking me for creating a place where they can ask so-called stupid questions and finally feel they aren't alone.

Advice for others just getting started in home improvement: Believe in the possibility that you *can* do this. All you need is for it to be *possible* in order for it to become a reality. Others will doubt you, and don't be surprised if you doubt yourself. In the end, you will be able to look at your finished project and say, "That's right, I did it!" Try it, and you'll know what I'm talking about!

just a matter of flipping a switch or pulling a trigger—and yes, even *you* can do that!

The Drill

The first power tool you'll want to invest in is a high-quality **power drill,** preferably a cordless one. Be prepared for the plethora of choices! Let's start with the basics:

■ **CORDLESSNESS.** This is both a blessing and a curse. Not being attached to a wall allows you to move around freely. (That's the blessing.) The curse is that often the batteries in a cordless drill are quite heavy, making the power tool harder to work with for extended periods, especially if you have to lift it above your head. But don't be fooled by the lighter models; be sure your drill has enough torque (power) to do what you want it to do.

■ **VOLTAGE.** This is the strength or torque of the drill. We have heard many stories from our fellow Janes about how the first drill they bought was a 6-volt drill because it was light-weight and seemed like a great deal (they're usually around $25). Then, within a few months, they had to go out and buy something with more power. We recommend that you buy nothing less powerful than an 18-volt drill, and if you feel that you can handle the weight of something more powerful, then go for it. One good trick is to try holding it over your head for a little while before buying it to see how quickly your arm gets fatigued.

■ **BATTERIES.** Most cordless drills come with rechargeable nickel-cadmium batteries. A newer and supposedly longer-lasting battery type is nickel-lithium. This combination allows the battery to remain fully charged for extended periods. Some can stay fully charged for up to 18 months. Regardless of the type of battery your unit has, make sure that whatever you buy has two of them, because you'll want to be charging one battery while using the other. This way, you'll never have to stop in the middle of a project because of a dead battery.

■ **SPEED CONTROL.** Think of the gas pedal in a car: Give it a little bit of gas and it goes slow, more and it goes faster. The benefit of speed control in a drill is the associated versatility.

Hammer Drill

While a regular cordless drill can be used to do the same jobs as a **hammer drill,** the hammer drill makes them go faster. A hammer drill uses a drill bit in the same way as a regular drill, but while it spins it also continuously hammers against whatever you are drilling. This function is great when you are drilling holes in concrete or masonry or in areas where you just can't create enough force on your own.

Electric Saws

Electric saws make any project go faster than if done by hand. There are many types of saws is on the market, but we deal with only a handful of them to keep things simple. Here are the ones you should know:

■ **JIGSAW.** Probably one of the most versatile machines you'll use, the jigsaw cuts in straight lines as well as in circles, making almost any cut possible depending on the blade you use. The cutting area looks like a sewing machine. The blade goes up and down like a sewing needle, and you have lines to follow like those on the plate of a sewing machine. When buying a jigsaw, get one whose blade can be replaced without an Allen wrench or other tool. Consider buying one with a blower attachment, which will keep your cutting field clear of sawdust as you work.

■ **RECIPROCATING SAW.** This saw looks like an electric carving knife, but bigger. It is great for cutting things that are firmly clamped down or overhead—just make certain to have a sure footing and, as when using any power tool, wear protective eyewear. It can come cordless,

> "My favorite power tool has to be my electric drill. I love the power I feel when I'm using it. I'm not afraid to make holes in my walls."
>
> Linda C.
> Escondido,
> California
> Age 25

> "I give cordless drill kits as wedding gifts and enjoy hearing stories of how the couples turn houses into homes."
>
> Jean C.
> San Clemente,
> California
> Age 53

and more expensive versions vibrate less than inexpensive models, which tend to shake a great deal.

■ **PORTABLE CIRCULAR SAW.** Your best bet if you want to buy only one power saw, this one does pretty much everything. It's similar to the jigsaw in its portability and the way it sits on the material it's cutting. The big difference is that its blade is actually circular, as the name suggests. Your ability to cut with this saw is limited only by the blade you put on it. With the right blade, you can cut almost anything. Take extra care when using a circular saw, as it is a powerful tool that cuts effectively, efficiently, and, most of all, *quickly*.

■ **COMPOUND MITER SAW.** This saw allows you to position the blade at exact angles to make precise cuts. The blade is positioned over the wood to allow the perfect mitered (or angled) cut. This is the electric version of the miter box and back saw, and can cut your work time in half.

Router

Cutting wood is an important part of building the framework for any project, but being able to *shape* wood is what separates carpenters from builders. The next tool we discuss is the **router,** and it does exactly that: shape wood.

The most common type is a **fixed-base router,** which many people prefer to attach to a **router table.** This way, your only concern is with the shank (or cutting piece) and how it is affecting the piece of wood you are shaping. This tool can plow grooves through wood, shape edges, add a bit of décor, and much more.

Finishing Nailer

If you've gotten a black thumbnail from using a hammer and nail one too many times, you will absolutely adore the **finishing nailer.** While it's perfect for attaching molding on the interior of your home, it is also

Jane Tip:

When using a palm sander or any other device likely to generate dust particles, be sure to wear safety glasses and a **sanding mask** to minimize the potential for injury.

Jane Tip:

Employ ear protection when using a finishing nailer, as it can be very loud, especially in smaller spaces.

perfect for jobs on the exterior. It is technically a power tool, but it derives most of its power from air pressure, making it a pneumatic tool. It's lightweight and easy to use and makes what would otherwise be a laborious job fun!

Palm Sander

If you've ever sanded something by hand, you will quickly learn to love an **electric palm sander,** also known as an **orbital** or **finishing sander.** These units are relatively lightweight, and their square shape allows you to sand into corners in a way that you can't with that round sander. The distinguishing characteristic of this sander is that its sanding face is one-quarter the size of a sheet of sandpaper. The sandpaper attaches easily with clips or Velcro. Many models have collection bags that help minimize dust.

A FINAL THOUGHT

Don't Be Cheap.

Quality counts in tools. You'll want to buy tools that will last for years, not weeks. There's nothing more frustrating than buying a tool that falls apart midway through a project. Find and buy those tools that have the perfect mix of quality, warranty, and, most of all, comfort level for you. After all, these are your tools, so buy what feels right and not what some expert tells you works best for them. But also, buy the best you can afford. Period.

The tools described in this section are just the first layer of those you might find at your local home improvement center. Owning these tools is an excellent start to building your own tool collection, and they will help make upcoming projects much easier and more enjoyable. If you can afford the whole set, we recommend it.

Jane Profile

Don't give up!

Shannon "Jane" Tucker

Age: 45

From: Smyrna, Georgia

Favorite tool: My tile saw: It's efficient and gets the job done quickly, with smooth cuts!

Projects accomplished: I remodeled my powder room. I gutted everything, including the commode and the cabinet, and even removed the linoleum. To finish the room I tiled the floor, wallpapered with a small, small leopard print, installed a pedestal sink with a new faucet, and even installed a new commode (yes, by myself). I also did a kitchen remodel, but there isn't enough room on this page to tell you about it! My before and after pictures are phenomenal, and I am extremely proud of this one!

Inspiration for starting home improvement: My inspiration is the ability to be creative. I'd also gotten fed up with calling repairmen and their excessively high quotes for something I knew I could do myself. I enjoy doing it and like learning new things. I find it keeps my mind fresh. Besides, it's fun seeing how something can go from blah to "That's amazing!"

Fears about home improvement: The thing that freaks me out is cutting crown molding because you have to be so precise, and even if you're a professional it never seems to work exactly the way it should.

How has doing home improvement affected your life? It makes me feel like I can do anything I put my mind to! I get a great sense of accomplishment, so much so that I wish I could do it full-time. I love it so much that I am starting a business where I go into people's homes, help them dream up their own room, and then make it a reality. Until I can support myself with this full-time, I will have to do it on evenings and weekends, but at least I get to do what I love.

How has doing home improvement affected others in your life? They want me to do more projects for them. I've also inspired some people to take on their own projects. My mom is now in the midst of remodeling her master bath because of what she's seen me do in my home.

Advice for others just getting started in home improvement: Don't give up, and be sure to learn something new every day in the skill that you're interested in! Read and learn all you can. Ask questions of all different kinds of people. You learn so much that way.

Safety Basics

While home improvement projects can be extremely enjoyable, not to mention gratifying, do not forget that *safety is absolutely Job One!* Everyone, whether a beginner or a licensed professional, can get a nick or a scrape now and then. The trick is to avoid the possibility as best you can.

We don't want to scare you. No, wait a minute. Yes we do—that is, if fear will make you safe. Just as our kids have to wear a helmet while riding a bike or wrist guards and knee pads while in-line skating, we have to behave safely while doing home improvement.

Through experience, we have identified excellent gear that will help you walk away from your next undertaking with all of your digits intact. Patience and alertness are essential components of successful home improvement.

BE PATIENT

When it comes to home improvement, patience is an absolute necessity. It is always best to take your time with any project, especially if it's the first time you've done anything like it. In addition, never start a project you will have to rush to complete. Not only do you drastically increase the probability of injuring yourself, but the quality of your work will probably drop off as well.

> "Don't work too fast—it's a ticket to cuts and bruises and worse."
> Susan W.
> Boise, Idaho
> Age 32

> "Don't forget to eat and hydrate! I get going on projects and the day just passes, and then I'm exhausted because I haven't had enough fuel!"
> Peg A.
> Seattle, Washington
> Age 45

BE ALERT

One of the easiest ways to injure yourself while working on your home is to do it when you're tired, stressed out, or distracted. If you have any of these feelings, consider taking a break to give your motor time to properly recoup. Stay well hydrated and eat regularly. If you have animals or small children, be sure to wrangle them out of the way. Remember, an injury or a mistake can happen in a fraction of a second, so it's crucial that your mind is on what you're doing.

EQUIP YOURSELF

Now it's time to become the director of your own Homeland Security and equip yourself with the proper protective gear. Obviously, your need for each of these items depends on the project. Familiarize yourself with each so you'll know *when* you should be wearing *what*.

■ **SAFETY GLASSES.** You never realize how fragile your eyes are until you get something in them. Protecting the windows to your soul should be of the utmost priority when working with tools that may create flying debris. Wear

How to Stay Girly and Still Do Home Improvement

Here are some tips that can help keep you looking and feeling your best during your project and after it is completed:

1. **Lips.** When you're creating a great deal of dust with an electric saw or sander, lip gloss is a fashion *don't*—unless you need a lip exfoliant! (And trust us, sawdust does *not* taste or feel good). Anything that can attract dust or other grime is not a good idea.

2. **Hands.** The particles and chemicals used in many home improvement projects can be drying to the skin, so you should take steps to protect your hands and nails. Work gloves add a layer of protection while you do rough work. Latex or nitrile gloves are the perfect way to safeguard your hands and nails while painting. Gloves also protect your hands from harsh chemicals that can dry and damage them.

3. **Hair.** Especially while painting or sawing, be sure to pull your hair back into a baseball cap and/or a do-rag. A shower cap will also work to help prevent paint chemicals and sawdust particles from creeping into your hair follicles and drying them.

   Even if you protect your hair, it's a good idea to wash it after working to remove the chemicals or sawdust, and then moisturize it with a super-duper conditioner. Hair oil, three-minute conditioners, and leave-in conditioners are all excellent choices.

4. **Face.** Unfortunately, you can't cover your face completely, or you won't be able to see your project. You can, however, put on safety goggles and a mask or a handkerchief. These precautions help prevent particles from floating into your pores. Be sure to wash your face with a gentle soap (especially if you were around chemicals) after working. Use a gentle astringent like witch hazel to cleanse the pores and a moisturizer and restore moisture.

5. **Other exposed skin.** If you're going to be working outdoors, be sure to use sunscreen. After one traumatic incident, we wholeheartedly recommend slathering on at least an SPF of 15—not forgetting your ears.

6. **Clothes.** Obviously you don't want to wear your little black dress while installing baseboard; coveralls and an old, ratty T-shirt are the perfect attire. If you don't have coveralls, then an apron, an old, long shirt, or even a trash bag (put on with the opening toward your legs and holes cut for your head and arms) can protect your clothes. You may even want to purchase some cheap, comfy clothes so stains won't stress you out. In the end, the few dollars you spend on work clothes will save you money on the nice clothes you might otherwise destroy.

---

safety glasses for painting, sanding, sawing, hammering, and other tasks. One way to avoid trouble is to put them on the moment you think of doing any home improvement project.

■ **GOGGLES.** Like safety glasses, goggles are usually fully enclosed and strapped to your head, so they are excellent eye protectors. The major difference between goggles and safety glasses is that goggles offer a more comprehensive form of protection. They are less likely to fall off during a project because they have a heavy-duty adjustable headband. Goggles are a good choice when you work with toxic chemicals or anything that creates fine dust particles.

■ **DUST MASK.** A dust mask is aptly named; it keeps dust, sawdust, and other particles out of your mouth and lungs. Most are disposable and offer great protection. Make sure, however, that you get masks sized for your face. The mask should fit snugly around your nose and mouth. Higher-end models have a metal bracket above the nose that helps the mask

> "I complained about wearing my safety glasses until they blocked a flying wood chip. I love them now!"
>
> Marci K.
> Orlando, Florida
> Age 29

conform to your face, making it even more effective.

■ **RESPIRATOR.** Think of a respirator as a mask on steroids. Doing everything a mask does and more, a respirator often comes with a replaceable charcoal filter that does a phenomenal job of preventing the inhalation of hazardous fumes. You don't need a respirator for an everyday sanding job; reserve it for jobs where you might be exposed to toxic chemicals. Be sure the filters you are using are appropriate for the job. If you're not certain what you'll need, don't be shy; ask your local home improvement center representative. Explain the types of chemicals you'll be using, what you'll be doing with them—and where—as well as the expected duration of the project. The rep can then recommend the best model for the job.

■ **GLOVES.** Gloves are made in a variety of materials, each of which safeguards your hands differently.

• **Leather.** Extremely durable and versatile, leather gloves work best for jobs involving wood or whenever your hands are at risk of getting roughed up or splintered.

• **Latex or Nitrile.** These highly economical disposable gloves guard your hands against dirt and stains and keep your nails from cracking. They are an excellent choice for painting and staining but do not protect from punctures or certain chemicals. People who are allergic to latex should use nitrile gloves instead. Being both latex and powder free, they are a great alternative.

• **Basic Work Gloves.** Usually made of a combination of materials (cotton, nylon, leather, pigskin), these gloves protect your hands during most everyday tasks. They can be used for a multitude of projects from gardening to carpentry. The major difference between all-leather gloves and combination-material work gloves is that

Jane Tip:

If you want to keep your hands feeling soft and smooth, pick up a box of disposable gloves that give off aloe while you wear them. Your house will look great and so will your cuticles.

Jane Tip:

For better air circulation when working, open more than one window or door to get a cross breeze.

the leather or pigskin is normally just on the palm and the cotton or nylon is on the back of your hand, creating a much better fit.

■ **CLOSED-TOE SHOES.** Whatever you do, don't mess up that pedicure! And nothing will quicker than spilling paint or dropping a heavy object on your foot. If you're painting, almost any type of tennis shoe or other closed-toe shoe offers adequate protection. Be sure, though, to choose a pair you don't mind getting paint on. For projects that call for heavy or sharp equipment, consider investing in a pair of steel-toe work boots to protect your feet properly.

■ **COVERALLS.** Coveralls do exactly what their name implies: They cover you all up. They are an absolute necessity for protecting clothing and for packing countless items in their numerous pockets. A number of brands offer disposable versions that make the problem of getting paint out of your clothing a thing of the past. Consider these the superhero's suit for home improvement.

A Word on Instructions

We put this topic in the safety section because this is one area of home improvement you *must* pay attention to. Everything from paint to chainsaws comes with some sort of instructions. We can't urge you more clearly: Read *all* of the manufacturer's instructions before beginning to work. They are there for a reason. No one knows the product better than the company that makes it. Instructions cover the best ways to use the product as well as the ways to *never* use the product. Once again: Read all manufacturer's instructions on all products. You'll thank us one day—that we can assure you.

Jane Profile

Make sure you know what you are doing before you get started.

Cris "Jane" Willig

Age: 48

From: Inver Grove Heights, Minnesota

Favorite tool: The electric miter saw is my favorite tool. It saves a lot of time on many projects. I'm also a small person and don't have hand-sawing endurance.

Projects accomplished: My favorite project was probably my most recent. I painted my kitchen walls, cupboards, wainscoting, countertops, and tin ceiling. I also stenciled the outside cupboards and hand-painted chickens and kitchen items on the center island. To finish off the cupboards I installed crown molding. All my friends say how great it looks. I took an out-of-date, dark kitchen and turned it into a light and airy room with a French country feel.

Inspiration for starting home improvement: Believe it or not, my inspiration was a nonelectric drill my father owned when I was a child. I wanted to get my hands on that drill and go to town.

I've been interested in doing stuff since I was a kid, but when I was first married we moved into what we lovingly called our slum home. We were twenty-one and didn't have much money. So we fixed it up, but then we realized we needed more room!

Fears about home improvement: I used to have a "perfection" fear. I was afraid of trying something because what I would end up with might not be perfect or might fall apart. But through trial and error and listening to experts, I've come to realize no one is perfect.

How has doing home improvement affected your life? That's hard to say. It hasn't really had an effect because it's always been a part of my life. For me it's kind of like, you breathe, you do home improvement. My parents lived in a home that was a hundred years old, so it was all I ever saw. If you live in a home you don't have the cash to fix up, you just do it yourself—though I must admit, I have told my husband that before I die I would like to live in a home that doesn't need any work.

How has doing home improvement affected others in your life? I think some of my projects have put smiles on their faces. Many have said I can do anything I put my mind to. My answer to that is so can *they*. People get in their mind that home improvement is extravagantly difficult, but it doesn't have to be. My friends come into my home and are amazed at how simple, little things can have such impact.

Advice for others just getting started in home improvement: Read, read, and read about your home improvement project. Make sure you know what you are doing before you get started. Being prepared could mean the difference between a $10 mistake and a $1,000 mistake. Also, check your measurements three times. If and when you get frustrated, take a break. Never give up, because the outcome will raise your spirits along with your self-confidence.

■ **HEAD PROTECTORS** (or hard hats). You may not need a hard hat often, but when you do, please don't forget it. Anytime you will be working above your head with power tools (attaching crown molding, installing a ceiling fan, etc.) or when entering a construction site, where anything can happen (and usually does), a hard hat is a wise safety precaution.

■ **VENTILATION.** The hardest part of taking ventilation seriously is that fumes are invisible and thus do not seem threatening. However, sitting in a room full of fumes and chemicals is not your lungs' idea of a good time. Be sure to open doors and windows when possible and always run a fan to help with air circulation. Remember, even if you can't smell fumes it doesn't mean they're not there—so be proactive in protecting yourself.

■ **TOOL BELT.** A tool belt is more than a fashion accessory and a reflection of your self-confidence; it is eminently practical. When you carry your tools and supplies in a tool belt, you eliminate the risk of tripping over them on the floor or dropping them from a ladder or a table. You keep them out of your way and your path free and clear.

■ **BACK SUPPORT BELT OR BRACE.** If you plan to do heavy lifting, stand on your feet for a while, or bend over, a back support is a must. Wearing one reduces stress to the lower back, which will thank you for it in the morning!

■ **KNEE PADS.** These are vital while working on the floor, roof, or any other place you might have to kneel. Anytime you will be on your knees for an extended amount of time, be sure to gear up and save yourself a trip to the orthopedist.

■ **EAR PROTECTION.** When you are using loud power tools like an electric saw, a finishing nailer, or a compound miter saw, earplugs may literally save your hearing. Avoid hearing loss with high-quality earmuffs or earplugs.

Jane Tip:

Even if you use a back support, *always* remember to lift heavy objects with your legs. Keep a straight back and bend at your knees. Your back will thank you!

■ **CAPS AND PONYTAIL HOLDERS.** Loose hair can catch on any number of things, so be sure to tie it back or wear a protective cap that will keep your hair out of your face and out of your way.

The important thing to remember from this section is to be safe. Home improvement is exciting and a lot of fun, but it can be a little dangerous as well. So take caution. Be patient, be well rested, and use the steps and equipment described here so you are at your best when you're doing your best.

Be Jane.
Products for Home Empowerment

paint
color

1 Gallon (3.78 Litres)   22-04

Painting Basics

Paint is the ugly wall's best friend. Actually, paint is *every* wall's best friend. Paint can hide imperfections, accent an architectural feature, create illusions of height, create illusions of space—it can even create the illusion of being on a sandy beach! Perhaps one of the most impressive things about paint is that it can make anyone who uses it look like a pro.

It is perhaps the easiest, fastest, and least expensive way to make over any room in your house. In fact, even if all you did was paint, you would immediately see a dramatic and long-lasting difference in a previously dull and lifeless room.

There are many types of paint and just as many ways to apply it: exterior painting, interior painting, faux painting techniques, murals. The good news is that anyone can do it—and do it well.

This section introduces you to the basics of painting. We cover everything from the tools you'll need to accomplish just about any painting task to the skills and techniques that will help make any painting job easier.

Although the painting process is relatively simple, knowing a few tips and tricks can make it even easier.

PAINT TYPES

There are two types of paint: **oil** and **latex.** Oil paints are much thicker and, some might argue, better stand the test of time. Using them also requires extremely good ventilation. Latex paints have come quite a long way in recent years, however, and because of their ease of use and durability are often the paint of choice. The biggest difference is the cleanup. Latex cleans up with soap and warm

water, while oil cleans up with turpentine or mineral spirits.

Remember these two things if you use oil paints: (1) Oil can only cover over oil. Oil and water don't mix, and because latex paints are water-based, you must properly prepare the surface to receive the new paint if you are covering oil with latex. You must sand the old oil paint off and use an appropriate **primer** to help the new paint stick. (2) White high-gloss oil paints tend to yellow over time. Avoid this by using high-gloss latex paints instead.

PAINT SHEENS

Once you've chosen the type of paint, the next decision is **sheen.** There are more than a few choices; here are a few of the most common:

Flat. This type of paint sheen is as described: completely flat, without any reflective properties at all; it is most commonly used on ceilings.

Eggshell. Paint with an eggshell sheen is the next step up from flat. It has only a slight amount of reflection in it. When it dries, its texture is like that of an eggshell. Like flat paint, it hides imperfections well, but it has a bit more pizzazz. It's a common choice for interior walls.

Satin. This paint sheen adds a glow to your walls without being too shiny. A satin finish helps spread light along the walls. It's commonly used in kitchens, bathrooms, and children's rooms. It's also a great choice for trim or woodwork, as it's durable and easy to clean.

Semigloss. This paint reflects 35 to 50 percent of the light that hits it. While this adds a great deal of light to any room you use it in, it does a poor job of hiding any imperfections on your wall. Semigloss is more commonly used on cabinets and trim, as it is quite durable and even easier to clean than a satin finish.

High-gloss. The sheen provided by high-gloss paint is like the reflective quality of a candied apple. This is used on areas you specifically want to highlight—for example, crown molding or window trim. Be aware, though, that any imperfections such as dents or dings in your wood will show through this type of paint.

CHOOSING A COLOR

Now it's time for the hard decision: paint color. We have received thousands of e-mails from people across the country asking us what color they should paint their rooms. While we would love to give you an easy rule of thumb for choosing paint colors, there really isn't one. But here are some basic pointers:

■ If the room you're painting is small, choose a light color to make it feel airy and large. Dark colors tend to shrink a room. The same can be said for a large room. If you're looking to make it feel a bit cozier, consider a warm, deep tone rather than a bright white or beige.

■ Consider using two colors for each room— one for the walls and one for the trim or woodwork. Try to make them complement each other by choosing colors within the same family. Strong color contrasts can be distracting.

■ Don't choose a color simply because it's popular. Instead, try to choose colors that make *you* happy. Remember, even if your bedroom ends up on the cover of *Architectural Digest,* it means nothing if you're not happy living in it.

Jane Tip:

If you're still having trouble deciding on a color, purchase a small paint sample of each color you are considering and paint a 2 x 2-foot square on the wall of the room you are going to paint. Leave it there for a few days and see how you feel about it. Remember to look at the paint square in all different types of light, as paint tends to change appearance with the light it's in.

Jane Tip:

Proper sanding before painting helps ensure a long-lasting paint job. Paint usually flakes or cracks off when the surface underneath was not properly prepared to accept the new paint.

"I used to worry about coloring in between the lines. Now I just mask it all and go crazy!"

Lisa J.
Phoenix, Arizona
Age 41

The Ins and Outs of Paint Preparation

Before getting started, prepare the room and walls for painting. The easiest way is by removing all furniture from the room or, if the furnishings are too heavy or too numerous, pushing all of them into the middle of the room and covering them with drop cloths.

Protect your floors from getting paint on them by covering them with drop cloths and taping down the edges. Trust us when we say it is way too easy to trip over an unsecured drop cloth!

PROPER PREPARATION

Masking. Think what else in your room needs to be masked (protected) before starting to paint. Use blue painter's tape to cover any areas you don't want to get paint on. (Just remember, painter's tape becomes difficult to remove if you leave it in place over time.)

Repairing. Once you've protected everything you don't want painted, it's time to properly prepare your walls. First, check for small holes or cracks that need to be filled in. Use a flexible putty knife to fill holes with **spackle.** This is as easy as spreading cream cheese on a bagel. Just scoop some spackle onto the affected area, scrape away the excess, and let it dry according to the manufacturer's recommendations. Then lightly sand the area with a fine-grit sandpaper. That's it! Sometimes spackle shrinks when it dries, so reapply if necessary.

Sanding. Typically you won't have to sand an area unless you are covering over either semigloss or high-gloss paint. If you are, then you need to sand the entire surface area with a fine- to extra-fine-grit sandpaper using either a sanding block or an electric palm sander. The goal isn't to sand down to the bare wood but rather just enough to break through the sheen to allow the new paint to adhere to the surface.

Cleaning. Be sure your painting surface is clean before applying a primer. If you're painting walls, one of the best ways to accomplish this is by wiping down the entire surface with a mixture of warm water and **TSP** (tri-sodium phosphate). TSP helps remove dust and sanding particles as well as grease or dirt buildup that might be present. Keep in mind that TSP and skin don't exactly love each other, so be sure to protect your hands with rubber gloves when using this product. Also, be sure you properly rinse the walls with a clean, damp cloth or **tack cloth.**

Priming. Priming is essential if you want to do a top-notch job. A **primer** is nothing more than a way of ensuring that your paint adheres to whatever surface you're applying it to. A primer can also enhance the sheen of the paint you've chosen, create a uniform surface, and prevent wall stains from bleeding through the paint. The right primer depends on what you plan on painting, the type of paint, its sheen, and what you're painting on top of. If you give these variables to your local paint store clerk, he or she can steer you toward the right primer for the job.

Painting. Paint can be applied any number of ways. Some techniques make your painting go faster and more easily and efficiently.

Painting ceilings. When you are painting ceilings, start by edging in from the corners with a brush. Use a roller on larger surface areas, but do it in 4 x 4-foot sections. This limits the strain on your back and shoulders and ensures proper paint coverage. Be sure to use **ceiling paint,** which is specially formulated a

Jane Tip:

We can't stress enough the importance of wearing protective eyewear when you are painting above your head. While you're at it, you should cover your hair to protect it from the paint, and wear a pair of disposable gloves.

Jane Tip:

Never wait to clean up after a painting job. Once paint has had a chance to dry, it is difficult, if not impossible, to remove. If you're not finished with your project, but finished for the day, you can simply wrap your paint-filled brush in plastic wrap and place it in the refrigerator.

bit thicker than other paints, making it less likely to splatter on you while you are painting. Also be sure to use a splatter shield on the roller to protect you from paint that tries to escape. For just a few dollars extra, you can buy a roller with a handle that enables you to draw paint up into the handle itself. This prevents you from having to make constant trips to and from the paint roller tray.

Painting walls. Painting walls is a lot like painting ceilings, although you can use regular wall paint. Be sure to edge in from the corners with a paintbrush and work in 4 x 4-foot sections with a roller until complete.

Painting cabinets. Depending on the amount of surface you need to cover, think about using a **paint sprayer** to paint your cabinets. For smaller jobs, you can use either a paintbrush or a paint roller, but be aware that cabinetry wood is a bit unforgiving and more likely to show brushstrokes or roller marks. Wipe away drips as they occur or they will permanently dry on the surface.

Painting woodwork (windowsills, door frames, etc.). The best way to apply paint to woodwork is with an **angled brush.** Make sure you get the paint into all the cracks and crevices, but make sure it doesn't drip. Masking those areas you don't want to get paint on will speed the overall painting process.

Cleaning up. As we mentioned earlier, clean-up varies depending on the paint. Latex paint only calls for warm soap and water, while oil paint requires mineral spirits or turpentine and plenty of ventilation. Keep in mind that your pots and pans have nothing in common with your brushes, so don't soak them. Soaking can actually ruin the chemical makeup of paintbrushes.

The hardest thing about painting is the time it takes to complete it. But, as you'll quickly see, it can turn drab into fab faster than almost any other home improvement project.

PART II

The Projects

Although the section that follows contains a number of how-to projects, we want you to look a bit deeper. We want you to begin to think about the purpose of doing these projects—the **why-to.** It's the why-to that will inspire you to start each project, and it's the why-to that will help you get to the end. Think of the projects as recipes that will enhance your overall happiness. But as with any recipe, you can deviate a little to make it your own.

We present this collection of projects in a manner we hope will inspire you to reassess your current situation and how much you love where you live. We give them to you within the context of a promise, a promise we hope you will feel has been answered.

We delve into five rooms in a typical home: kitchen, bathroom, bedroom, family room, and dining room. Your home might be similar, or slightly different. For example, your dining room might very well be your family room. The important thing to remember is to try. The very act of changing out a single pillowcase can have a dramatic effect on a room. We know you will see, as we have, that even small changes can make a huge difference.

The projects we've included range from beginner to intermediate, but nothing we don't think you're capable of handling your first time out. We measure the level of each project via the **JQ**, or **Jane Quotient.** The JQ is a quick way for you to discern how much experience or skill a project calls for and how much effort is needed. Although the JQ ranges from 1 to 5, we don't like to say that 1 is the easiest and 5 is the hardest. We know you are 100 percent capable of completing

any project in this book. We just want to give you an idea of how much work is involved with a given project. If you've never tried this type of work before, or if you simply don't have a lot of time on your hands, try a few projects with a JQ of 1 or 2. We can almost bet that the satisfaction you get from accomplishing those tasks will lead to your completing projects with JQs of 3, 4, and 5.

We know your time is valuable, so we include an estimate of the time it should take to complete each project as well. Keep in mind, however, that we use the word *estimate* because every project tends to take a bit more time than you expect. If this is the first time you've ever done any type of home improvement, expect to need time for your learning curve. We also want you to be aware that you may start one project that will spawn two or three others. Don't be concerned if this happens, as it is very common. Just take a deep breath and keep moving forward. You can do this, and you will.

As you'll see, we separate the projects by rooms in your house. We want you to *want* to do these projects, so to make them feel usable, comfortable, and personal, we introduce a bit of reasoning for each. After all, why do all of this work if you don't know why you're doing it?

Another goal is to show you five to ten quick changes you can make in the most important spaces in your house today to make a difference you can see immediately.

Many of these projects are interchangeable. Just because one project is placed in the dining room section doesn't mean it wouldn't be good to do in the living room or possibly even the bedroom. Most of these projects can be done anywhere in your home (with the exception of plumbing, unless you have a toilet in an unusual location).

"As a woman, you either learn you do it yourself or it usually doesn't get done."

Pam H.
Mesa, Arizona
Age 53

"Give a woman a tool and a project and it'll get done."

Carolyn J.
Cleveland, Ohio
Age 39

It's important to note that the results of your efforts will not always meet your expectations. Sometimes you will make mistakes, and sometimes things will go wrong. The important things to remember are to always take proper safety precautions no matter what you do and that *any* mistake you make can be fixed. The more you do, the more you'll know. You'll learn to love phrases like "Caulk and paint will make it what it ain't" or "If it's dark and dented, then paint becomes my saint." You'll learn from your mistakes and you'll solve your problems, and each time it will be easier to do so.

Often the hardest part of home improvement is getting started—hitting the first nail, drilling the first hole, painting the first stroke. With experience comes confidence. With every stroke of your brush, every time you drill a hole, every time you drive a nail with a hammer, your confidence will grow. It may not seem evident in the moment, but you'll soon discover it.

Last, and to reiterate, remember to allot the time necessary to complete a project but to take into account that most projects yield surprises.

Take a few moments and dream up your ideal home. Over the next few weeks and months, do your best to make it a reality. Your house shouldn't be a storage center for your stuff; it should be the place that reflects who you are and how you live your life. You *exist* in a house, but you should *live* in a home. It's time to turn your house into your home.

What are you waiting for? Get started!

Making a Cookable Kitchen

You don't have to be a gourmet chef to enjoy cooking, but you should at least have a cook-friendly kitchen to want to cook, eat, or hang out in. After all, your kitchen is supposed to be the place where you create nourishment for your whole family, both literally and figuratively.

To transform your current kitchen into a *cookable* one, think about the things that might inspire this transformation.

There are four keys to a cookable kitchen. Making your kitchen **aesthetically pleasing** is the first. After all, if you absolutely hate being in your kitchen, how often do you think you'll use it? First and foremost, you should add colors, textures, and a style that will make your kitchen *your* kitchen. Cooking is a process, so make the kitchen a place you enjoy spending time.

Cooking is much more of a pleasure when you can find what you need when you need it —and have the space to store it when you don't. That's why a cookable kitchen is **organized.** Most kitchens don't have enough space. The trick is to utilize the space you have as efficiently and as creatively as possible.

"I used to hate our kitchen— it felt so uncomfortable. I didn't even like to cook in it. It has such a warm feeling now. It gives you a good vibe the minute you walk into it."

Tania T.
Meriden,
Connecticut
Age 35

A cookable kitchen is also **functional.** You need proper lighting, stain-resistant floors, true cutting surfaces, sturdy appliances, and fresh water supplies. Without functionality, cooking is less of a joy and more of a chore.

Last, but most important, your kitchen should be **safe.** Your kitchen is a place of gathering—a place where your family and friends join you while you work. You want to be certain the environment promotes an air of responsibility and care.

The following projects are just a start to help you make your kitchen truly cookable. Try a few—because once you see how they start to improve your culinary cubicle, the thought of going out to dinner might remain just a thought!

Jane Profile

Eden "Jane" Jarrin

Age: 30

From: Vancouver, BC, Canada

Favorite tool: Anything with power! But really—at the risk of sounding boring, I'd say a cordless drill. It's like the little black dress of home improvement; no matter what the project, you nearly always end up using a drill.

Projects accomplished: I have done many types of jobs, from framing a house to removing walls, replacing electrical outlets, and installing dimmer switches and light fixtures. I've redone my kitchen cabinets, constructed and refinished furniture, built a bar, installed baseboard and crown molding, done extensive painting, installed faucets and other kitchen appliances, and more!

Inspiration for starting home improvement: My parents always encouraged me to try anything—at times, much to their regret. No matter what the project was, my mom always used to say, "That's easy! We can do that ourselves!" At age seven, I was redecorating every surface of my tree house (stealing colorful towels and nailing them to the walls). At age nine, I tried building my own four-poster bed (using branches and twigs from the forest, mind you). At age fourteen, my parents let me wallpaper our bathroom (which had to be redone shortly thereafter!), and in college I was redoing my friends' dorm rooms. Each project was an accomplishment that inspired me to continue. When I finally bought my first home, it was like having one giant blank canvas just waiting to be messed with, and I haven't stopped since!

Fears about home improvement: None! Okay, that's a lie. I still have fear at times, mainly when I'm doing a project I've never done before. There's always that feeling of what if I mess this up, what if my husband, Eddie, disowns me, and I have to spend hundreds of dollars to fix it? But now I feel that no matter what it is, I know I can at least give it a try. More often than not, I surprise myself and end up with a project I'm proud to say I did.

How has doing home improvement affected your life? It's given me the belief that if I can do this, then there are other things I can do that I never believed possible. That if someone says I can't do something, that doesn't mean it's true. Just because something is labeled as what I shouldn't or can't do doesn't mean it's off-limits. I also don't feel as powerless as I did before. I'm less afraid of when things go wrong. I'm not at the mercy of some contractor.

How has doing home improvements affected others in your life? I love having the ability to help others see that *they* can create spaces they love to live in. Whether it's my family, friends, or now the hundreds of thousands of Janes who are part of our Be Jane community, I've been able to share the feeling of empowerment that comes from doing home improvement.

Advice for others just getting started in home improvement: Don't worry about "not knowing" or asking "stupid questions." Every professional contractor started at the beginning. So take that first step! If you're a brand-new do-it-yourselfer, try visiting a home improvement store and looking through the aisles, or start by painting something small—a side table or a small room. With each project you take on, your confidence will grow and you'll realize you *can* do this! Next thing you know, you'll be renovating your entire bathroom and wondering, "Why did I ever think I couldn't do this?"

Making Your Kitchen Aesthetically Pleasing

How your kitchen looks affects more than how you feel when you cook in it. After all, how do you think your food will taste if your kitchen doesn't have anything pleasing to feed the other four senses!

Even a few simple changes will make a dramatic difference in the overall feel of your kitchen. You'll not only enjoy cooking in it but you also might even enjoy eating in there, too!

Start by thinking about the focal points of your kitchen. Usually the first things you notice when you walk into a kitchen are the appliances. The refrigerator, the stove, the oven—they all make a statement about the room as a whole.

If your appliances are a little out of date but still functional, you can spruce them up in many simple ways.

Choosing new appliances is never easy. Aside from all of the feature choices you're faced with, there's price, warranty, quality, and possibly just as important, color.

"I desperately need to paint my appliances. I've bought a vacation home that has an UGLY green fridge and yellow oven and stovetop."

Carolyn M.
Pataskala, Ohio
Age 51

Kitchen appliances today are built to last for ten years or longer. But how can you possibly know how your tastes will change over the next seven to twelve years? Well, you can't. Eventually, you're forced to choose a color. But just because your favorite color is red doesn't mean you want it all over your kitchen. Now you know why so many appliances are white.

If you happen to be one of those who chose an avocado green fridge oh so many years ago and now find yourself thinking, "It still works. Do I have to buy a new one?" the good news is that the answer is no. By painting your appliances, you can turn beige to white, or white to green or whatever color you choose.

You can go with solids, or you might decide to become a little artistic. Break the rules. After all, your parents don't live here—and even if they do, this is your kitchen. Make it what *you* want.

Project: Give Your Old Appliances the Look of Stainless Steel!

Jane Quotient: ❶ ② ③ ④ ⑤

Estimated Time: **1 to 2 hours (varies with number of appliances)**

A wide variety of films can be applied to the surface of your appliances to create the look of a vast number of finishes from wood grain to stainless steel. These films are as easy to apply as shelf paper and can last the life of your appliance.

MATERIALS

Tools
- Tape measure
- Utility knife
- Sponge
- Squeegee

Supplies
- PVC or other laminate appliance film
- Degreaser (such as Formula 409)
- Paper towels
- Small needle or pin

1 Measure the surface you would like to cover and add an extra ½ inch to 1 inch to all four sides. We recommend purchasing a roll of film wide enough to cover the face of your appliances in one piece so you won't have obvious seams. Using a utility knife, cut a piece to your specifications.

2 Degrease the surface of the appliance. In order to be certain the film will stick properly, wipe the surface with a solution of mild dish soap or Formula 409 and warm water. Be sure the surface is not oily or greasy to the touch. Once it feels clean, thoroughly rinse the area with clean water and let dry.

"We used to refer to my fridge as the 'ugly duckling.' Now it's the silver swan!"

Kathy M.
San Francisco,
California
Age 31

Review the manufacturer's instructions for any other steps required prior to application.

3 Wipe down the surface with a damp sponge and begin to apply the film by pulling off some of the protective backing. Begin at the top and work your way downward.

STEP 3 Apply the film to the front of the appliance by removing the backing and smoothing it in place, working from the top down. First, go over the surface with a damp sponge; the moisture will temporarily delay the adhesive backing from setting in place, giving you more time to position it correctly.

Remove enough of the protective backing to allow you to work across the entire top of the appliance. The trick is to take it *slow*. Move down the appliance 1 inch at a time. As you apply the film, use the squeegee and the sponge to remove air bubbles. This is key, as air bubbles can affect the outcome.

4 Once the film is applied to the face of the appliance, trim any excess with the utility knife. Remove any visible air bubbles that remain on the surface by pricking them

"My dish-
washer and
my fridge
finally match!"
Susan O.
La Mesa,
California
Age 44

with a pin or a small needle, and then use the sponge or the squeegee to squeeze out any remaining air.

5 Using the same process as above, finish the sides of the appliance, trimming away excess as needed.

Let the film set for 24 hours to give the adhesive time to stick. The good news is that if you don't like the results, you usually have enough time to remove the film before the adhesive sets completely.

Project: Paint Your Appliances

Jane Quotient: ① ❷ ③ ④ ⑤

Estimated Time: 4 to 6 hours (varies with number of appliances and varying drying times)

The following project steps can be applied to a wide variety of appliances, but because it's the most prominent appliance in your kitchen, we focus on the refrigerator.

MATERIALS

Tools
- Screwdriver set (Phillips and flat head)
- Paint sprayer (optional; can be rented)
- Respirator

Supplies
- Drop cloths (plastic and cloth)
- Sandpaper/sanding sponges
- Tack cloth
- Blue painter's tape
- Primer suitable for epoxy paint
- Epoxy paint in your desired color(s)
- Latex or nitrile gloves

1 Before starting, completely empty your refrigerator and keep your food away from paint products.

2 Turn off your refrigerator. Pull up the leveling legs of your refrigerator; these are usually in the front corners and help keep the refrigerator level. Not all refrigerators have leveling legs, but if yours does, screw them up so they're no longer touching the ground. Now check on the bottom of your refrigerator for wheels. Most new refrigerators are on wheels, but few of us know this

Jane Tip:
To avoid hurting the cooling motor of your refrigerator, turn the interior cooling control to the "0" or "off" position prior to unplugging the unit.

little secret. Typically, when a refrigerator is delivered, it is put in its place and its wheels locked. Check underneath and unlock the wheels.

If your refrigerator does not have wheels, you can move it using a dolly or, if you have an old piece of carpet, place carpet strips under the front, pile side down. This will help you slide your refrigerator away from the wall.

Note: Be sure to protect the floor from the weight of the refrigerator by placing cardboard or thin pieces of wood underneath the wheels before moving it. Linoleum and tile floors can tear or crack if you drag your refrigerator across them.

If you have an electric ice maker, disconnect the copper tubing that supplies the water before rolling out the refrigerator. You'll want to be sure that you first cut off the water supply. This might be a valve behind the refrigerator in a designated water supply box or it could be under the sink. Either way, be sure to consult your owner's manual on how to do this, as the process differs by model.

3 Disconnect the power plug and place the refrigerator where you want to work. No matter where you choose, be sure to cover everything you don't want to get paint or dust on; this can be a messy project. In choosing your work area, find somewhere with a great deal of ventilation as the fumes can be toxic. A garage or even outside is ideal, if possible. Remember, though, that if you work in a garage, make sure it doesn't have a water heater or furnace inside. Fumes can quickly become flammable.

4 If possible, remove the handles from the doors, placing all of the screws into a plastic ziplock bag to keep them safe.

STEP 5 Sand down the shine of your refrigerator with either a palm sander or a sanding sponge. Make sure not to use anything rougher than a fine grit; you want to dull the surface and avoid leaving scratches.

5 Using either a palm sander with a fine-grit sandpaper or a sanding sponge, sand all of the areas you would like to paint.

Your goal here is to eliminate or at least

Jane Tip:

FOR STEP 4
If the handles of your refrigerator can't be removed or simply look too difficult to put back in place, mask them with blue painter's tape instead.

minimize the semi- to high-gloss finish of the current paint. This will allow the new paint to adhere properly. Make sure you sand down the finish anywhere you plan to apply paint.

6 Get rid of all of the dust before you begin to paint. Sweep up any on the floor and go over the fridge with a damp paper towel or a tack cloth to remove any dust residue.

7 Don't get paint on the rubber gaskets that seal the doors (it will make them brittle and prone to cracking) or inside the fridge; make sure to cover them with blue painter's tape. You might also want to cover the inside of the fridge and freezer as well as the interior of both doors with plastic. Don't forget to cover the brand's metal tag on the front as well. If you want your fridge to look like it came out of the factory in the new color, you'll want to leave it legible and clean.

STEP 7 Make sure to cover all of the areas of your fridge that you don't want to paint with plastic and painter's tape. Be especially careful not to get any paint on the door gaskets, as paint can affect their ability to make a tight seal.

8 If necessary, using a brush or roller, apply a coat of primer. (Not all epoxy paints require a primer.) Epoxy paints have better adhesive qualities than most paints, and if you properly sanded the area in which you're working, you might be able to skip the primer step. Be sure to read the manufacturer's recommendations on the paint can. If they suggest you use a primer, then you should probably do so, as it will help keep your new paint from flaking off.

When using the primer, be sure to cover the entire surface area, being careful not to create any drips in the paint. Remember, all drips will be visible in the final paint coat, so take your time here. Let the primer dry completely before proceeding.

9 You're ready to paint. When buying the paint, you'll be faced with a few options. Some—but not all—epoxy paints are suitable for painting appliances, and some paints are made specifically for this task. Most appliance paints come in a spray can, as they are usually meant for touch-ups and not a full paint job. You may want to consider using a paint sprayer to apply the epoxy. Doing so will not only minimize drips but make the whole job much faster.

If you've never used a paint sprayer before, be sure to test it out to give yourself the best chance of having professional results. Use an old piece of cardboard or wood to get the hang of the spray gun and perfect your paint stream. Try spraying side to side, keeping your wrist straight and the spray line perpendicular to the painting surface at all times. To avoid overspray and runs, start spraying outside the area to be painted and move

Jane Tip:

FOR STEP 8

If you do end up with a drip on your fridge, quickly wipe it away with a cloth dipped in mineral spirits. Be careful, though, as any texture created by your cleanup may show through in your final paint.

Jane Tip:

FOR STEP 10

If the tape and paint overlap, it might be a good idea to first score between the paint and the tape with a utility knife. This will help avoid pulling off any of the new paint when removing the tape.

across the surface until you are past the painting surface by several inches. Keep in mind, though, that you need to thin the paint before putting it in the sprayer. Ask your paint professional about what to thin it with and at what ratio.

👓 Safety Check

Remember that epoxy paints are highly toxic, so it is essential that you have proper ventilation as you work. Wear a respirator, not just a dust mask or a sanding mask. Wear eye, skin, and clothing protection, especially if using a paint sprayer. These paints are similar to those on your car, so take the proper safety precautions.

Be sure *not* to use a paintbrush, as it will leave brushstrokes behind.

The trick to applying an epoxy paint is to add several thin coats of paint, letting each coat dry before adding the next, instead of one or two heavy coats. Heavy coats tend to drip, and those drips are sure to end up permanently on your fridge. As you work, be sure to have a cloth dipped in mineral spirits at the ready should you need to wipe away any drips. Remember, use light and easy strokes, let each coat dry completely and, you'll do a beautiful job.

10 Once you've applied a few coats, you can let the paint job dry completely. Check the manufacturer's label on the can for drying time, taking into consideration that any humidity in the air will add to this. When the paint is dry, simply remove the masking materials, wheel the refrigerator back in place, and reattach the power and water sources. If you have leveling legs, screw them back down until they meet the floor. Put a level on top of the refrigerator and adjust the leveling legs as necessary.

Project: Paint Your Cabinets

Jane Quotient: ① ② ❸ ④ ⑤
Estimated Time: **5 to 8 hours (varies with number of cabinets)**

Considering that the cabinets are a major focal point of your kitchen, shouldn't they express something other than the fact that they haven't been updated since 1975? One of the most definitive ways to alter your kitchen is by adding a little flair to your cabinets.

Even if your existing cabinets are dented, dinged, and worn, you don't have to replace or resurface them. A number of projects can give them new life without costing a fortune. In fact, one of the quickest, easiest, and most cost-efficient ways to spruce them up is to paint them. By adding a bit of color to an otherwise drab kitchen, you might be inspired to prepare home-cooked meals the entire family will love!

MATERIALS

Tools
- Screwdriver
- Electric palm sander
- Roller or paintbrush
- Power sprayer

Supplies
- Mask
- Protective eyewear
- 120–150-grit sandpaper
- Tack cloth
- Drop cloths
- Blue painter's tape
- XIM primer
- Paint
- Cabinet door magnets

Note: Before starting this project, take a moment to think through your color choices. Remember, this is *your* kitchen. You are limited only by the limits of your imagination. What colors work for you? What about potential color combinations? What unusual colors might make your kitchen truly unique?

"The kitchen cabinets were old, brown, and just plain ugly. I read all the information on refinishing the cabinets and how to sand and paint them. A few days later, I had a brand-new kitchen. It looks beautiful, and my husband and I love it!"

Tania T.
Meriden,
Connecticut
Age 35

If you have some immediate thoughts on color choices but aren't sure, you might try painting a small area and checking it against the rest of the room. Of course, any color you choose means change, and it's human nature to resist change at first. See how the color grows on you. You might create something you never thought possible.

1   Take down all of your cabinet doors. This step is necessary to expose the entire surface area to be worked on: the doors, the door frames, and the cabinets themselves. As you remove the cabinet doors, make sure you mark or number them so you know which ones go where when you put them back up. We call this mapping your cabinets, and it will make the process of putting them back together much easier.

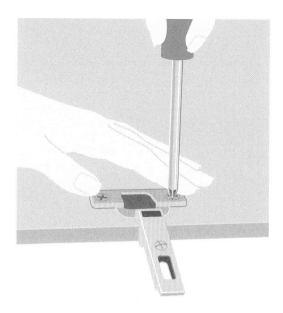

STEP 2 Remove hinges from cabinets and doors by removing the screws with a screwdriver.

2 Remove all of the hardware, such as handles and hinges. Be sure to put all the screws, hinges, and handles you intend to reuse in a safe place.

👓 **Safety Check!**

For the next few steps, make sure you use the proper mask and protective eyewear.

3 Lightly sand the surface with 120-grit sandpaper. This will help the paint stick to the surface (paint retention). After all, you don't want your paint peeling six weeks after you complete the project! If you're working with a Formica laminate, consider using an electric palm sander with 120-grit sandpaper. This will not only drastically speed the process but make the job more fun, too! Remember, though, you don't have to sand down to the wood grain. The idea is to create a surface just rough enough for the paint to stick to. If you don't need to remove a lot of existing material from the face of your cabinets, then use sandpaper with a higher grit number.

Jane Tip:

FOR STEP 2

It's easy to misplace handles and screws, so we suggest using a strong plastic ziplock bag to hold them. If by chance the handles for each door are vastly different from one another, consider marking the bags with the coordinating number you assigned to the cabinet doors and drawers so you'll know which knob belongs where.

Jane Tip:

FOR STEP 3

If you absolutely hate sanding and your cabinets are covered with a smooth laminate, you may not have to sand at all if you can find a primer made for use over laminates. This type of product is a favorite of many do-it-yourselfers because of its ability to go right over smooth surfaces such as clean Formica laminate and even glass. However, as much as we like this product, the best way to ensure solid paint retention is always to lightly sand prior to painting.

STEP 3 Sand the surface of the cabinets with an electric palm sander. Make sure to wear gloves, goggles, and a dust mask to protect yourself, and keep your hair away from your face.

This will prevent you from creating heavy scratches in the wood that will be hard to cover with paint.

4 After sanding, clean the surface with a *clean* tack cloth (a cloth that removes dust, dirt, lint, and sanding residue before and between coats when painting, staining, or varnishing; it usually costs less than a dollar). Now the area is ready.

5 Tape or mask off all of the areas you don't want to get paint on with blue painter's tape. Try not to use anything other than the blue tape, as the adhesive of most masking tapes is too strong and will either pull up the paint or leave a residue that could ruin the job! Protect your floor with drop cloths, attaching them with blue painter's tape.

6 Using a roller or paintbrush, add a single coat of primer. If you have Formica laminate as mentioned above, make sure the primer you use is meant for high-gloss surfaces even if you sanded. Primer goes on just like paint, so whether you use a paintbrush or a roller is up to you. Keep in mind, however, that a roller may not leave the brushstrokes most paintbrushes do. Additionally, using a roller on flat surfaces allows for a more even coat than a paintbrush does. You will still need the paintbrush for detail areas, corners, and edges.

Watch out for drips, as they can dry into the paint and be visible when you are finished.

Safety Check!
Be sure to have proper ventilation in the area you're working in.

7 Let the surface areas you just primed dry the amount of time specified on the primer can—usually 2 to 4 hours, depending on the humidity of the room you're working in. A small fan can sometimes speed the process. Consider lightly sanding with a 220-grit sandpaper to provide a nice surface for your final coat.

With respect to paint sheen, we suggest staying away from flat paints, as most are a pain to keep clean. And aesthetically, they're just not as appealing. Try to stick with a satin or semigloss. In the short term, they're easy to apply, and in the long term, easy to keep clean.

Some people prefer the look of high-gloss paint. Keep in mind, though, that such paints show every mistake you make with the brush or roller as well as every dent or ding in the

Jane Tip:

FOR STEP 6

If you're going to paint your cabinets in a dark color, save a step by having your primer tinted. When purchasing your primer, simply ask someone in the paint department to add enough of the paint color you've chosen, sometimes referred to as the **dark-value base coat** (paint is described in values of colors), to the primer to turn the normally white primer into what's known as a **medium-dark value.**

Jane Tip:

FOR STEP 7

To provide a truly smooth surface for your final coat of paint, consider lightly sanding the paint surface (once dry) between coats with a minimum 200-grit sandpaper.

door. If you go this route, consider applying the paint with a power paint sprayer to help guarantee the best finish possible. If you do use a power paint sprayer (you can rent one at most home improvement centers), be sure to practice with it first to get a feel for it. Also, make absolutely certain you use it with excellent ventilation and while wearing appropriate safety gear (a respirator, goggles, and gloves).

8 Once the primer is dry, apply 2 coats of the paint color of your choice to the cabinets as well as the inside and outside of each door. Allow enough time for drying between coats—usually an hour or two, depending on the type of paint; ask your paint professional or check the can for the recommended drying time.

9 Try to wait at least 24 hours before reattaching the hinges and handles. The paint on the doors and cabinets should feel hard, not rubbery. If you do this task too early, you may dent or otherwise damage your new paint.

10 Using your map, replace each cabinet door and drawer in its respective frame. You may also want to consider purchasing interior door magnets to help keep your cabinets closed. Door magnet sets are typically $1.50 per door, and they add a professional feel to the result.

Project: Add Molding to Your Cabinets

Jane Quotient: ① ❷ ③ ④ ⑤
Estimated Time: **30 to 40 minutes per cabinet**

In a lot of older homes, kitchen cabinets were installed with functionality in mind, but rarely with aesthetics. They were usually nothing more than flat pieces of wood with handles. Adding color to your otherwise drab cabinetry will certainly spruce them up, but to give your cabinets a true sense of flair, add a bit of molding too. This will quickly change the overall feeling of your kitchen. Your cabinets can go from boring flat slabs to beautiful paneled showpieces.

MATERIALS

Tools
- Tape measure
- Electric miter saw or a miter box with a back saw
- Phillips head screwdriver
- Countersetter
- Hammer
- Paintbrushes

Supplies
- Pencil
- Molding (enough linear feet to cover your doors)
- Protective eyewear
- Brad nails
- Spackle or wood filler
- Paint or stain

Jane Tip:

FOR STEP 2
Whenever you are working on a molding project, add an extra 10 percent to your total. This will help you avoid making extra trips to the store in case of mistakes.

1 Start by looking in magazines or at home improvement centers to see what type of finished look you would like your cabinets to have. There are more choices than you might think. This research will not only help you choose your look but also determine the quantities of molding you will need and the types of cuts required to create that look.

2 Purchase the molding. If you prefer a mission style (square and flat), then purchase a 1-inch flat molding and cut it to match the outside edge on the front of the door. If you want a traditional panel look, purchase molding with a more detailed shape. Figure out the placement you prefer (inset an inch or two or along the edge of the door, or get creative and design your own look); this is a matter of taste. Measure the lengths of molding needed for each door, multiply that by the number of doors, and calculate the linear footage needed to cover the doors.

3 If you plan to paint or stain your cabinets a different color, start the process of preparing the surface as discussed in the previous project.

4 To cut the molding, you need either a miter box or an electric miter saw. Remember to use protective eyewear. You may have a bit better control over your cut when

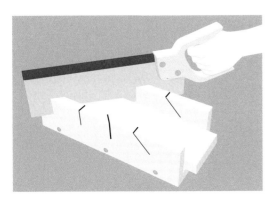

STEP 4 Use a miter box and a back saw to cut the corners at either a 45- or a 90-degree angle.

you do it by hand with the miter box, but the miter saw will be much faster.

The types of cuts you'll need to make depend on the look you are trying to achieve. For example, for a mission look using a flat molding, you should make all cuts at a 90-degree angle, then butt the pieces up against each other using the straight edges.

If you are going for the more traditional panel look, you probably need a raised molding. For precise corners, cut this type of molding at a 45-degree angle. This will create a beautiful finish and allow the edges to come together properly.

5 Attach the cut pieces of molding to the cabinet door. To guarantee proper placement of the molding, it's best to lay the door flat, so use your Phillips head screwdriver to remove the door. The best way to adhere the molding is to nail it in place with brads. A brad is a small headless nail that can be sunk below the wood's surface and covered with wood putty or spackle to hide it completely. This is called **countersetting** your nail. If you use an electric brad/nail gun, this will be automatic, or you can use a tool called a countersetter. You use a countersetter by first hammering the nail as far as you can without

Jane Tip:

FOR STEP 4
Consider gluing the miter cuts together to keep the mitered corners together as the wood settles.

Jane Tip:

FOR STEP 5
If you plan to paint over the molding, consider purchasing molding made of MDF (medium-density fiberboard). MDF molding usually comes primed, which saves you a step, and it's lighter and typically costs less than pine.

marring the surface of the molding, then placing the smallest end of the countersetter on top of the nail and gently hitting it with the hammer.

All you should have left is a small hole to be filled with spackle (paint over it) or wood filler (stain over it). Make sure to fill in any gaps at the corners of the molding with one of these before painting.

If you are staining, apply the first coat of stain before filling the nail holes. This will help them blend and disappear.

STEP 5 Using a countersetter, countersink the nail below the surface, then apply wood putty or spackle to fill in the hole.

6 Complete your project by putting on the finish coat of either paint or stain. If your plans include staining your molding, purchase a higher-quality wood molding with a better-looking grain. Check to see if you prefer the look of your stain on pine or oak, as the same finish will appear differently on each of these woods. If you're not sure which to use, purchase a small piece of each and test the stain to see which you like best. Be aware, though, that stains affect different woods differently. If your cabinet doors are made of oak and you use a pine molding, you might see a slight difference in the color.

Project: Update Your Old Tile Countertops with Concrete

Jane Quotient: ① ② ③ ❹ ⑤

Estimated Time: 6 to 8 hours

Drying Time: Between each coat drying and staining and sealing, close to a week

Another focal point in a kitchen, and probably the most important, is, of course, the countertops. The amount of counter space is obviously crucial, but secondary to how it looks. We discuss ways to increase counter space in the next section.

No kitchen is truly cookable if the countertops are hardly something you would consider putting your food on! If your current kitchen counters are subpar, you can improve them without breaking the bank or hiring a contractor.

Tile counters are common in many kitchens, but tiles break, crack, or get scratched, and usually the grout gets rather dated. Replacing your grout is a great way to spruce up a tile countertop. We do this project a bit later in our Spa-licious Bathroom section.

But sometimes you just want to get rid of your tile all together. Kitchen tile is susceptible to problems such as mold and bacteria growth that make the job of keeping your grout clean almost impossible.

Concrete is a recently popular way to update a countertop. It has been featured in

many magazines and television shows as being both beautiful and functional but usually expensive and requiring a professional to install. But not always. We found a great way to add a thin layer of concrete to an existing tile countertop!

MATERIALS

Tools

- Screwdriver
- Right-angle grinder
- Electric mixing paddle
- Buckets (two 5-gallon, one 1-gallon)
- Drill
- Cement finishing trowel (2 ½ x 12 inches)
- Hammer
- 2-inch paintbrush for stain

Supplies

- Drop cloths
- Brown kraft paper
- Blue painter's tape
- Protective eyewear
- Earplugs
- Respirator
- Heavy-duty cloth or leather gloves
- Portland or hydraulic cement, white and gray
- 90-mesh sand
- Concrete polymer
- Heavy-duty rubber gloves
- Spray bottle with light mist adjustment
- 220-grit sandpaper
- 1-pound coffee tin and lid
- Concentrated concrete stain
- Tile sponge
- Water-based sealer
- Large fan

Jane Tip:

FOR STEP 1
For extra safety, you may want to consider turning off power to the area you'll be working in.

1 Remove all of the outlet and switch covers along the backsplash areas. Mask the outlets and switches themselves with blue painter's tape. Protect the bottom cabinets with plastic drop cloths, attaching them with the painter's tape as well. The floor should be protected too; for this we suggest using brown kraft paper and, again, securing it with painter's tape.

⬯ Safety Check!

Before moving on to step 2, protect yourself. You'll be working with some rather loud machines and potentially harmful chemical dust, so put on protective eyewear, hearing protection, and heavy gloves, and get your respirator ready as well. Ventilate the area by opening the windows. If you have one, bring in a large fan.

2 You need to texture the tile surfaces so the concrete will stick. Use a grinder to remove some of the tile's smooth, glazed surface. We can't stress this enough: Be properly protected *before* getting started, as

STEP 2 Using a grinder, roughen the surface of the tile. Make sure to wear protective eyewear, gloves, and a respirator.

the tile dust is not something you want in your eyes or lungs.

Move the grinder's surface over the tile at a 30-degree angle, going over any area you can reach with it. You can leave a few smooth areas, but there should be more rough ones than smooth. For areas the grinder can't get into, scratch them with the clawed end of a hammer.

3 Mix up a batch of concrete, starting with the dry ingredients. In a bucket, put in $^1/_5$ coffee can of gray cement and 2 cans of white cement. Mix these together well, but don't stir them too vigorously, as the powder can easily go everywhere.

4 For this step, you'll need only 2 cans of the $2^1/_5$ cans you just mixed; the rest can be thrown away. In a 5-gallon bucket, mix the 2 cans of concrete with 2 cans of 90-mesh sand and stir well. In a second 5-gallon bucket, mix 1 can of concrete polymer and 1 can of water. Incorporate the cement and sand into the wet ingredients and stir until the mixture is smooth and without lumps.

5 Before beginning work on the backsplash, lay a piece of brown kraft paper on the countertop below where you will be working. This is to keep the counter's surface free of cement. Put on your heavy-duty rubber gloves and, with the cement trowel, apply the base coat of the concrete to the backsplash. The surface area you should be working on at any one time shouldn't exceed 2 feet. Smooth the areas at the edges to create a uniform look. Your goal in this coat is not an overall smooth finish; this is just the base coat. Expect to see some of the tile definition as well as the grout lines of the tile underneath, but make it as smooth as you can. Making it *completely*

Jane Tip:

FOR STEP 3
One way to get the color you want with more crack and scratch resistance is to buy a pre-measured mix for concrete counter-tops. Quite often these are carried at concrete suppliers in designer colors.

Jane Tip:

FOR STEP 4
Mixing up any type of cement-based substance can be tiring if done by hand. Try using a **mixing paddle;** simply attach it to your drill and blend. Think of it as a really large cake mixer. Make sure your drill has at least a $^1/_2$-inch chuck to fit the paddle and is at least 18 volts, as cement can be taxing to a less powerful drill.

STEP 5 **Apply the base coat of cement to the backsplash, putting a piece of kraft paper down to protect against drips.**

smooth is the purpose of the second coat. Keep the coat as thin as you can while still covering the existing tile.

Once you've completed the backsplash, remove the brown kraft paper and do the same thing to the countertops, but not all the way up to the edges.

6 Here's where you need both creativity and patience: the edges. Begin by putting concrete all along the trowel, holding it faceup and against the vertical edge of the counter-top. Your next move depends on the type of edging you currently have.

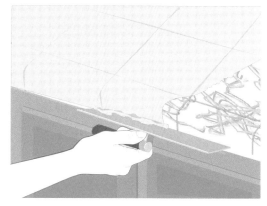

STEP 6 **Begin applying the cement to the edge by dragging the loaded trowel up and over the bullnose. If your counters aren't bullnosed, pull the trowel straight up.**

Bullnosing, or rounded edges, will require you to begin to apply the concrete and follow the shape of it by rounding up and around the edge. While square corners begin with the same approach, do not roll over the edge; instead, pull the trowel straight up, and then do the same thing with the top part of the edge to fully cover the corner.

Let the base coat dry completely. It's best to wait overnight before going on to the next step.

7 To make sure your finished countertop is smooth, sand the base coat with a 220 fine-grit sanding sponge or sandpaper, focusing on areas that are rough. Then moisten the base coat by spraying a light mist of water over it to help the next coat adhere. Mix up a second batch of cement and apply it to the backsplash and countertop in the same manner.

8 Cover the edge with the same technique you used when you worked on the first coat. If you have rounded edges, once you've applied the cement to them, use a flat piece of plastic from the coffee can lid or a plastic milk carton, wrapping it around the corner and dragging it down the counter toward you. This will help you create a smooth, rounded

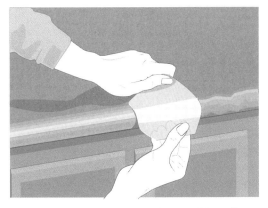

STEP 8 Using the flat part of a coffee can lid or milk container, round the cement over the bullnosed edges for a smooth, rounded finish.

Jane Tip:
FOR STEP 6

An easy way to dipose of the extra cement is to leave it in the bucket until almost set, and then flip the bucket over and hammer the cement into pieces if it's too heavy to get rid of as it is.

Jane Tip:
FOR STEP 10

Don't freak out if the color of the stain isn't the color shown on the container. Applying this stain to the cement precipitates a chemical reaction between the cement and the stain that causes the right color to appear. You should, however, see how intense you want the final color to be by trying out a bit of the stain on cement leftovers. If you want a softer look, add a bit more water. For a more concentrated look, add less water. Remember that this is a stain and not paint, which means the surface will have a patina, or a mottled look to it. It works like a stain on wood; some areas thus appear deeper than others.

finish. If the cement is too tacky and the plastic won't move smoothly, spray it just enough for a slight sheen and then finish the edges. If you have the opposite problem and the cement is too wet, wait a few minutes for it to slightly dry out and then continue.

9 Let the second coat dry overnight and then sand any areas that feel rough to the touch. If the coverage is yet to be complete, or if the finish isn't exactly how you want it, mix up a third batch and put it on in the same manner you did the first two coats. Let it dry overnight and sand any areas that need it. Remember, this is a surface you will be cooking on for quite some time, and the results of skimping on it will be with you for years to come, so take your time and work to a point you're happy with.

10 Using a glass bowl that won't be used in the kitchen for food, mix the concrete stain with water at a ratio of 1 part water to 10 parts stain.

👓 Safety Check!
Remember, most concrete stains are highly toxic, so be sure you're wearing the proper eye, skin, and lung protection and that you have as much ventilation as possible.

11 Begin the staining process by covering the countertop with plastic and applying the stain to the backsplash in a circular motion. Then move on to staining the countertop itself and the edges. Make sure you are wearing heavy rubber gloves and have a bucket of water with a tile sponge nearby. Any drips will be visible in the final product, so you may want to ask someone to help you while you stain by watching for drips and wiping them up with a well-rinsed sponge as soon as they happen.

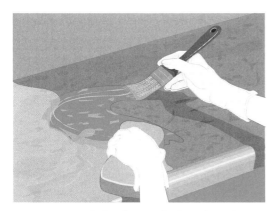

STEP 11 Use a paintbrush to apply the stain to the concrete in a circular motion.

12 Wait 48 hours, and then remove any residue by wiping down the surface with a damp sponge. All that's left to do is to seal the countertop with a sealer you can place food on. This is typically water based and is available at most home improvement retailers.

"It sounds silly, but I recently realized I could change the color of my home to fit my tastes. The fact that I did it myself without any help made me feel so good!"

Tamara C.
Easly, South
Carolina
Age 28

Project: Add a Backsplash

Jane Quotient: ① ② ❸ ④ ⑤
Estimated Time: 2 to 4 hours (depending on surface area)
Drying Time: 3 to 5 days

One of the least appetizing things you see in many kitchens are walls near the sink or stove that have all kinds of food, filth, oil, and water stains on them. A lot of it is simply because it's not an easy area to keep clean, and it's usually an area that takes significant abuse.

One easy and creative project that will add both beauty and utility to your kitchen is to install a tile backsplash. This will protect against countertop spills that would otherwise stain or warp your wallboard and at the same time increase the cozy flair of a truly cookable kitchen.

MATERIALS

Tools
- Tile cutter (or wet saw)
- Tape measure
- Chalk line
- Notched trowel
- Level
- Rounded stick
- Float
- Rubber mallet or blue painter's tape
- Sponge

Supplies
- Plastic tarp
- Denatured alcohol
- Coarse sandpaper or sanding block
- Stone or porcelain tiles
- Mastic adhesive (use Thinset for stone)
- Spacers
- Grout
- Grout sealant
- Lint-free rag
- Gloves

"I love the way the backsplash in my kitchen gives it such a homey feeling."

Karyn M.
Vancouver, B.C.
Age 50

Note: Before getting started, look through magazines and go to showrooms to see what you really like. Get tile samples to take home to see how well they match your kitchen right now. Remember that this may not be an extremely difficult project, but it is one you probably won't redo for many years to come, so you'll want it to make you feel good about being in your kitchen.

You might consider getting a little creative and adding a mosaic or pattern to your backsplash. Draw your ideas and see what you come up with! If you have children, get them involved by painting a few of the ceramic tiles before you install them. Even though a backsplash is functional, it can also be fun.

Keep in mind that we're using ceramic tiles for this particular backsplash. Although you can use other materials, ceramic tiles are exceptionally durable and lightweight, meaning you won't have to install an extra support mechanism or be overly concerned about maintenance.

1 Remove everything from your countertops and cover them and your stove with plastic tarp to protect them while you're working. If there are electrical outlets or wall switches in the area you're working in, be sure to turn off the power to that area and then remove any electrical outlet covers and set them aside.

2 Go over the walls with denatured alcohol to remove any oils. For increased adhesion, sand the walls with a coarse sanding block or sandpaper. Wipe down the area with warm water and allow it to dry completely.

3 Lay out your tile pattern. Be creative, as you will probably be looking at this tile for quite some time.

Depending on the size of your tile and how extensive your design, you may need a tile cutter (which cuts porcelain), a wet saw (which is made for stone but cuts it all), or both. (You can usually rent a wet saw for $50–100 per day.) Score or cut your tile to size using the tile cutter. If you can't get a clean cut, use the wet saw. Be sure to score on the back side if possible, as you won't want your cut lines to be visible.

When laying out the pattern, start by deciding how high you want the backsplash to go, and then find the exact midpoint of the area you will be working on. If this is where you want your pattern focus to be, then move out from there. The easiest way to do this is with a tape measure and a chalk line. Snap a line at the very top so you know where you can put the adhesive up to, as well as at the exact middle. To find this, snap a horizontal line across in the middle and a second, vertical line in the middle. Where these two lines intersect is the exact center of the area.

Jane Tip:

FOR STEP 3

If you don't have enough counter space to completely lay out your pattern, buy a roll of kraft paper and cut a piece to the exact dimensions of the space you are working with. Lay out the pattern on the paper exactly as you plan on laying it, tile spacers and all.

If you plan to move your tile off of the kraft paper before laying it, then, using a pencil, draw an arrow indicating the orientation of each tile. Also, number each piece in the order in which it goes. Use the pencil on the back of the tile only, as it might not come off later.

Jane Tip:

FOR STEP 4

Spread only as much adhesive as you can cover with tile in 10 minutes (usually 3 x 3 feet). If you have precut your entire pattern, you can start from a corner. Otherwise, start from the middle. Don't forget to use spacers when putting your puzzle together on the wall.

4 Now you're ready for the messy stuff! The adhesive you're going to use is easiest to buy premixed, but it typically costs more that way. Apply the adhesive to the wall with a notched trowel like you're spreading peanut butter on toast. The notched trowel ensures even distribution and increased suction when you place the tiles—hence the reason for the square notches out of the edge. Hold the trowel at a 45-degree angle and spread a thin layer (approximately $1/8$ inch deep).

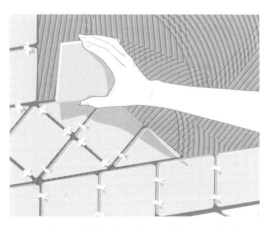

STEP 4 **After applying the Thinset with a notched trowel, place your tiles in it, using spacers to guarantee proper spacing. Lay them out the same way you did before.**

5 Position the tiles by putting the first tile in the center at the base of the backsplash, using a slight twisting motion. Once it is set, place a spacer at each corner of the first tile and then cut one end of the spacers off to fit them between the countertop and the bottom of the tile. You can then push the spacers into the adhesive. Be sure to wipe away any excess that squeezes up along the sides.

While you are putting the tiles on the adhesive, periodically check to see if they are level. Use your level for this task, even if the tile looks level. If you find your pattern isn't level, you can still move the tiles around until the adhesive sets. If you find the adhesive is set more than you would like, pull off the tile, scrape off and discard the adhesive below it, and put down some new adhesive. Then just try again.

If you're having trouble getting the tiles to stay up, gently tap them into place with a rubber mallet. This helps add to the suction you are trying to create with the adhesive. If that doesn't work, use blue painter's tape to keep the tiles in place until the adhesive is dry, then remove the tape. Leave your backsplash alone for 24 hours to allow the adhesive to dry.

6 Now you are ready to grout. First, remove all the spacers. Mix up the grout according to the instructions on the bag. Hold the rubber grout float at a 45-degree angle and move it diagonally across the tile face. This will force the grout between the tiles. You can apply this stuff all over the tile until the spaces are full. Run the rounded stick on top of the grout to help shape it.

If you've used a highly polished stone or ⅛-inch spacers between each tile, then we suggest using a nonsanded grout. If you've used anything larger, use a sanded grout. Be careful, though, as sanded grout can easily scratch a well-polished surface.

Jane Tip:

FOR STEP 5
Use an old paintbrush and cut off the bristles, leaving 1 to 2 inches of bristle. Dip the brush in water and use it to help clean out any excess Thinset between the tiles.

Jane Tip:

FOR STEP 7
In order to prevent cracking, especially with larger grout lines, spray the grout with water in a spray bottle twice a day for the first three days. This way the top won't dry fully before the rest does.

STEP 6 Once you've applied the grout, quickly remove any excess from the tiles before it fully dries. Do this with a damp sponge. If you wait too long, the grout will dry on the tile surface and ruin your beautiful new backsplash.

Use a clean, damp sponge to wipe off any excess grout on the tiles before it gets a chance to dry. This may take several passes. Rinse the sponge between passes.

7 The grout will take 72 to 96 hours to dry completely.

8 Grout can be extremely susceptible to stains, so be sure to seal it. Most sealers require a 7-to-10-day waiting period after you've grouted before applying.

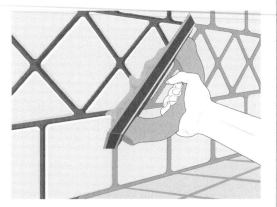

STEP 6 After mixing up the grout, apply it to the surface of the backsplash. Hold the grout float at a 45-degree angle to get the best retention in the grooves.

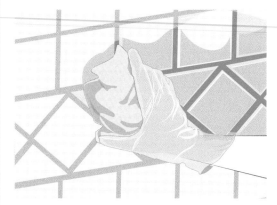

STEP 8 Apply sealer to the entire backsplash with a lint-free rag or a paintbrush. This will help protect it and allow you to enjoy it for years to come.

Jane Profile

> I have learned not to say "I can't" no matter what it is.

Juanae "Jane" Barkley

Age: 25

From: Detroit, Michigan

Favorite tool: I love my electric screwdriver the best. Sometimes when I can't find my husband to help me unscrew this or that, I use a power tool to be my strength.

Projects accomplished: When we bought the house, not only did we paint a few rooms, we also took wallpaper down and put tile up. For myself, I built my own version of a California Closet system in the master bedroom. One of our Christmas presents to ourselves was building our own fireplace mantel. Everyone else's favorite is my yellow-striped room.

Inspiration for starting home improvement: My husband and I bought our first home last year. When we moved in, there was a lot to do. Not only did we have the inside of the house to do, there was landscaping to complete in the front and back. Everyone kept telling us it would be a few years before we would have it all done, but I just couldn't wait that long. I began doing things even before we moved in. I had been watching all of those fix-it shows on TV, and I knew my house could be like the homes featured on the shows. What inspired me to do the things in my house the most was that I wanted to have company over and be able to show them a nice place that was truly *mine*.

Fears about home improvement: I was afraid that I would totally mess it up and not be able to fix it. Even more, I was afraid I would hurt myself, especially with power tools, or that my husband would come home and wouldn't like what I had done.

How has doing home improvement affected your life? It has made me feel like I can do anything and that I want to do more. It makes me want people to come over to my house and see all the work I've done. I love it when they come over and I get to tell everyone, "I did that!" It's even affected other parts of my life as well because no matter what it is, I think, "I can do it!" I have learned not to say "I can't" no matter what it is.

How has doing home improvements affected others in your life? No one could believe we were so young and still have accomplished all of the things we did to make our house a home. Our family is so proud of us. After visiting my house a few times and seeing how easy it was to change things, my aunt designed her own library with custom-built shelves. She says if I can do it, she knows she can too. My mother and her sisters tell everyone they need to see what I've done in my house. Friends and family come over to see what I've done and then want to do it themselves.

As for my husband, he always says it's "interesting" to come home to see what's different that I've done —though he's threatened to lock out all of the home improvement/decorating channels on our television so I won't get any more ideas!

Advice for others just getting started in home improvement: Read up on what you want to do. Make sure you know what you want the outcome to be, and even have an alternate if something doesn't go as planned. Make sure you clean up before, during, and after, and don't forget to take pictures before and after from the same angle. This way when people come to your house, you can show them exactly what you've done!

Figure out exactly what you want to do, plan what you want it to be when you're done, and then do it!

Creating a Functional Kitchen

Your kitchen must be functional to operate well. You need to have more than just running water or a stove that works. Start looking around your kitchen and find what's not working.

Functionality of a kitchen begins with light. Without proper lighting, it doesn't matter what you're cutting, chopping, or dicing—you won't be able to see it. Improper lighting in your kitchen can actually be hazardous.

But beyond the practical applications of light, there are aesthetic elements as well. You want a kitchen that's not too bright but not too dim either. You definitely want to be able to work, but you don't want to feel like you're in a hospital emergency room.

> "I have inspired my friends to do it themselves instead of hiring someone."
> Ana R.
> Worcester,
> Massachusetts
> Age 48

Project: Change Out Your Fluorescent Light Box

Jane Quotient: ① ② ③ ❹ ⑤
Estimated Time: **2 to 4 hours**

Many of the kitchens built in the 1970s and '80s feature a drop-down fluorescent lighting system. These units, although bright, don't offer much in the way of décor. They often make a kitchen look small and sterile, and the fluorescent light itself does little to improve the look of your food. The good news is that there is an easy way to remove these units without an entire structural redo.

With a little **cable lighting** (which can be purchased inexpensively at places like Ikea), you can design your own lighting pattern that not only provides direct lighting for specific task areas within the kitchen but also has the effect of drawing the eyes upward, thereby enlarging the overall sense of space.

MATERIALS

Tools
- Ladder
- Drill
- Electrical tester
- Power screwdriver
- Wire strippers
- Putty knife
- Sanding block
- Paintbrush or roller

Supplies
- Safety glasses
- Spackle
- 220-grit sandpaper
- Primer
- Paint
- Cable lighting kit

👓 Safety Check!
Before you begin, be sure the power to your kitchen light fixture is off. Don't just turn it off at the switch. As always, turn it off at the source—the panel box. Also, be sure to wear safety glasses during this project. Any time you work above your head, you run the risk of dust or other materials landing in your eyes. So take care, and be safe!

> "I love the look of natural light, especially in my kitchen. It does wonders for my cooking!"
>
> Stacey A.
> Dallas, Texas
> Age 36

1 Since you'll be working overhead, be sure to wear safety glasses throughout the project. Begin by removing the old plastic panels. You're probably never going to need them again, so you can discard them.

2 Most lighting systems of this nature have a metal grid holding the panels in place. Take out this metal grid support and then remove the metal surround that borders the soffit as well. Discard.

3 Using your electrical tester, check again to be absolutely sure that the POWER IS OFF. Then remove the old fluorescent bulbs and put them aside.

4 Remove the housing for the unit by unscrewing any screws holding the fixture in place. Be careful when removing the last two or three, as you don't want to misjudge the weight of the unit. Be sure you're on a sturdy ladder and can support the weight of the fixture prior to removing it. You may find you have to disconnect the wiring prior to removing the fixture as a whole. Untwist the wiring to remove the unit completely. Observe how each wire is connected—like color with like color. At this point, all you should have remaining is the wires coming from the ceiling.

5 Patch any noticeable holes with spackle and let dry. Once the spackle is dry, sand smooth all surfaces with 220-grit sandpaper in a sanding block.

Note: You might find that this area may not have been completely finished by the original builder. To properly prep this area for paint, you may need to apply a coat or two of drywall mud (sanding in between coats) to get a smooth finish.

6 Determine what color you want your new extended ceiling recess to be. You can go dark for a dramatic effect or lighter for a more subtle look. A lot will depend on the overall size of your kitchen. Once you've chosen a color, prime the space and then paint two coats, with ample drying time in between. Remember, however, that this is a ceiling, so be sure to choose wisely when it comes to the sheen of your paint. A high-sheen paint (such as a semigloss) will reflect the light, giving your ceiling a heavy glare. It's often best to use a flat paint on the ceiling. For more on setup and painting techniques, see the Painting Basics section on page 33.

7 Shop! Go to your local home improvement or home décor store and select a cable lighting system that suits your taste.

8 Remember in high school geometry class when you were saying, "Why do I have to learn this? I'll never use it!" Well, you were wrong. Because now you determine the pattern you want your for cable lighting system. You could simply do two parallel strips and direct the lighting to its desired destinations, or you could do something a bit more geometric such as an *X* shape or a diamond shape. It's completely up to you.

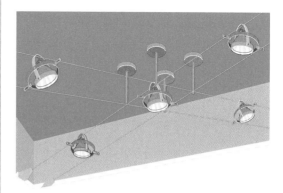

STEP 8 Try out different geometric configurations for your cable lighting system. Find the one that optimizes the amount of usable light.

👓 **Safety Check!**

Be sure to read the lighting manufacturer's recommendations on maximum cable length for your lighting system. Also, be sure to check the maximum number of units attached to a single unit. There is a potential fire hazard if you exceed the recommended limits, so check carefully.

9 Once you've determined the configuration, mark your cable contact points within the recess and begin stringing the cable using the wall hooks provided.

10 Install the transformer of your unit according to specifications on the package. The wiring to the transformer of the cable unit will be the same as it was to your old light fixture. Simply match like colors with like and if necessary, use your wire strippers to expose a bit of the copper wire. Then simply twist the ends together and cover them with a wire cap. Black wire to black wire (hot), white wire to white wire, and green or copper wire to green or copper (ground) wire.

11 Once your transformer is firmly in place, attach it to the cables you strung in step 9. Again, refer to the manufacturer's specifications for exact details based on the particular product you purchased.

12 Determine where and what the individual lights will highlight and position them on the cables. Puncture the cable plastic sheathing by tightening the screws on the lighting fixtures themselves. Again, your particular product might have slight variations, so be sure to check the

Jane Tip:

FOR STEP 10
Although most of the cable lighting systems work the same way, always be sure to review the manufacturer's instructions for specific tips and precautions you'll want to be aware of when installing your unit.

manufacturer's instructions. Position the lights to focus on specific areas of the kitchen.

13 Turn the power on and test your lights. If they're working, then jump for joy: You did it! If the lights don't go on, simply turn the power back off and troubleshoot by rechecking your wiring to the transformer.

14 One great way to finish off your lighting recess is with decorative molding around the border. This will frame your new lighting accessory. Paint or stain the molding to your liking. If you stain, be sure to finish it off with a few coats of polyurethane to protect the wood.

Project: Install Under-Cabinet Lighting

Jane Quotient: ① **②** ③ ④ ⑤

Estimated Time: 1 hour or less

The most common task lighting in a kitchen is under-cabinet lighting. This not only supports the functionality of your cookable kitchen but also adds that bit of flair that raises it above the everyday. And it's easier to install than you might think.

MATERIALS

Tools
- Cordless drill with Phillips head bit (or Phillips head screwdriver)
- Hammer

Supplies
- Plug-in light kit
- Pencil
- Screws
- Masking tape
- Horseshoe nails (brad nails) or picture-hanging nails

"I'm thrilled to have found BeJane.com because I need all the support I can get to take care of this big house of mine."

Mary R.
Bellingham,
Massachusetts
Age 55

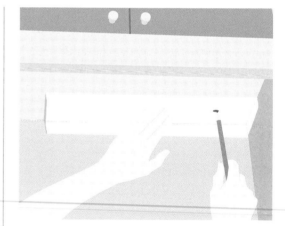

STEP 3 Hold the light in the position you would like to see it attached, and then mark with a pencil on the underside of the cabinet where the screws will go.

1   Remove everything from the cabinet where the light will be attached.

2   Pull everything out of the box with the plug-in light. Familiarize yourself with the components, and thoroughly read the manufacturer's instructions.

3   Place the light under the cabinet in the exact position you wish to install it. Be sure an available outlet is close enough before going any further. Once you've determined this, put pencil marks on the underside of the cabinet where the screws will go (see illustration). (There will be two to four obvious spaces on the light that the screws will be drilled into. If you have trouble finding these spots, refer to the directions included with the plug-in kit.)

4   Use your drill and the screws that came with the kit to drill small starting points on your marks. If you have hardwood, the power drill will make the job easier.

5 Align the light to the markings underneath the cabinet. Hold the light in place with one hand and use your other hand to drill the first screw into place.

Depending on the weight of the light kit, you might use a bit of masking tape to hold the light in place while you screw it in.

6 Put in the rest of the screws to firmly secure the light to the cabinet.

7 Run the electrical cord to the outlet. Before plugging in your new light, secure the cord to the wall. If no clips or horseshoe nails (small nails in the shape of a horseshoe that have sharp points at both ends) were included with your lighting kit, you can use small picture-hanging nails.

Try to tuck the majority of the cord out of view. Usually you'll be able to secure it behind the lighting unit either on the underside of the cabinet itself or against the back wall where it meets the cabinet. Use the nails to secure the cord by placing them just underneath and then bending them over the wire to hold it in place. Be careful not to puncture the cord or to squeeze the wire with the nail. The goal is merely to hold the wire against the wall and out of the way.

Jane Tip:

FOR STEP 5
Many screwdriver head drill bits are slightly magnetized to help you hold the screw on the drill as you work.

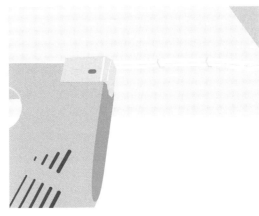

STEP 7 Keep the cord out of sight by attaching it underneath the cabinet with horseshoe nails. You can put them in with a hammer or an electric staple gun that shoots horseshoe nails.

If you're using horseshoe nails, place the cord where you want it, set the nail over the cord, and hammer it into the cabinet or the wall, being sure to leave a little space (the thickness of a pin) between the cord and the top of the nail. Should you make a mistake, use a pair of pliers to remove the horseshoe nail, and put it in another place. Continue nailing the rest of the cord until you get to the outlet. Let the wire drop straight down to the outlet.

8 Plug in your new unit and flip on the switch!

Project: Install a Garbage Disposal

Jane quotient: ① ② ❸ ④ ⑤
Estimated time: 1 to 3 hours

One luxury that makes cooking easier is being able to put your scraps down the drain. There are few things worse than digging food out of your sink and drain basket, and the smell of decomposing food in the garbage can is no better.

Installing a garbage disposal can take care of many of these issues, and you can do it in a few hours. The only prerequisites are a normal-size drain opening, enough room below the sink for the disposal to fit, and an electrical plug below the sink that is attached to a toggle switch (most homes are built with one).

If you've got all three of these, then the toughest part is deciding what type of disposal you need. If you have a septic system, make sure you buy a disposal that is compatible with it. We recommend buying a 1 horsepower disposal rather than a $^1/_2$ horsepower model. Not only will it work better but also it typically has more insulation and is less noisy.

MATERIALS

Tools
- Pipe wrench (water pump pliers will also work)
- Bucket
- Screwdriver
- Putty knife

Supplies
- Plumber's putty
- Garbage disposal with all the parts
- Appliance cord (most units do not come with one)
- Wing nuts

Jane Tip:

FOR STEP 2
If the parts don't come off easily, use a large set of channel lock pliers to pry them loose.

1 Make yourself room to work. Clear out anything you don't need from under the sink. Remove the P-trap under your sink by using a pipe wrench (or water pump pliers) to loosen the two connections—one just past the P-trap and the other just before it. Once they are loose, pull off both the P-trap and the drainpipe leading to it from the sink. Have a small bucket handy to catch any excess water.

2 Unscrew the nuts holding the strainer body in place under the sink. The strainer body should come off easily, as should the sink flange, which is the piece sitting in the sink itself. Use a flat head screwdriver to pry it up and then scrape up the old plumber's putty left behind with a rigid putty knife.

STEP 3 When installing the mounting ring, alternate tightening each screw to create a good seal.

3 Apply a bead of plumber's putty to the underside of the new drain flange. Press it in place using even pressure. Attach it with a fiber gasket, backup ring, and mounting ring; some also have what's called a *snap ring*. These items probably go on the flange in this order, but follow the manufacturer's instructions included with your kit if they are different. The mounting ring should have three screws in it to screw all of these items down.

4 Attach the disposal to the mounting ring while keeping the disposal outlet directed toward the drainpipe. To lock it in place, turn the lower part of the disposal ring clockwise until the lock catches and the weight is fully supported by the sink. Remember, there are three rings that the disposal clips in to. Make sure all three engage or you will have leaks!

Jane Tip:

FOR STEP 3

Screw each screw in slightly and continue around until the mounting ring is securely seated at the base of the sink. If you tighten one screw all of the way and then try to do the others, you won't end up with a proper seal.

Jane Tip:

FOR STEP 4

If you have a dishwasher, make sure to purchase a disposal that has a knock-out for it. Make sure you knock it out with a screwdriver and attach the discharge line from the dishwasher.

STEP 4 When you are attaching the disposal to the mounting ring, make sure the outlet is facing the drainpipe.

5 Attach the disposal's discharge tube to the P-trap. Cut the pipe to the right length and attach it with wing nuts. You may need to offset the garbage disposal drainpipe a bit to get the pipes to fit again. Make sure all the pipes slope toward the drainpipe in the wall, otherwise the sink will not drain properly.

6 Tighten the mounting lug with the special wrench that came with the disposal. This will lock it in place. Check to make sure all of the screws are tightly in place. Then plug in the disposal and turn on the water to see how it works and to check for leaks.

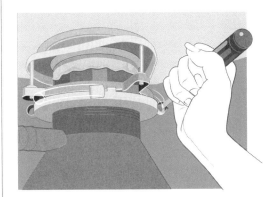

STEP 6 Tighten the mounting lug with a screwdriver of the special wrench that came with the disposal to lock it in place.

Project: Install a Wood Laminate Floor

Jane Quotient: ① ② ❸ ④ ⑤

Estimate Time: 7 to 10 hours

One area of a cookable kitchen that is often overlooked is the floor. The problem with many types of flooring is that no matter how often you clean, they never seem to *look* clean. The floor in most kitchens takes quite a bit of abuse, not only from the walking back and forth from stove to fridge but also from the food, utensils, plates, and glassware we drop on it from time to time. Needless to say, the floor in your cookable kitchen must be prepared.

MATERIALS

Tools

- Tape measure
- Utility knife
- Pry bar
- Protectant polyurethane film
- Wood floor planks (laminate)
- Circular saw with a carbide blade
- Installation spacers (¼ inch)
- Miter or chop saw
- Tapping blocks (commercially purchased or cut from a piece of 1 inch x 1 inch)
- Hammer
- Pencil
- Jigsaw (possibly)
- Chalk line
- L-iron (or specialized hook iron, designed to tap the laminate into place in tight corners or against the wall; most efficient when purchased commercially)

Safety Items

- Safety glasses
- Knee pads
- Tool belt
- Gloves

Jane Tip:

FOR STEP 2

Allow laminate planks to acclimate to the temperature and humidity of the room they will be laid in. To do this, leave the planks in the room, opened, for at least two days. This will allow the planks to expand or contract *with the environment.*

1 Nowadays, most laminate floors come in planks. To know how many planks are needed, measure the area of the room. To do this, measure the length and width of the room and then multiply. This gives you the square footage of your room. If your room is not perfectly square or rectangular, calculate the square footage of the inset by multiplying its length and width, then subtract that square footage from the total area of the room.

2 Purchase enough flooring to cover 110 percent of your floor. For instance, if you have 200 square feet, purchase enough planks to cover 220 square feet. The box of laminate flooring tells you how many square feet it will cover.

3 If you are laying your laminate where carpet currently resides, remove the carpet, the padding, and the tack strips (use the pry bar for this). If you are laying your flooring onto cement, wood, or tile, sweep clean the surface.

4 Remove the existing baseboard. The baseboard is the wood at the base of your walls that frames your flooring. It is attached to the wall with nails and, sometimes, caulk. If yours has caulk on it (caulk is a white toothpaste-like substance that fills the space between the wall and the baseboard), cut it off with the utility knife. Face your knife down and press it on the caulk. Move the blade parallel to the floor, starting in one corner of the wall and finishing at another.

Place your pry bar (preferably one with a thin lip) between the wall and the baseboard. As when cutting caulk, start in one corner and work your way to the other. Next, pry the wood away from the wall by pushing the bar toward the wall. It's best to start from a corner to avoid damaging the parts of the wall that aren't backed by a stud. If you want to save these baseboards and reinstall them after laying the laminate, be careful not to break them during the prying-out process. About every 10 inches, pry the baseboard away from the wall. Do this until you come to the corner. Once you've finished one wall of baseboard removal, continue until all of the baseboards are removed.

5 Lay the protectant polyurethane film (also called underlayment) on the floor. You will need to measure and cut the film to fit the floor. Some laminate floors come with the protective film already sealed to its underside. It's worth your time and money to purchase this type of flooring, which will save you both the time to install the protective film and the cost of purchasing it. When it comes attached to the planks, purchasing the exact amount needed is guaranteed. If you do purchase the laminate with the polyurethane protectant film attached, you won't need the protective film—that is, unless you are laying your laminate flooring over cement. In this

Jane Tip:

FOR STEP 4

While working on your baseboards, try sitting on a skateboard and pushing yourself from one side to the other. It makes the job go by quicker and is a lot of fun!

Jane Tip:

FOR STEP 8

Due to the different temperatures and climates your home experiences during the year, you need to leave a $1/4$-inch gap between the floor and the wall. (Your baseboard will go over the flooring and attach to the wall, thus covering this space.) This $1/4$-inch gap allows the floor to expand and contract without buckling.

case, the extra polyurethane protection helps block the moisture the cement gives off.

6 Now you'll have to determine which direction you want the floor to run. Most are laid lengthwise, which is the direction of the longest part of the room. However, you can choose differently based on preference, the design of the space, or necessity.

7 Stand in the center of the room facing one of the walls the floor will run perpendicular to. Look to the left corner in front of you: That is where you will lay your first plank. Make sure to read the instructions that come with the flooring, as they will help you with this step. Also, some flooring instructions call for starting in the right corner.

8 Use a circular saw to remove the tongue from the first plank so it can lie against the wall. Lay down your first plank. As this is a floating floor, lay it directly on top of the existing flooring (or protective film)—no screws, nails, or glue needed! Remember to leave at least $1/4$ inch between the wall and the first plank. The easy way to guarantee this is to use $1/4$-inch installation spacers. Make sure that the flooring is completely parallel to the longest wall in both directions. If the floor starts to drift, the angle will become more apparent as you move down the line.

9 Attach the second plank to the bottom of the first plank. Push the top of the second plank into the bottom of the first (you may need to push a little harder than you expect). Place the second plank lengthwise at a 45-degree angle to the first plank; push into the first plank's end and then lay it on the floor. Remember to leave a $1/4$-inch space between the side of the second plank and the wall it runs parallel to.

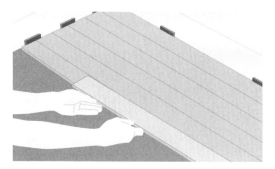

STEP 9 Insert each plank at a 45-degree angle to the one previously laid.

10 Continue this process with more planks until you reach the end of the row, meaning you run into the wall opposite to the wall you started on. Until you hit the end of the row, you should not have to cut any planks. You may get lucky and be able to lay down exactly seven planks, but it's unlikely.

11 Cut the last plank of the first row to size. First, of course, you have to figure out how long the plank should be. (Remember—measure twice, cut once.) Measure the distance of the space between the last plank you laid and the wall. Subtract $1/4$ inch from that length (to allow for the $1/4$-inch space from the end of the plank to the wall) to calculate the length of the last plank. If the total distance is $12\,1/2$ inches, cut your last plank to $12\,1/4$ inches in length. This is a job for your miter saw.

12 Lay your second row. Because planks come in predetermined lengths of about 48 inches, make sure the seams alternate from row to row. The seams run perpendicular to the planks and are the space between the bottom of one plank and the top of another. Alternating the seams is more aesthetically appealing. Because your planks run lengthwise and the seams are perpendicular to them, placing the same size planks at the top of each row would create a line across the width of the room.

Jane Tip:
It's not mandatory, but wearing canvas or leather work gloves when working with wood laminate floor planks will keep your hands free from injury.

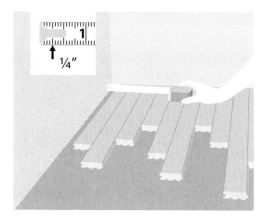

STEP 12 Make sure to alternate the seams of the pieces so you don't end up with one long seam. Be careful to lay the wood $1/4$ inch away from the wall.

To prevent the seams from lining up, use the leftover piece of the plank you cut at the end of the first row to begin the second row. Using the same example as above, if you cut off and used $12\,1/4$ inches of a 48-inch plank, the remaining plank would measure $35\,3/4$ inches. Use that $35\,3/4$-inch plank as the first plank in the second row, leaving $1/4$ inch between the wall and the top of the plank. Connect this plank to the very first plank you laid. Angle the plank beginning the second row by placing it at the side, pushing it into the first plank, and then laying it on the ground. Remember, you may have to use a bit of force to lock it into place.

13 Lay the second plank in the second row. (This is the first plank of many that must attach to two or three planks at the

STEP 13 Use a tapping block and a hammer or rubber mallet to help force all of the pieces of wood together.

same time, meaning it will attach to two sides—its top and left.) Angle this second plank down toward the first row, on its left. Attach it to its side partner and then to its top buddy. Before inserting this plank into its left neighbor, make sure you get its top as close to the one above it as possible. Push the angled plank into the planks on the first row. Lay the plank flat, parallel to the floor, and push it into the top plank on the second row.

14 Continue laying the planks until you finish the room, being sure to fill in doorways at least halfway—that is, if you have another type of flooring outside the room. Otherwise, you can fill in the doorways completely and keep going.

15 When you get to the last row, you will have to do some cutting. The best way to know what to cut is to place the planks in a row all the way across. They won't fit, so you'll have to lay them on top of the last row you laid. Create a template to know the width you'll want the planks to be; use a piece of scrap. Pencil in where you want the cut to be. Remember to take into account the width of the tongue, so place it against the wall when you measure

Jane Tip:

FOR STEP 13
These planks attach together using a bit of force. They don't just lay together like Lincoln Logs or pieces of a puzzle; they attach more like LEGOS. If you are having trouble pushing a plank into the plank above it, try using a tapping block, a rubber mallet, and some elbow grease. Place the tapping block on the bottom lip that will be inserted into the next plank. (Don't tap on the top laminate part because you could damage the flooring where it would be seen.) Hammer the block with a few forceful blows until it locks into the plank above it.

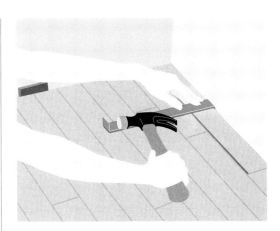

STEP 15 Placing the last piece of laminate flooring can be tricky. One great Jane tip is to use an L-iron and a hammer to help all the planks join together properly.

Cut with your circular saw on your pencil line. This will be your template for measuring the rest of your pieces for the last row.

Having laid laminate flooring ourselves, we can tell you what a gratifying sensation it is to look at a gorgeous floor and say, "Hey, I did that!" If it's too intimidating to start on a 200-square-foot kitchen, try the hall closet and work your way up. It's so much simpler, though, showing off a floor in an open space than closed up in a closet. So, go ahead—have faith in yourself, grab your miter saw, and get flooring.

Jane Profile

Be patient, and don't be afraid to try something new.

Lydia "Jane" Contreras

Age: 25

From: Escondido, California

Favorite tool: My favorite tool has to be my electric drill. I love the power I feel when I'm using it. I'm not afraid to make holes in my walls. I love putting furniture together just to use my power drill.

Projects accomplished: My former roommate and I bought a house together when we were 24. We did some small home improvements, including painting one bedroom and both bathrooms. But my biggest and most recent home improvement occurred after she bought a house of her own and left me the one we had bought. I had to get rid of some gross, dingy carpet, and I decided to lay laminate wood floors. After being quoted a price and then having it almost double during the estimate, I decided to take on the project myself. I bought all my materials from Home Depot and did a lot of research on the Internet. I called on some friends and my boyfriend to help. We started on the Saturday before Memorial Day and didn't finish until the following Saturday. We moved furniture, pulled out the carpet, got rid of the popcorn ceiling (as all the furniture was out of the way anyway), painted, rolled out mats, measured and cut boards, and laid out a beautiful new floor. It's not perfect, but I am very proud of myself and the wonderful work we did.

Inspiration for starting home improvement: My own perseverance, but female superheroes also inspired me. They could defeat the bad guy, just like their male counterparts.

When I bought the house, it was a nice house, but it needed work. I wanted to make it a nice home, possibly for a future family. It's as simple as the fact that I wanted to beautify my home.

Fears about home improvement: My biggest fear was that it wouldn't come out right, that it would be completely messed up and I would have to hire a professional to come in and fix it.

How has doing home improvement affected your life? I feel empowered by it. Growing up, I would ask my mom for help, and she would always say, "Wait for Dad." It made me mad because I felt like I needed her and she wasn't there for me. It may seem trivial to most, but that changed when I moved out and had to put together my first computer desk. Being able to put it together really made me feel empowered. The little stepping-stones of putting together my furniture helped me along the way, and now I have my own home and I don't need my dad or the help of a man to get things done. I would have to say it is empowering across all levels of my life.

I work in an office of all women, and when they need manual labor done they come and get me.

How has doing home improvement affected others in your life? I never would have expected that my doing home improvement would have added a new level of respect between me and my fiancé, but it has. He is proud of me and impressed by what he's seen me accomplish. He knows that I am with him because I want to be, not because I need to be.

Advice for others just getting started in home improvement: Be patient, and don't be afraid to try something new. It may take time, but it can be done. You get such a sense of accomplishment once you've finished a project!

Organizing Your Kitchen

For many of us, organization is the key to success. It helps us locate what we need when we need it and not spend a lot of time wishing we could find something that has seemingly disappeared.

Most restaurant kitchens have clear systems in place for everything. Restaurant chefs know their kitchens inside and out, including the location of everything in them, or else the evening's shift will be harried indeed. For your kitchen to be cookable, you need the same sense of efficiency.

There have been many developments in organizational systems lately that make them easy to install and customize to your needs. We think you'll find that a little organization

"I'd probably cook at home more often if I could find my cookware. Or my plate. Or my food!"

Ginny K.
Norfolk, Virginia
Age 33

goes a long way toward making cooking enjoyable.

Accessible counter space is crucial in a cookable kitchen. Unfortunately, there is all too often not enough of it. Many of us have small, cramped kitchens with limited counter space. Much of this is due to clutter—utensils, small appliances, spice racks, and the like.

One of the fastest ways to improve your cooking ability is to give yourself ample room to work. Because much of the clutter on our countertops is the result of poorly organized cabinets or drawers, this is easier to fix than you think. Organizing and rearranging your kitchen items can have a dramatic effect on the amount of space you thought you didn't have.

Project: Install a Pot Rack

Jane Quotient: ① **②** ③ ④ ⑤
Estimated Time: 1 to 2 hours

As we mentioned earlier, an organized kitchen is a successful kitchen. If every object in your kitchen has its own place, you're more likely to use it and never misplace it again.

Hanging a pot rack is a great way to maximize storage in a small kitchen. In a larger kitchen, a pot rack gives a bit of flair and can focus an otherwise empty space. All of those pots and pans eat up valuable cabinet space that can be used for food, spices, and utensils. A pot rack is a simple solution with great aesthetic appeal and installing it is easier than you think.

When shopping for your pot rack, you will find countless options. Be sure to take into consideration the style and size that will work best in your kitchen. Should you have a very traditional kitchen, then a stark, sleek, modern rack will look out of place. If your kitchen is the size of a coat closet, an extra-large pot rack will not be a good choice either.

MATERIALS

Tools
- Tape measure
- Stud finder
- Power drill with screwdriver bits
- Screwdriver

Supplies
- Safety glasses
- Pencil
- Hanging ceiling pot rack kit
- Cardboard sheet (the box the pot rack comes in should suffice)
- Blue painter's tape

Jane Tip:
Be sure to ask the salesperson how much weight your pot rack can hold.

1 Decide where you want the pot rack to go, taking the following factors into consideration.

- Make sure you have enough space from the ceiling. Obviously, if you have an island, above it is the ideal place for installation.

- How high are your ceilings? You don't want your pot rack hanging too low. Not only is it a hazard, it could make your kitchen less attractive.

- A pot rack is quite heavy when fully loaded, so be sure to properly secure it to the ceiling joist (see step 3) and not just to the drywall.

2 Since you'll be working above your head, remember to wear your safety glasses. Once you've decided where to place your rack, measure the area and take these measurements into the store with you when you buy your rack. This will ensure that you purchase a pot rack kit that will fit into the space.

3 Use the stud finder to find the studs—which, in the ceiling, are called ceiling joists. You will be attaching the hooks to these to help support the weight of the pot rack. Do not hang a pot rack into plain drywall. Drywall will *not* support the weight.

4 With a pencil (so you can erase it later), mark the location of the ceiling joists. Use the stud finder and mark off where the joists start and end, widthwise (usually 1½ inches). Once you find one, you can measure 16 or 24 inches in either direction to find the next one. You'll also want to determine which way the joists run.

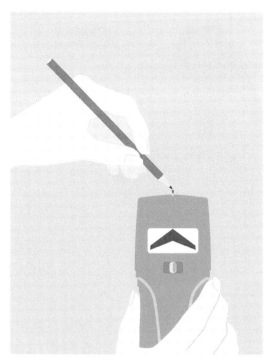

STEP 4 **A stud finder can also find the joists in the ceiling.**

Jane Tip:

FOR STEP 5
Preassembled kits are often missing a key piece, such as a screw or nut. Be careful if replacing these pieces that they have the same strength and durability as the pieces the manufacturer included.

5 Take the pot rack components out of the box and get familiar with them. Look at the bits and pieces in the kit and make sure you have all the pieces the instructions say you should have. Read through the instructions to learn what each piece is and what it does.

6 Lay out the rack on the cardboard. Draw a template of the rack on the cardboard. Then, make holes on the template where the hooks will be hung. To do this, place the rack on the template. With a pencil, mark on the cardboard where the hooks are located; this is where you will make the holes in the cardboard template. The holes should be large enough for your pencil to go through.

7 Tape the template to the ceiling where you intend to install the pot rack. Line up the holes on the template with the center of the width of the ceiling joists. Mark the spots on the ceiling with the pencil through the holes on the template. Remove the template from the ceiling. You should also find a reference wall and measure equal distance from the wall to the two holes on one side of the pot rack. This way the rack will be parallel to the wall and not look crooked.

8 Create holes for the hooks to go into by drilling starter or pilot holes in the ceiling using the recommended size drill bit. Check the instructions to know which size you'll need. Drill the holes slightly smaller than the size of the screw.

9 Screw the hooks into the pilot holes in your ceiling. This can be a little tough, as you can't drill them in. When the going gets tough, try to slide a screwdriver through the opening of the hook, and with one hand grab the handle and with the other grab the screwdriver end and twist the hook into place.

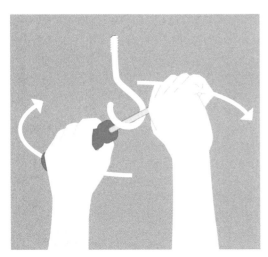

STEP 9 A trick to screwing a hook into your ceiling is to place a screwdriver through the hook and use the handle and metal piece to twist it into place.

10 Attach the chains, and then attach the rack. Because the rack itself may be quite heavy, don't be afraid to get someone to help you lift it. Let go of the rack slowly to ensure it is properly supported.

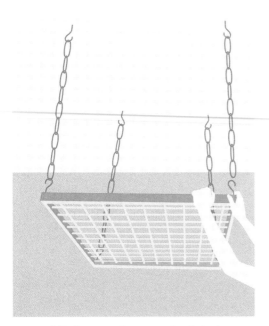

STEP 10 Lift the pot rack up on to the chains by attaching them to the hooks. You may want to ask for help when you do this, as the rack can be heavy.

Jane Tip:

FOR STEP 11
To help keep your cookware clean and ready for display, consider purchasing a cleaning product called Barkeeper's Friend. It doesn't scratch your cookware and does a fantastic job of removing burned-on foods and stains.

11 Hang the pots, and admire your handiwork!

You are now officially allowed to go shopping for beautiful cookware to show off on your new rack!

Put a Lid on It!

Now that you've got your pot rack in position, think about this: What the heck do you do with the lids? Just putting them in a drawer is annoying and chaotic. They sit one on top of the other, jam the drawer, and end up requiring a huge effort just to pull out.

The good news is, a number of lid holder organization systems are available that can slide right into an existing drawer or cabinet. They might be as simple as a wire rack that stacks your lids vertically, or sophisticated systems attached to gliders that let you slide the drawer in and out of your cabinet. Either way, these are easy systems to install, usually no more labor than attaching a few screws. Which one you choose will depend largely on the cabinet or drawer space you have available.

You can take measurements and even a photo of the area you're thinking about and bring them into your local home improvement center so one of their experts can lead you to exactly the product you need.

Jane Profile

Make it your own—put your signature on it, and be proud to tell people "I did it myself!"

Kyra "Jane" Randall

Age: 46

From: Lake Charles, Louisiana

Favorite tool: A drill! I can put anchors in the wall to install shelving and hang just about anything on the walls.

Projects accomplished: I redid the guest bathroom, taking out the old vanity and replacing it with a pedestal sink. I replaced the light fixtures in the bathroom, and then retextured the walls and painted. I also recently put in solar lights.

I am currently redoing my bathroom. I am changing out the sink and updating it to my tastes.

Inspiration for starting home improvement: To be honest, it was mainly money reasons. When I bought my first house, I didn't have the finances to hire someone. I figured this way I can get exactly what I want and I don't have to pay someone $500 to do it.

Fears about home improvement: My biggest fear was that I would really mess something up or that it wouldn't turn out right and I won't like the end product. That I would be totally wrong and not be able to finish what I started.

How has doing home improvement affected your life? I definitely have more confidence in myself now. And it's really empowering to know that if there's something about my home that I don't like, I can change it!

How has doing home improvement affected others in your life? My best friend and I bought houses at the same time. While she's married and can ask her husband to help her, I told her a lot of it is pretty simple if you just read the directions, go to the stores, and read some books. She took my advice and put a fountain in her living room and finished painting her house lots of bold colors. While she's had the most obvious effects from it, I recently watched my daughter take down the wallpaper in her room (by herself) in a matter of a few hours. She's since gone to the home improvement center and picked out the wall color she wanted. She approaches her projects with a "Yeah, we can do this, it's not a big deal" attitude. I love that!

Advice for others just getting started in home improvement. Know your limitations. Know when to get help. Other than that, have fun! Make it your own—put your signature on it, and be proud to tell people "I did it myself!"

Just do what makes you feel good. You can always fix something you don't like and it's often easier than you think, so just go for it!

Creating a Safe Kitchen

Study after study has shown how many accidents happen in the home every year. The kitchen is often the source of many of these avoidable incidents.

Safety in the kitchen should be a top priority. There are so many simple things you can do to minimize the potential hazards in the average kitchen, such as cleaning up spills when they happen, using proper protection when handling hot food items (and no, a wadded-up dishtowel is not

"We used to refer to our kitchen as the little house of horrors."

Navarra O.
Chicago, Illinois
Age 34

proper protection), and using your oven and stove only when you're in their immediate vicinity.

Cooking and home improvement are similar in that you must pay attention to what you're doing. Cooking while you're tired, emotional, or distracted adds to its potential dangers.

A cookable kitchen is a safe kitchen, so look around, assess the hazards, and see what can you do about them right now.

Project: Install a Knife Drawer Organizer

Jane Quotient: ① ❷ ③ ④ ⑤

Estimated: **2 to 3 hours**

There are smaller hazards you might not at first consider, such as the storage of your knives. Are you blindly reaching into a utility drawer to find a knife when you need it? Eventually, the odds will catch up with you. Remove that danger right now.

If you don't have a butcher block knife set, or you have one but would like your counter space back, a knife drawer organization system is perfect. It will help protect both your hands and the blades of the knives themselves.

MATERIALS

Tools
- Tape measure
- Clamps
- Circular saw

Supplies
- 1-inch-thick maple, oak, or cherry wood
- Safety glasses
- Gloves for woodworking
- Wood glue
- Sanding block
- Tack cloth
- Polyurethane/primer and paint

Jane Tip:

FOR STEP 1
Use a C-clamp or a bar clamp to hold the wood in place while cutting.

1 Measure the inside of the drawer that will house your knife organizer and then transfer the measurements to the wood. Once you're sure, clamp down your wood and make the cuts with your circular saw. Make sure to wear both safety glasses and proper-sized gloves while cutting. You may also want to use a sanding mask, as circular saws tend to raise quite a bit of sawdust.

2 Measure, mark, and cut 2-inch-wide strips from the wood with the circular saw. They should be half the length of the drawer you are making this for. Glue these pieces down with wood glue, keeping them all on one side of the base. They should be attached on the 1-inch side and stand up 2 inches. Decide how many openings you want and will fit your drawer. Glue the pieces with about $\frac{1}{4}$ inch in between each.

To guarantee proper drying, place a second piece of plywood on top and clamp the top and bottom together.

STEP 2 **After applying the wood glue, clamp a second piece of wood on top with two clamps.**

Jane Tip:

FOR STEP 2

You may want to leave a gap on one of the sides large enough to hold kitchen scissors or other utensils with sharp blades that won't fit in the ¼-inch openings you made.

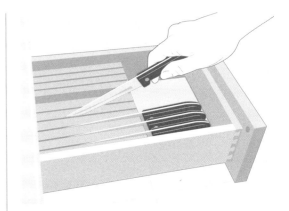

STEP 4 **Place your knife organizer in the drawer with the wooden pieces toward the back.**

3 Once the glue is dry, sand all of the edges smooth with a fine-grit sandpaper and sanding block. Decide if you want to urethane or paint; the choice typically depends on the finish of your cabinets. For the organizer to look like it came with the cabinets from the factory, the finish should match. Go over the surfaces with a tack cloth before applying urethane or priming.

If you plan to use urethane, apply 2 or 3 coats, letting each coat dry before applying the next. Be sure to use a natural bristle brush to apply it, as urethane can melt some synthetic brushes. If you plan to paint, begin by applying a coat of primer and then 2 coats of paint.

4 Place your new knife organizer in your drawer with the wooden pieces at the back. Insert the knives with the blades toward the back and enjoy easy access to the handles.

If you have high-quality knives that call for more than an everyday sharpening, check with your local hardware store for someone in your area who professionally sharpens knives. You can also check with a local restaurant to find out who sharpens its knives, as most restaurants use this service. If this is the route you choose, don't forget to bring along your scissors, too!

Keep Your Knives Sharp

One of the things that adds to the enjoyment of cooking is having sharp knives. This doesn't mean you need to go out and buy a new set of expensive knives; there are other options. First of all, you can sharpen knives yourself. Most knife sets come with a rod sharpener. Simply hold the blade against the rod, blade facing you, and drag it along the rod by pulling it away from you. To extend the life of your blade, make sure you do this in only one direction. Flip the knife over and do the other side for an even sharpening. Wipe any residue off the blade with a clean, damp cloth before using.

Many electric can openers come with a knife sharpener in the back. All you have to do is run your knife through it a few times. Be careful not to push too hard, as you don't want to damage the blade.

Project: Install a GFCI Outlet

Jane Quotient: ① ② **❸** ④ ⑤
Estimated Time: 1 to 2 hours

One of the biggest dangers in a kitchen is that you are often around water and electricity at the same time. You can remove the danger of an accidental shock simply by installing what's known as a **GFCI outlet.**

GFCI stands for "ground fault circuit interrupter," which means there is a small circuit breaker in the outlet that will trip the switch—instantly cut off the supply of power—anytime there is a surge of electricity. More than likely, you've already seen these outlets if you've stayed at a hotel in the last few years. They look just like regular outlets, only they have Test and Reset buttons (usually red and black) on their face that "pop" should a surge occur.

GFCI outlets are easy to install and can be installed in any room where water and electricity coexist and may meet.

If the idea of protection isn't enough to motivate you, this fact may: Most state building codes now require GFCI outlets in the vicinity of a water supply. Not that you have to worry that a building inspector will randomly come into your house, but if you're looking to sell your home, you may be required to complete this project before putting it on the market.

MATERIALS

Tools
- Electrical tester
- Screwdriver
- Lineman's pliers
- Needlenose pliers

Supplies
- Electrical tape
- GFCI outlet

"Electricity still scares me, but at least I know it's something I can work with."

Patty A.
La Mesa,
California
Age 37

1 As with any electrical project, begin by turning off the power to that outlet and ensuring that it's off. You can do this by flipping the breaker into an off position or, if you have a fuse box, removing the fuse completely. Be sure to either lock the electrical panel or tell everyone in the house not to turn on the power while you're working. That's a surprise you can do without.

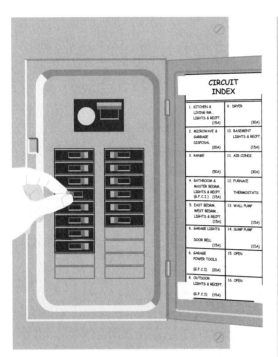

CIRCUIT
INDEX

1. KITCHEN & LIVING RM., LIGHTS & RECPT. (15A)	9. DRYER (30A)
2. MICROWAVE & GARBAGE DISPOSAL (20A)	10. BASEMENT LIGHTS & RECPT. (15A)
3. RANGE (50A)	11. AIR CONDI. (30A)
4. BATHROOM & MASTER BEDRM., LIGHTS & RECPT. (G.F.C.I.)	12. FURNACE THERMOSTATS
5. EAST BEDRM., WEST BEDRM., LIGHTS & RECPT. (15A)	13. WALL PUMP (15A)
6. GARAGE LIGHTS DOOR BELL (15A)	14. SUMP PUMP (15A)
6. GARAGE POWER TOOLS (G.F.C.I.) (20A)	15. OPEN
8. OUTDOOR LIGHTS & RECPT. (G.F.C.I.) (15A)	16. OPEN

STEP 1 Begin by turning off the breaker or removing the fuse from your electrical panel.

2 Go back to the outlet you'll be working on and double-check to be sure the power is off using a voltage or electrical tester (we prefer a penlight electrical tester, which is easier to use and safer overall). Once you are *sure* that you've turned off the power, it's time to get started.

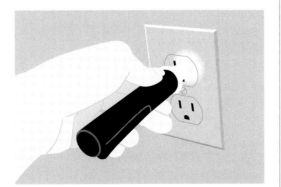

STEP 2 Before getting started, use an electrical tester to make sure the power to the outlet is off. We prefer a penlight tester, as all you need to do is insert the tip into each of the two slots; if the tester doesn't light up or chirp, then the power is off. But if the light goes on, as in the picture, it's *not safe* to begin your project.

STEP 2 If you prefer to use a regular electrical tester to check that the power is off, you can use it with the outlet still in or with the wires exposed. Regardless of how you check for the power, if the tester lights up, it's *not safe* to proceed.

3 We know working with electricity is scary. The good news is that, as we mentioned earlier, electricity works like water; once it's turned off, it's off, and the area is safe.

Begin by unscrewing the outlet plate and the two screws that hold the outlet itself into the wall. They are easy to find once you take off the outlet plate. There is one on the top and on the bottom. Once you've removed them, the outlet should be loose. Pull it out of the junction box (the plastic or metal box it's sitting in). The tension you might feel is normal; it's just the stiffness of the copper wiring. Remove the outlet by loosening the

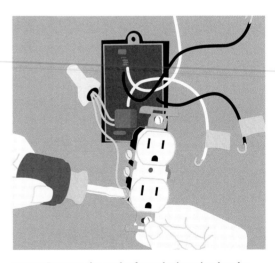

STEP 3 Remove the outlet from the junction box by unscrewing the screws from the top and the bottom. Make sure to mark the hot black and white wire with a piece of tape to make installing the GFCI easier. Release the wires by unscrewing the terminals that hold them in.

screws that hold the wires in place. Make a note to remember what terminals the existing wires are connected to. This will make installing the new outlet much easier.

4 This is where you'll find out if the outlet is in the middle of a series of outlets and switches, or at the end. The easiest way to tell is by the number of wires attached to it. If it has only three wires, it is the end of a run of outlets and/or plugs. The other possibility is five wires, which tells you that your outlet is in the middle of the series.

Find out which of the sets of white and black wires are hot, or the source of electricity for that outlet. To do this, pull apart the wires that were attached to the outlet so that none are touching (even green or bare copper ones). Then turn on the switch at the breaker box.

Now *very carefully* check with your electrical tester to see which wires are hot. *Never, under any circumstances, touch the wires with your fingers unless you're absolutely certain there is no power running through them.* Once you've figured this out, return to the breaker box to *switch it off again.* Put small pieces of electrical tape on each of the wires so you won't get confused when you are installing the new outlet.

5 To wire a GFCI, there is a "line" and a "load" marking on the back or side. The bottom screws are the line, meaning this is

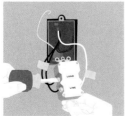

STEP 5 Place the hot and neutral wires on the terminals marked "line," and if you are working with five wires, place the other two on the "load" terminals.

Jane Tip:

FOR STEP 6

Don't be surprised if this is harder than you expect. Copper wires are quite hard to move around. Have patience and get the outlet mostly pushed back into the box. Unless you have a really deep electrical box, it probably won't go in easily and you will have to finish by screwing it in place. Make sure to lightly tighten one screw and then go back to the other. If you screw one in completely and then try to do the other one, it won't work.

Jane Tip:

FOR STEP 6

One way to prevent shorts is to wrap electrical tape around the entire outlet and across the screws before placing it in the electrical box.

Jane Tip:

FOR STEP 7

If your outlet was in the middle of a string of connected outlets, check to make sure they all still work. If they don't, turn off the power to the outlet and go back to step 4.

where power should be coming in. There is a spot for the black wire (copper screw) and the neutral or white wire (silver screw). The load is the top of the GFCI and that allows anything down the line to be covered by one GFCI breaker.

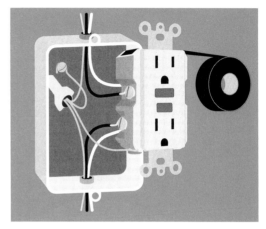

STEP 6 To help the wires remain in place, wrap electrical tape around the outlet and across the screws.

6 Put the new GFCI outlet into the electrical box and put in the two screws to hold it in place. Don't forget the outlet cover to make the job complete.

7 Check to see if the outlet works by turning the power back on and then pushing the red Test button on the outlet. If all is well, you should hear a small click or pop that is the noise of the small circuit tripping inside the outlet. Push the Reset button and plug in a small appliance or radio to see if the outlet works.

After completing a project like this, you've truly accomplished something. After all, electrical work can be scary. We hope that by getting through this project you start to develop a sense of confidence, which will help carry you through to your next big project. But remember, be *confident*—never cocky. Cockiness leads to carelessness, and when you're doing home improvement, carelessness can be dangerous.

Creating a Bedroom for Romance

Ah . . . romance. The word conjures images of being swept off your feet and whisked away to an enchanted evening of starry-eyed love. Silk sheets, rose petals sprinkled across your pillow, magnificently scented candles, and your favorite music playing gently in the background while you gaze lovingly into the eyes of your mate. What more could a girl want?

These days, most of us are lucky if we have enough energy at the end of the day for a goodnight kiss. But what if you were able to create an atmosphere that fostered a romantic mood? After all, it doesn't matter if you're single, in a relationship, married, or divorced, your own space in which to indulge in romance is good for the soul.

Because the bedroom is usually where you experience your most intimate moments, it's also the place where romance likes to live. Whether you want to heat up your love life or create a place to indulge all on your own, a romantic bedroom is a luxury every woman should have.

Most people need to be comfortable to feel romantic. A room that is dirty or cluttered can be distracting rather than inviting. The lights need to be able to dim, the bed needs to feel welcoming, and the room should be orderly.

"My husband and I seem to cuddle a bit longer in the morning ever since I repainted our bedroom. Makes me wonder what'll happen if I put in a dimmer!"

Michelle L.
Mountain View,
California
Age 40

A romantic bedroom should represent who you are either as a person or as a couple. You can start making it do so by painting the walls a color you both enjoy. And because there's nothing like the fear that your child will barge in unannounced, make it a private enclave by adding locks on the doors. How about your windows? The idea that your neighbors might be able to see in can kill a romantic moment in a hurry.

Ultimately, though, a romantic bedroom has to be *romantic*. It must be a place that fosters the growth of romance and then maintains it. It is a retreat, a place you can both go to get away from the rest of the world and get back to focusing on each other.

Remember, romance doesn't just help to build love—it preserves it.

Jane Profile

Don't be afraid to try it.

Wendy "Jane" Waldrep

Age: 53

From: Rochester, Michigan

Favorite tool: Router. It turns a piece of wood into an object of art.

Projects accomplished: I gutted three bathrooms, took them down to the 2x4s, and redid every element of them. I also redid my kitchen. I put in new countertops and cupboards (although the cupboards still need to be finished). I am very proud of the 7-foot oak wet bar I built. I live in a condo with no fireplace, so I designed and put in a direct vent fireplace with a marble surround and oak top.

Inspiration for starting home improvement: My inspiration was really just the need to get things done. I was always fascinated by tools and watching my uncle, who could create everything and anything. My father didn't know which side of a hammer to use.

Fears about home improvement: That little bit of dread of when you go ahead and cut copper pipes. I knew that if I didn't get it perfect, someone might not be taking a shower later on. I always had that little voice in the back of my head saying, "I hope I put things back together how they should be."

How has doing home improvement affected your life? There is a saying I really like that goes, "If you can conceive it, you can achieve it." I can visualize taking a room or project to the next level. I have no formal plans, no blueprints, just a vision in my head. So by living by that quote and seeing my vision come to life, it has made me more confident that whatever obstacle comes my way I can most likely overcome it. There are high mountains in life, but there are paths that we can take to overcome them and be successful.

How has doing home improvement affected others in your life? Because at least half of their lives I've been a single mom, it has taught my kids that there's really nothing they can't do. They aren't afraid to tackle any home improvement job—electrical, plumbing, fencing. They even helped put in drywall. I don't think there's anything they are afraid to try. They've never seen anything they'd be afraid to tackle.

Advice for others just getting started in home improvement: Don't be afraid to try it. Hey, I didn't come from a father who was handy. But I learned that the only way to guarantee failure is not to try. When someone asks you, "What makes you think you can do this?" answer them with, "What makes you think I can't?"

Creating a Personal and Private Bedroom

Many of us have busy, fast-paced lives, and it is difficult to find our romantic side. We need a place that reflects who we are at our core. All day long we rush from here to there, getting done what needs to be done, rarely taking the time to think of what *we* might need.

A romantic bedroom is more than just a place to share with your significant other. It's a place to be safe, to reconnect with who you are at the most intimate and personal level.

When you create a romantic bedroom, you create a place that reflects your tastes in a way that reminds you of you through each of your senses. You reawaken parts of you that are often forgotten. This will become your private hideaway.

Whether you're staring into your neighbor's kitchen, the sun wakes you up every morning at five, or you want a little flair for your bedroom, putting up curtains is a quick and simple project you can do in less than an hour.

One of the many wonderful things about curtains is the wide variety of styles and colors available in fabrics from over-the-top silk crepe fit for a queen to basic cotton. But the choices don't end there: You still have to decide how you want to hang them. The standard way is with a basic curtain rod—although we say "basic," we don't mean it literally. Today you can choose curtain rods made of painted wood or brushed metal, rods with ornate finials (end pieces) that act as jewelry for your room, and many more sorts and styles.

Project: Add New Curtains to Your Bedroom

Jane Quotient: ❶ ② ③ ④ ⑤
Estimated Time: 1 to 2 hours per window

The key is to determine your needs and the style of drapery that suits you. Are you looking to add a bit of romance or glamour? Do you want to soften the look of the room with floor-to-ceiling fabric? Or do you just want to black out your windows so you don't wake up before the roosters? Whatever the reason, you'll love the look and functionality of your new curtains.

MATERIALS

Tools
- Tape measure
- Stud finder
- Cordless drill
- Level

Supplies
- Pencil
- Curtain rod
- Hardware (included with curtain rod)
- Curtains

Note: If the manufacturer's instructions are included with your curtain rod kit, be sure to follow them closely throughout.

"Blinds are great because they keep people on the outside from looking in. But curtains are better because they look great when you're on the inside looking out!"

Kimberly A.
Denver, Colorado
Age 51

STEP 1 Measure your window, allowing an extension of at least 2 to 4 inches on both sides.

1 Before you set out on your shopping spree, measure the width of your window at the top as well as the height. If you're installing the curtain rod outside the window frame, you'll want it to extend 2 to 4 inches *past* the width of the window. Decide if you want your curtains to hang from just above the window to the floor, to just cover the height of the window, or to dramatically fall from ceiling to floor. In any case, measure the height you want to cover. Once you have these measurements in hand, you're ready to shop for curtains.

2 The best place to install the brackets that hold the curtain rod in place is into the wall stud that surrounds your window. By anchoring the curtain rod in the wood stud instead of just screwing it into drywall or plaster, you won't have to worry about the weight of the curtains pulling out the curtain rod over time.

Hold up the curtain rod in the location you want to place it, then use a stud finder to locate the wall studs. With any luck, the wall studs will coincide with the screw holes of the curtain rod brackets. If so, simply mark the spots through the screw holes of the bracket where you need to drill the pilot holes. (A pilot hole is a small hole you pre-drill to make the screw go in easier. It should be just smaller than the circumference of the screw you'll be using.)

3 Hold up your curtain rod mounting bracket to the marked holes and secure it to the wall by driving in the screws.

Secure the second bracket to the wall, making sure it is level with the first bracket. When both brackets are secure, hang the rod (without the curtains) on the brackets and use your level.

4 Now—hang your curtains! Run the curtain rod through the material and then carefully place the entire piece on the brackets. Make sure you use a sturdy ladder, and be aware that the weight of the curtains can throw you off balance.

STEP 4 Hang the rod with the curtains attached to the brackets.

Jane Tip:
FOR STEP 2
If you end up having to install your brackets directly into drywall, use what are known as molly bolts. A molly bolt is a type of fastener that can help support heavy objects held in by the drywall. Be aware, however, that molly bolts are limited in the amount of weight they can carry. If this is the only way to install your curtain rod, choose lightweight curtains.

Jane Tip:
FOR STEP 3
For most windows there are two 2x4's on each side of the window called the trim and king stud. If there is no trim on the window, you are almost guaranteed to find solid wood within 3 inches of the window opening.

Treat Your Windows to Something Special

Another way to create a designer look in a romantic bedroom is to add window treatments. Not only can they soften the room—important when you're going for a romantic look—but they can also shield you from bright light and keep out cold air and drafts. You can also match the fabric to your bedroom and create a fully finished look.

If you don't have a sewing machine, or frankly just don't know how to sew and have no desire to learn, then we have great news: Using an iron and a heavyweight fusible adhesive such as Stitch Witchery, you can forget the sewing machine altogether!

Project: Install Privacy Blinds

Jane Quotient: ① ❷ ③ ④ ⑤
Estimated Time: 30 to 45 minutes per window

While curtains on bedroom windows are great to keep others from peering in at night, what can you do for privacy during the day? You can always draw the curtains, but is it necessary to give up daylight in exchange for privacy? We're happy to say no.

An easy solution is to add privacy blinds to any window. You will be able stop others from peering in by tilting the blinds for day and night. This is a fairly easy project, and one that can make a big difference very quickly.

MATERIALS

Tools
- Tape measure
- Drill
- Drill bits
- Screwdriver bit
- Level

Supplies
- Privacy blinds
- Pencil

1 Decide where the blinds should go. The choices are:
- Within the frame of the window
- Outside the window so the valence of the blinds sits above and outside the frame

For most rooms, you will probably want to attach the blinds within the window frame so you can add more romance with fabric curtains that match the style of the bedroom.

Jane Tip:

FOR STEP 1
Take a look at how the window is currently trimmed. If you have molding around it or curtains or valances that make the room more beautiful, you'll want to draw as little attention to the blinds as possible.

2 Measure the inside of the window frame. Take the measurements to your local home improvement center to purchase blinds to fit the window.

When looking for the right size blinds, the biggest determining factor is the height of the window. If the window is 22 inches tall, get blinds that are either the same length or slightly longer, such as 24 inches tall. The reason is that the last 2 inches can always remain on the windowsill and no one will be the wiser. As for the width, you'll want a blind that is slightly larger than that of the window.

If you can't find the right size for your window, take the blinds to the person in charge of that section and often they'll cut it to fit your measurements.

3 Typically, blinds come with brackets to hold them in place for use in either type of placement. When hanging them within the window, place each bracket in the upper

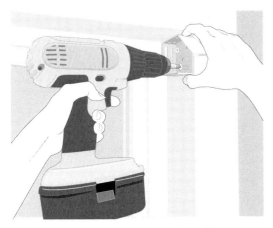

STEP 3 Attach the brackets to the inside of the window frame using a drill and the screws that came with the blinds.

corners of the window frame so the openings face out. Attach them with the screws that came with the blinds to either the sidewalls or the top of the bracket, depending on the manufacturer's instructions.

4 Many blinds come with small valances to cover the head rail. These are usually attached with valance clips to the head rail. Slide them on before installing the blind on the brackets, and then place the head rail within the brackets.

STEP 4 Slide the head rail of the blinds into the brackets you have installed.

Jane Tip:

FOR STEP 3

If your window is wider than 4 feet, consider adding a middle bracket to support the extra weight. You should be able to find these in the same section where you purchased your blinds. Put it up with 2 screws, attaching it to the top of the inside of the window frame.

Jane Tip:

FOR STEP 4

When placing the blinds in the brackets, be certain the cord is facing you so you can adjust it properly once it is installed.

Jane Tip:

FOR STEP 7

Before attaching the hold-down brackets, check the markings with a level to see if they are level. If you don't, it will be obvious when you attach the blinds to them.

5 To lock the blinds in place, close the bracket doors by folding them down and snapping them in place. They should close easily, as most of them are hinged.

6 The tilt wand, for opening and closing, may already come attached. If yours isn't, simply attach the wand by hooking it in place in the small extension with a hole in it; this is typically to the left of the blind. Some blinds come with a small piece of plastic just above where the hook should go. Pull this piece down on top of the hook to keep it in place.

7 To finish off the window, snap the blind valance into the attached clips. For specific details on how your valance attaches, check with the manufacturer's instructions. **Note:** The way to install blinds above or outside the window frame is to attach the brackets to the wall above the window on either side of the blind. Attaching them this way also offers the option of hold-down brackets, which keep the bottom of the blind from moving. This is especially good for French doors.

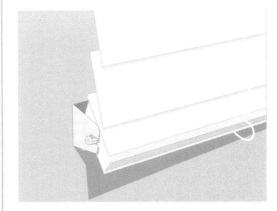

STEP 7 Attach the brackets to the wall where you would like the blinds to hang using a drill, screws, and a level. Once they are attached, simply slide the blind edges in place.

Project: Install a Locking Doorknob

Jane Quotient: ❶ ② ③ ④ ⑤
Estimated Time: 1 to 2 hours

One thing you don't want to have to worry about while in the sanctity of your bedroom is someone barging in uninvited. One of the easiest ways to keep this from happening is to install a locking doorknob on your bedroom door.

Changing out the doorknobs in your home is a simple and inexpensive way to not only enhance your sense of privacy but also to dramatically update and improve the overall look of your doors. Doorknobs and door handles come in a wide variety of styles and colors from ornate to modern, gold to brass, brushed nickel, polished chrome—whatever you like.

Last, replacing your old doorknobs is usually easy because new ones are generally sold in standard sizes, almost assuring your new knob will fit where the old one is now.

Although this project outlines how to change out the doorknob and latch of an interior door, the same steps can be applied to doors that lead outside as well.

MATERIALS

Tools
- Flat head screwdriver
- Eyeglass screwdriver

Supplies
- New doorknob and hardware

Jane Tip:
When looking for a locking doorknob, be sure to get one that can be opened easily in case of an emergency.

1 Remove the trim (also known as the rose cover). The trim is the round-shaped piece of metal behind the doorknob. There should be trim on both sides of the door and attached directly to it. The screws are fairly obvious, but if you can't find yours, look on the side of the trim for two tiny screws securing it in place (they are embedded in the side of the trim and because they're so small, you may need to remove them with an eyeglass screwdriver). Some newer models may not have screws. If this is the case, pry off the trim with a flat head screwdriver or a small pry tool. Be careful not to damage the wood behind the trim when you do.

2 Once the trim is removed, you'll notice two screws (usually on a rose insert). When you start unscrewing them, you'll find they are quite long. Their function is to hold the two doorknobs in place. Remove these screws one at a time.

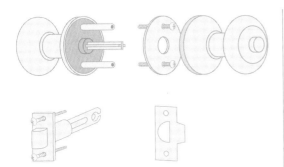

STEP 2 Doorknob anatomy.

3 Pull the knobs apart and out of the door completely.

4 Once the doorknobs are out, you'll note two screws holding the dead latch in place. It's simple to take this out: Remove both screws and pull out the unit.

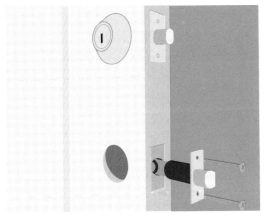

STEP 4 Remove the screws holding the dead latch in place using a screwdriver or a cordless drill.

5 If you'd like to replace the strikeplate (the small metal plate that catches the bolt or lock in the door frame), remove the existing one from the frame of the door now as well. The way to do this is by removing the two screws and pulling it out.

6 Insert the new bolt. Set it in its hole and then screw it into place. Do this with the latch for the doorknob as well. The slanted

Jane Tip:

When purchasing your new doorknob, check to see who manufactured the one you are replacing. Try to find a new one made by the same manufacturer—it will make replacing it easy!

side of the latch should always point in the direction the door closes. This is what makes it so the door can't be pushed open.

7 Place a trim piece flush against one side of the door surrounding the hole where the doorknob will go. Place the doorknob in its hole. Do the same on the other side. The only difference is when you place the second doorknob in its hole, you need to make sure the two doorknobs align properly and that the holes for those two long screws line up.

How to Purchase a New Doorknob

Know ahead of time what you're looking for. Questions to consider:

- Should the doorknob have an internal locking mechanism (for bathrooms, your bedroom, etc.), a deadbolt (for doors to the outside), or no lock at all (for your kids' rooms)?
- Would you prefer a round knob or a lever-type handle?
- Do you need to match the knob with others in your home, or are you looking for decorative door handle sets to add some style?
- What color are you looking for—gold, brass, chrome, brushed nickel, or maybe even glass? You might even consider purchasing an antique model!

Make your decisions ahead of time and always keep your receipt . . . just in case!

STEP 8 When attaching the second doorknob to the first, make sure all of the pieces line up properly. They should fit together so the two long screws will hold the two halves together.

8 Attach the two handles together using the two long screws, alternately tightening each side until you have a solid fit and the knobs come together evenly. Make sure the screws are tight together.

9 Test your work and make sure that both handles twist easily, the knobs don't rattle up against the door (if this happens, the screws are too loose), and the door cannot

Jane Tip:

FOR STEP 6

If you are having trouble getting the new doorknob back in and you can't remember if you're doing it right, try partially removing another doorknob in the house and use it as a model to follow.

be pushed or pulled open from either side without using the handle.

Tips and Tricks

■ If you have installed a new bolt and strikeplate and the latch still feels loose or insecure, replace the original screws with longer wood screws.

■ If you still find additional slack or airspace between the strikeplate and the door trim, fix the problem with a narrow piece of cardboard. Unscrew the strikeplate, fit the cardboard or shim (a small piece of wood used to fill gaps), and replace the screws.

■ One thing to consider when purchasing your new doorknobs is that lever-style door-knobs are easier for small children and adults with physical disabilities to open—clever cats, too.

■ When you remove the old doorknob and lock, place the pieces on the ground in the order you removed them. This should help you know in what order they should go back in.

Jane Profile

It's a lot easier than people think.

Susan "Jane" Lewis

Age: 41

From: Camarillo, California

Favorite tool: My favorite tool is my cordless screwdriver. I like the power it gives me!

Projects accomplished: I laid linoleum tiles in my kitchen and bathroom. Of course, first I had to dig up and rip out three layers of linoleum before I could get started. I also painted my kitchen cupboards perfectly!

Inspiration for starting home improvement: It was when I was on my own, and I had moved into a duplex. I asked the owner if I could do the repairs on the apartment and take it out of the rent, and he said yes. I just started taking on projects and realized I could do it. That's how it started.

Fears about home improvement: When I bought my first electric saw, I was nervous about using it. I was afraid I would hurt myself.

How has home improvement affected your life? Knowing that I can fix just about anything in my home has taken the fear and the cost out of the words, "Oh no! The toilet is broken! What am I going to do?!" Also, I have learned that the word passion can mean a whole lot more than romance. Passion has empowered me to fix things myself!

How has doing home improvements affected others in your life? My teenage daughter tells her friends that her mom can fix anything! It's also affected my home life because my husband doesn't know what end of a screwdriver to use. So the rule around our house is he does the housework and I do the repairs.

Advice for others just getting started in home improvement: Read the instructions! It's a lot easier than people think. Go to Be-Jane.com! Ask a lot of questions. Get a lot of advice. Ask friends who have a background in this work or have done it before.

Creating a Romantic Environment

Even though the idea of what is romantic to each person is subjective, there are a few things most of us would consider romantic. Adding some of these simple touches to your bedroom will help create an ambiance that fosters romance.

But romance is something that needs constant attention. Like a sensitive plant, romance must be cared for and nourished in order to thrive. To make sure romance thrives in your life, you must create an atmosphere that encourages it to grow.

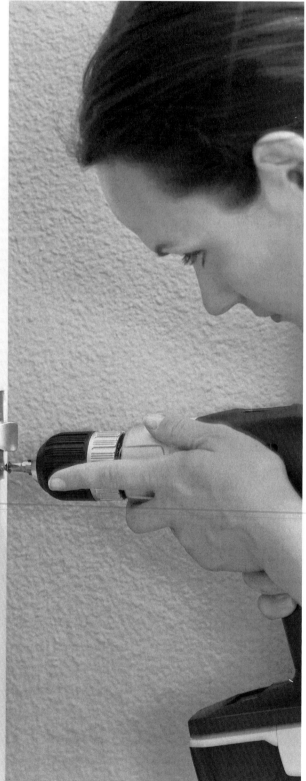

Project: Create a Romantic Fabric Tent Canopy over Your Bed

Jane Quotient: ① ❷ ③ ④ ⑤
Estimated Time: 3 hours

The centerpiece of a romantic bedroom is the bed. The second you step into your room, you should feel it's the one piece you splurged on and makes the rest of your furnishings jealous. Just imagine a bed that makes you feel like a queen (or a princess!) and allows you to feel special every time you climb in it. One way to get this feeling is by creating a canopy for your bed. There are several types: tented canopy, box canopy, ring canopy, and others. They are an easy way to add a sense of romance and elegance to your bedroom.

MATERIALS

Tools
- Tape measure or string
- Scissors
- Sewing machine
- Drill

Supplies
- Fabric
- Pencil
- Pushpin dry-wall anchors
- Curtain rod
- 2 tiebacks or smaller curtain rods
- Fringe or beaded edging (optional)
- Matching thread

"We love how our canopy gives our whole bedroom a new look."

Gina C.
Washington, D.C.
Age 30

1 Decide if you would like the same fabric showing on the top of the canopy as the bottom. Some fabrics look good from both sides, but others need a lining. Consider mixing colors or fabrics for more interest.

2 Decide on the height at which you will place the curtain rod over the center of your bed. Make a mark on the wall and place a pushpin or very thin temporary nail. Next,

decide on the location of the tiebacks on the left and right sides of the bed. They should be no more than 3 inches past the edge of the bed and at least 30 inches above the floor. Mark these spots and place a small pushpin.

To determine how much fabric you'll need, start at the floor and run a long piece of string or soft measuring tape up over the placeholder pushpin for the tieback, over the one for center rod, then back down over the other tieback placeholder to the floor. Allow the string to hang softly with some slack between the tiebacks and the center rod so as to leave room for swagging.

Cut off the string and measure it. Add an additional $1/2$ to $3/4$ yard of fabric for pockets and hems. Ideally, you want the fabric to lightly pool on the floor. Decide on the depth at which your fabric will hang out over your bed on the center curtain rod. Usually $1 1/2$ to $2 1/2$ feet is plenty, although with a slightly wider fabric you can gather it for a thicker, pleated look.

3 Install the curtain rod on the wall, exactly above the center of your bed. Make sure to secure it to a stud or use dry-wall anchors to secure the rod.

Attach the two tiebacks to the wall on either side of your bed, no more than 3 inches past the edge of the bed. These should be at least 30 to 35 inches off the floor.

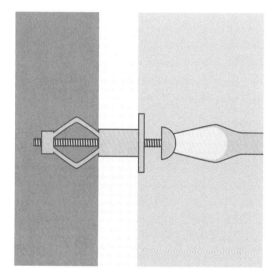

STEP 3 Use wall anchors if there isn't an accessible wall stud.

4 If you have chosen two types of fabric for the inside and outside, sew the panels together, adding fringe or beaded edging as desired. If you have a single piece of fabric, turn it over and sew the edges to create a hem on the sides, top, and bottom.

5 Once your fabric panel is complete, fold it in half to find the center point. Make a pocket for the curtain rod and prevent your fabric from slipping off the poles by sewing a line with matching thread approximately 4 inches down from the center point.

6 Slide the center pocket over the curtain rod and drape the fabric over the tiebacks. Adjust the swag as necessary.

STEP 5 Sew a line approximately 4 inches from the center point to keep your fabric from slipping.

Romantic Color Schemes

When it comes to romance, most people think red is the color of choice. But there are many others you can use to create a romantic setting.

First, think of the type of romance you are attracted to. Do you prefer a soft, willowy romantic novel that sweeps you off your feet? Or are you a hot-blooded romantic with a fiery passion? If the former, consider a monochromatic color scheme using light colors such as white, ivory, or soft pink. Use a variety of textures and sheer, lightweight fabrics for a soft romantic look, but try to stay within a few hues of your color choice. On the other hand, if you want to create a warm but intense romantic bedroom, consider vibrant colors like red, orange, or even purple. Red come in a variety of hues ranging from bright apple red to deep burgundy wine. Add luxurious fabrics that feel great to the touch—velvet, chenille, silk, suede—and your room is on its way to being a destination for romance.

Jane Profile

Make sure you get the right tools for the job.

Yvonka "Jane" Hodges

Age: 43

From: Boyton Beach, Florida

Favorite tool: I love them all, but forced to choose I would have to say my hammer. I have had it longer than any other tool, and it makes me feel in control.

Projects accomplished: My most recent project is my kitchen remodel. The cabinets are hung, and now I am working on the mundane task of prep for the painting. In the past I have built furniture, built walls, changed lighting fixtures, installed ceiling fans, broken down walls, moved electrical outlets, laid a ceramic tile floor, tiled a kitchen counter and backsplash, and much more. In the near future I will be installing my first laminate floor, building a closet, building a new wall, creating built-ins, and revamping two bathrooms.

Inspiration for starting home improvement: I started tackling home projects because it seemed like it would be fun. My philosophy has always been "What's the worst thing that will happen? If it doesn't work, I can always call someone." I think I was brought up to do things for myself at an early age and grew up thinking I could do anything.

I think that my inspiration was I had no one around to do it for me and I was broke. If you want to have things done and you don't have the money, the only option is to do them yourself. I wanted to have things look a certain way, so I thought, "I can do this."

Fears about home improvement: I always have fears when I'm starting a new project, especially if I've never done it before. Most of my fears are related to tool safety. Some of the tools I have, such as my impact nailer, can be pretty scary and take all my nerve when I use them. With every project I do there is at least one fear, but I always seem to get through them.

How has doing home improvement affected your life? I have a tremendous sense of empowerment. It's built my confidence level, and I feel much more empowered. Now I look at a project, and I think, "I can do that." I think, "I'm not paying money for something I can do myself." I can do anything I want to do. The confidence I developed from doing home improvement helped me go back to technical school at age 40. Now I'm in a new career, and it's from the confidence of learning I can do things on my own.

How has doing home improvements affected others in your life? I think more than anything my friends and family have started to believe that women really can do anything. It's been a good example to see that a woman can do these things even if she hasn't done them before. They are impressed, and it gives them a little bit of courage to try new things they hadn't considered trying before.

Advice for others just getting started in home improvement: If it looks scary, it is worth trying. The details really do matter. Make sure you get the right tools for the job. Measure twice, cut once. Just believe in yourself and try it. You'll not only get a home you love, but more self-confidence. Take it one step at a time to get through the project, and if you need help, call me!

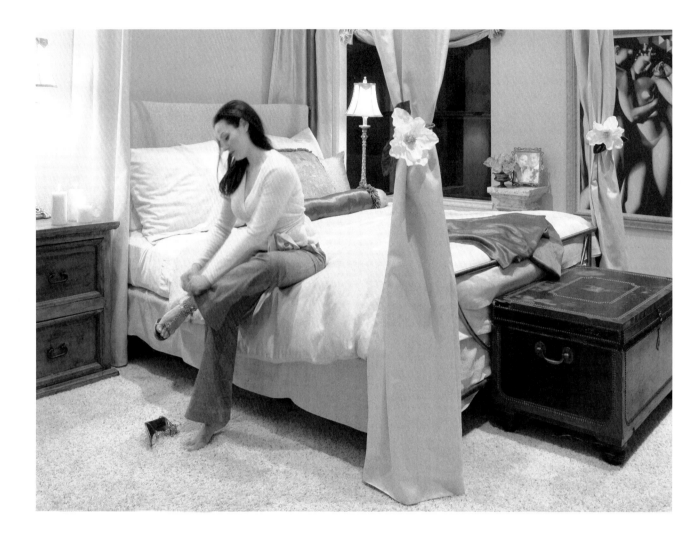

Keeping Your Bedroom
Comfortable and Uncluttered

Nothing kills romance faster than when you feel you can't relax. If something is making you uptight and irritable, chances are you aren't feeling romantic.

When creating your romantic space, your comfort level is absolutely essential. If either you or your loved one isn't comfortable because of the condition of the furnishings, or because the room is cluttered, or the lighting

"Happiness is my homemade shoe tree."

Colette M.
Bakersfield,
California
Age 32

of the room is off, the fragile connection needed for romance to thrive is potentially lost for the night.

It's important to take these things into consideration. What items seem to break you or your loved one out of the moment? What can you do to fix them? The more attention you give to resolving these issues now, the more attention you'll have for other matters later.

Project: Build a Plush Upholstered Headboard

Jane Quotient: ① ❷ ③ ④ ⑤
Estimated Time: **2 to 4 hours**

One key to making a bedroom romantic is to create a bed you find warm and inviting. Unfortunately, many of us can't afford to purchase a brand-new bedroom set to achieve this. But making your own upholstered headboard is an easy and inexpensive way to add new comfort to any bedroom.

Visually, the possibilities are almost endless. You can choose any size, shape, or fabric you want—cotton, linen, velvet, silk. Or why not try fake fur, denim, or even leather! Keep in mind, of course, that the fabric you choose should make you feel comfortable, because you are going to see it every day. You might make it match existing draperies in your room, or try coordinating it with your wallpaper or bed linens. Don't feel limited; the overall look is completely up to you!

This project is fun, simple, and easily completed in a single afternoon.

Get creative with the fabric and decorative accents, and use a jigsaw to give it a unique and fun shape. Remember, the only limits on this project are your own.

MATERIALS

Tools
- Tape measure
- Scissors
- Jigsaw (if you will be cutting the plywood yourself)
- Utility knife or electric c arving knife
- Staple gun (manual or electric) and matching 1/4-inch staples
- Hot glue gun
- Drill
- 3- to 4-inch upholstery needle

Supplies
- 1/4-inch plywood (use 1/2-inch for extra stability)
- 2-inch foam
- Batting
- Upholstery fabric (make sure it isn't see-through, and the thicker the better)
- Large pieces of paper for template (if cutting it yourself)
- Pencil
- Safety goggles
- Heavy-duty rubber gloves
- Mask
- Ball buttons (the metal type you can cover in fabric, found at most fabric and craft stores)
- Strong upholstery thread (it looks like string—white and relatively thick so it won't snap when you pull it tight)
- Small wood dowels or disposable chopsticks for holding the thread
- Polyurethane

Choose among any number of shapes and sizes to add flair to your bedroom.

1 Determine the size and shape of your new headboard. You have two options here:

■ You can go to a thrift store and find a basic headboard to upholster that fits your bed and your style.

■ You can build your own headboard from scratch with a bit of plywood and only a little more time.

The great thing about option 2 is that *you* determine the exact shape and size of your new headboard.

If you're a beginner, you can choose a basic rectangular shape that is easy to cut (you can even have your local home improvement store cut the wood for you). If you're confident in your woodworking abilities, think outside the box—or rectangle—and choose a different shape. Romantic? Try a curved top. Modern? Try a triangle or notched side. Sketch your vision before getting started. A rectangle is the easiest and quickest shape to complete, but it's not the only one.

Plan to make the headboard a bit wider than your mattress. We recommend adding at least 1 to 3 inches on either side.

Determine the height. This is up to you; however, you'll want to know the purpose of the headboard. Is it solely to add a bit of comfort and romance to the room, or will you

Jane Tip:

FOR STEP 1
Don't forget—wrapping the batting and foam padding around the sides will also add slightly to the width, but usually less than 2 inches.

Jane Tip:

FOR STEP 2
Remember, if you're going for a basic rectangular headboard, your home improvement retailer should be able to cut it for you, often at little or no cost.

want to rest up against it to read or watch TV? Be sure you make it tall enough to accommodate your needs.

2 If you don't already have a headboard you plan to cover, you'll need to pick up some plywood to use as your base. Use basic $1/2$–$1/4$-inch plywood, available at any large home improvement retailer. Stay away from particleboard, which may have an odor from all of the chemicals it contains and may not stand the test of time.

Make a fabric, craft, or upholstery store your next stop. It may save time to call ahead and find out what types of foam and batting the store carries. Here's what you need:

■ **FOAM PADDING.** For comfort, you want foam at least 2 inches thick. If your headboard is rectangular, the store should be able to cut the foam to the exact size for you. For a more decorative shape, you can cut it yourself. Believe it or not, we find it's easiest to do this with an electric carving knife. Be careful! The foam handles a bit differently than a turkey.

■ **BATTING OR FIBERFILL.** Batting comes in large rolls and is a thin, white gauzelike substance. Be sure to purchase at least 12 extra inches of batting, both lengthwise and widthwise. You need the extra when you wrap it around the foam padding and wood base.

■ **FABRIC.** Keep durability in mind—it's always best to opt for a slightly thicker and durable fabric. Choose a fabric that's strong and that, once stretched across the headboard, completely obscures the foam. Other than that, your options are wide open! As with the batting, add at least 12 extra inches to the length and width of the fabric to make sure you have enough to wrap it around to the back side.

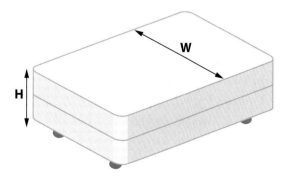

STEP 1 Measure the width and height of your bed to make your headboard an appropriate size. Add 1 to 3 inches to the edges and make it as tall as you desire.

3 If you want to make a decorative or curved headboard, it is a great idea to make a template out of paper (like kraft or butcher paper) first. After drawing your headboard style and cutting it out, try it out behind your bed to see if you like the shape. If you do, tape the template to the plywood, trace the edges carefully using a pencil, and start cutting. For straight cuts, use a circular saw or a handsaw; for curves, use a jigsaw. Remember to wear safety goggles, a mask, and gloves.

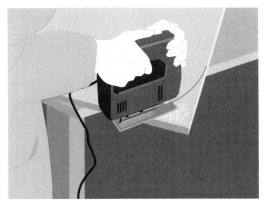

STEP 3 Use a jigsaw to cut the shaped edges of your headboard. Pay special attention to where you place your hands while cutting.

Place the freshly cut wood template on top of the foam and trace the edges with a marker. Cut the foam using a utility knife or an electric carving knife. Finally, cut the batting, leaving at least 12 inches to wrap around the foam and plywood.

4 On a large, clean, flat work surface, perform the next steps in order.

■ Lay down the fabric, right side down. You might want to iron it first.

■ Place the batting on top of the fabric. The two pieces should be approximately the same size.

■ Lay the foam on top of the batting.

■ Place the plywood on top for a stack of four layers. Check that the foam and plywood are properly aligned and that you have plenty of

Jane Tip:

FOR STEP 3
Be sure to wear safety goggles and a mask—sawdust is not good for contact lenses or lungs! It's always a good idea to wear gloves as well to avoid splinters.

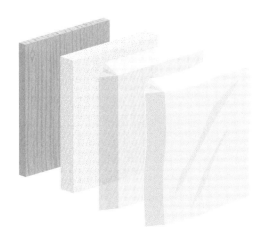

STEP 4 Your headboard will be layered, with plywood at the bottom, then foam padding, batting, and fabric.

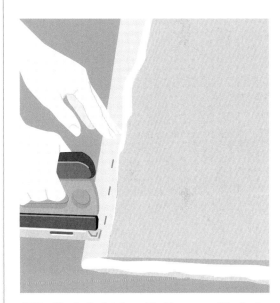

STEP 4 Staple the fabric and batting around the back of your headboard with a staple gun.

Jane Tip:

FOR STEP 4
Start with a few staples in the center of the right and left sides; then place a few in the center of the top and bottom. Work your way out from the center, alternating from side to side and top to bottom. If you've chosen a patterned fabric—especially one with stripes—be careful not to pull too hard while stapling, which can throw the lines off center. Once the initial staples are in, you may want to lift the headboard and sneak a peek to make sure it's wrapping correctly.

fabric and fiberfill around the edges to pull up and around the back of the plywood.

■ Pull the fabric and batting around the foam and plywood. Using a staple gun loaded with heavy-duty staples, secure the fabric and batting with $\frac{1}{4}$-inch staples every 2 inches.

■ Trim excess material and batting from the back with scissors or a sharp utility knife.

Note: Skip to step 6 if you are not adding buttons.

To add upholstered buttons to your headboard, cut circles of the same or a contrasting fabric and attach them to the buttons with a hot glue gun.

Measure where you want the buttons to go and mark the spots on the back of the headboard.

Using a drill with a ⅝-inch drill bit, drill holes where your marks are. It's okay if the drill hits the foam, but don't let it go through the fabric. Thread a long, thick upholstery needle with strong thread. Starting at the back of the headboard, push the needle through the foam, batting, and fabric until it comes out the front. Thread on the button and push the needle back through the fabric and through the hole in the back. Don't be surprised if the needle is difficult to get back through the hole in the wood.

5 Repeat the last step one or two more times. The button should now be well secured and the thread hanging out the back of the hole. Place a small piece of wood such as a dowel or chopstick across the hole. Tie the thread around the wood as tightly as possible, pulling the button in. The dowel will hold the thread in place so the string does not wiggle back out.

6 Covering the legs is necessary only if you cut out legs on the bottom of your plywood. Repeat the process, covering the two leg pieces of wood with lining or decorative fabric by stapling it to the back of the leg. Alternatively, you can leave them bare, considering they'll be behind the head of the bed.

Stand the headboard against the wall behind the bed, using the mattress to stabilize it. You can also drill holes in the legs and attach them to the frame of the bed with long screws and bolts.

Jane Tip:

FOR STEP 4
Pull the thread as tightly as possible to form an indented look on the front (if desired). This is where strong thread is important!

Thread Count Counts!

In a romantic bedroom, your bed should be the focal point. The bed represents the warmth and feeling of comfort in your room and is the ultimate place for treating yourself to a romantic night.

The key is to make the bed as cozy and luxurious as possible. The elements you need to consider are the sheets, pillowcases, throw pillows, comforter, bedspread or duvet, and bedskirt. While bedding can range from inexpensive, low-thread-count sheets to over-the-top luxury fabrics that cost thousands of dollars, you can save money and still create the romantic bed of your dreams.

The place *not* to skimp is the sheets. You should buy sheets with the highest thread count you can afford. A good idea is to shop discount or clearance stores and online outlets and warehouses, which often sell high-thread-count sheets and pillowcases for up to 75 percent less than a traditional retail store.

Project: Install a Closet Organization System

Jane Quotient: ① ❷ ③ ④ ⑤
Estimated Time: 3 to 4 hours

If your lounge chair is covered with clothes, your underwear is in your shoe rack, and your shoes are in your dirty clothes hamper, then this project is for you. Don't worry, we aren't going to channel your mother and tell you to clean your closet. Instead, we'll show you how to *make* a new closet—one you're not afraid of.

Most people leave things out because they never designated a place to put them. Especially in your bedroom, nothing looks more unappealing than a pile of clothes on the floor. You don't want to feel like you're sleeping in a storage closet.

There are companies that charge thousands of dollars to help you organize your closet. The good news is that now there are just as many companies supplying the world with easy-to-install closet organization kits.

For a small investment and a little bit of work, you can finally put your mess to rest and get your romantic life back on track.

MATERIALS

Tools
- Tape measure
- Drill
- Paintbrush
- Hammer
- Stud finder
- Pry bar

Supplies
- Spackle
- Sandpaper
- Paint
- Pencil
- Hanging rack system

Jane Tip:

FOR STEP 1
Consider giving the interior of your closet a fresh coat of paint at this point. If you decide to paint, follow the painting techniques outlined in "Painting Basics" on page 33.

1 Empty your closet. By doing this you will get a better grasp of exactly what type of closet organizer will work best for you. Not only do you need to take everything out but you'll also need to take down the existing shelving. You may need a pry bar, hammer, and drill for this. Remove all nails and screws.

Fill all the holes with spackle. Let the spackle dry, and then sand it down.

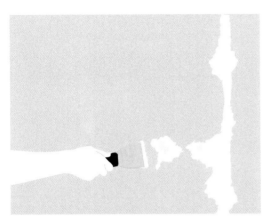

STEP 1 Once you've completely cleaned everything, including the racks, out of your closet, fill in the holes left behind with spackle. You will create your closet from scratch.

2 Measure the width, length, and height of your closet. If it isn't square, draw a blueprint with the measurements on it. Take this to your local home improvement store or any other place that sells closet kits. If you feel comfortable, pick out the new shelving system yourself based on the measurements. If you are lucky enough to find someone who really knows about closet organizers, it will be worth your time to chat with him or her about what you need.

Try to purchase a system that hangs on the wall and doesn't touch the floor. This way you won't have to remove it if you change out the carpet or flooring.

Keep these few points in mind while buying a closet system:
- Long hanging space is needed for dresses, long coats, and so on.
- A double-hanging system helps double your hanging space. These are perfect for hanging shirts and jackets on top and pants on the bottom. Or, if you prefer to hang your pants lengthwise in the long hanging space, you can divide your long-sleeve and short-sleeve tops on the bottom and top racks.
- Inserting drawers and open shelving for

Jane Tip:

FOR STEP 2
When trying to figure out a closet organizational system, you can always have a closet organizer come to your house and draw up the best options for your closet. Many companies will come out to give you a free estimate in the hope that you'll buy the system from them. This can be valuable information if you try to do it yourself. If your effort doesn't work out, all you have to do is call the company back—though our money is on you.

folded clothing might eliminate the need for a dresser in your bedroom.
- Attaching hooks will help you hang housecoats, belts, and scarves.
- One of the most important things to remember in a woman's closet is space for shoes! There are numerous shoe solutions, from cubbyholes built into the closet unit to shoe holders that hang on the back of the door, and floor units that consist of a metal rack or a flat shelf. Make sure the style you choose fits your particular shoe size and that you're able to easily see and get to your shoes.
- Some closet systems include cabinets small enough for jewelry.
- Don't assume you're too short for top shelves. Even if you need a stepladder to reach them, they are perfect for storing out-of-season clothing, hats, and so on.
- You can install armoire-type shelving units as well. These are great for hiding your intimate items.
- Refer to the lighting section in this book for help should you decide to install a new fixture to brighten up your new space.

3 After getting your closet kit home, pull out all the parts to make certain nothing is missing. Take out the instructions that came with the kit and keep them handy. While we give you guidance here, you will need to follow the manufacturer's instructions that are specific to your kit.

4 Your next move is probably to attach the mounting brackets. For best support, attach them directly into the wall studs, which you can find using your stud finder.

Once you've marked with a pencil the spots on the wall where the mounting brackets will go, screw the brackets into the studs with your cordless drill. If you need to put a few screws where a stud isn't available, predrill a

STEP 4 Attach the brackets to the studs in the wall of your closet with wood screws to support your new closet system.

hole and put in a drywall anchor before attaching the shelving to the wall. While drywall anchors do help, make sure most of the bracket screws are drilled into studs.

Jane Tip:

FOR STEP 4

Make sure the mounting brackets are put in level. The last thing you want is your clothes sliding off your new rack and onto the floor.

5 Most kits are assembled before being attached to the mounting brackets. Arrange the racks and shelves according to your own needs and desires, being certain to follow the instructions included with your kit.

6 Once your shelving is in place, you can put everything in the closet. (Now's your chance to get rid of those old clothes you're keeping for no good reason. Take advantage of it!)

With your new closet—which you successfully installed yourself—you won't have to slam your bedroom door shut when visitors drop by. Another real treat with this home improvement project is that the moment you find the perfect black dress, you'll be able to locate it after you bring it home.

Project: Install a Dimmer Switch

Jane Quotient: ① ② ❸ ④ ⑤
Estimated Time: 1 to 2 hours

If we had to name one item that adds more ambiance to a room faster than a dimmer switch, we would come up empty. A dimmer switch on any light in your room is a remarkable romance enhancer.

The hardest part of this project might be which dimmer to choose, as a number of dimmer styles and types are on the market. Most dimmer switches range in price from $12 to $40, depending on the features. Some have a toggle you push up and down, or there are new finger touchpads that dim the lights when you drag your finger across the plastic face. Some have a nightlight embedded in the switch or even the ability to connect to your home computer system for remote access!

Whichever route you go, we know you'll soon agree that a dimmer switch is the king of romance.

MATERIALS

Tools
- Electrical tester
- Screwdriver
- Wire cutters or lineman's pliers
- Wire stripper
- Wire caps/nuts

Supplies
- Dimmer switch with plate (may have to be purchased separately)
- Wire connectors
- Electrical tape

Note: Before you remove your old switch, you need to know what type of switch you are dealing with.

■ **SINGLE-POLE SWITCH.** This is a switch in which the electrical wires affect one light and do not continue on to other switches or receptacles.

Jane Tip:

Dimmers cannot be used on most fluorescent lighting. They should also not be used on ceiling fans unless you get a dimmer made specifically for a fan/light combo.

■ **THREE-WAY SWITCH.** This type of switch works in pairs to control a light from two locations. For example, you can turn on one light fixture from either end of your hallway. We don't recommend installing a dimmer switch here, but if you do, don't install more than one dimmer—the other end needs to be a toggle switch (the basic on-off switch we're all used to).

■ **FOUR-WAY SWITCHES.** These are rare but sometimes found in very large rooms. They are used in combination with a pair of three-way switches to control lights from three or more locations.

Identifying your switch type is easy: Just count the screws! Single-pole switches have 2 screw terminals, three-way switches have 3 screw terminals, and four-ways have 4 screw terminals.

Safety Check

- Do not install a dimmer switch that is connected to a receptacle (plug or electrical outlet), as you can blow out your vacuum cleaner or other appliances if you don't have the switch up to maximum power.
- Make sure the new dimmer switch is rated for the total wattage of the fixture. For example, a chandelier with five 100-watt bulbs would be too much for a 400-watt dimmer. This information is generally found on the packaging of the dimmer switch.
- First things first: Make sure to turn off the circuit breaker that feeds the switch. If your circuit breakers aren't labeled, flip them on and off, one at a time, to see which goes to which switch (or set of switches). It's best to do this with a partner who can call out when the light goes off. Turn off the breaker (and label it). Once back in the room you're working in, if you're removing an old toggle switch, flip it on and off before removing it to make sure there's no power feeding it. Once you remove the faceplate, use an electrical tester to be 100 percent certain.

1 Use your electrical tester to be certain no power is flowing to the switch. Remove the screws from the top and bottom of the old

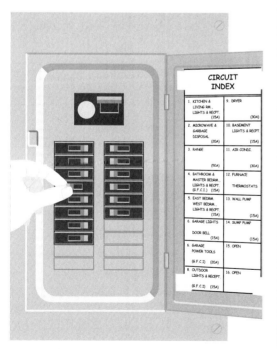

STEP 1 Make sure to turn off the correct breaker for the switch you will be working on. Use your circuit map to know which is the right one. If you don't already have a map, ask someone else to stand in the room you will be working in to let you know if the light goes off. This way you won't have to go back and forth.

Jane Tip:

FOR STEP 1
Always let everyone in your house know when you're working on anyting electrical. This will help prevent your family members or roommates from inadvertently turning the power back on.

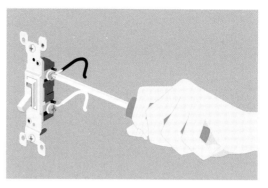

STEP 1 Remove the toggle switch by using a screwdriver to unscrew the terminal screws holding the wires in place.

toggle switch. Take off the faceplate and pull the entire switch box out of the wall. You'll see the wires from the switch box connected to wires coming from the wall. Unscrew the plastic wire connector caps. Untwist the wires. Toss the old toggle switch in the trash.

2 Using a wire cutter, cut off the bare wire just below the plastic insulation on all three wires. Then use a wire stripper to strip off about 3/8 inch of the insulation. This will give you a clean piece of wire for the new connection to the dimmer.

If necessary, strip the wires attached to the dimmer switch to give you room to twist the two sets of wires together.

3 Connect one of the black wires (these are the hot wires) coming out of the wall (also known as the workbox) to one from the dimmer switch by placing the bare wires next to each other and then twisting on a wire connector nut—these are plastic caps that should have come with the dimmer switch. Make sure the bare wires are completely encased in the wire nut. Do the same for the other set of black wires.

4 Connect the white (neutral) wires and cap them with a wire nut as well. Some

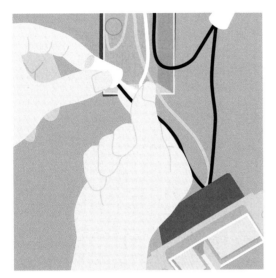

STEP 3 Attach the wires coming from the wall to the correct wires on the dimmer switch with wire nuts. Hold the wires together and twist the nut clockwise over the tips.

of the new dimmer switches don't have the white and black wires on them, but the hot wire should be marked. If you can't tell which wire in your house is the hot one, check how the wires were connected to your old switch. If that doesn't work, get out your electrical tester. Remember, if you happen to put the wrong wires together, you reverse the flow of electricity and risk blowing out the dimmer switch. If you do, you'll have to buy a new one, so try your best to get it right the first time. Be sure to tie together all the ground (usually green) wires as well. Ground wires are there to ground out the electricity in your home so that if it does get hit by lightning, it won't blow out the entire electrical system.

5 Now you'll probably have more wire than you started with, so bend the wires in a zigzag pattern so they easily fold into the workbox in the wall. Make sure all the caps are tightened and that no bare wires are exposed (use electrical tape to cover them). Once you stuff the wires back into the wall, push the new dimmer switch into place.

6 Adjust the switch so it is perpendicular to the floor. Tighten the two screws that hold it in position in the workbox.

7 Insert the mounting screws (which attach the dimmer to the wall). Before fully installing them, go back to your circuit breaker, turn the power back on—or as we like to say, "Hit it, Jane!" If the switch is working just fine, finish attaching the dimmer to the wall and put on the face plate. If the switch is *not* functioning, make sure power is coming to the dimmer with the electrical tester. If it is, turn off the power and recheck the wiring to make sure you've connected the wires correctly.

Soften Your Nightstand Lighting with the Touch of a Finger

Lighting makes a big difference to romance in a bedroom. Dimmers work great on softening overhead lighting, but what can you do about bright nightstand lights?

A great and innovative product that helps with this is called a **tabletop full-range electronic dimmer**. While it may be a mouthful to say, all you have to do is plug the light into the dimmer and then plug the dimmer into the wall. Once it is plugged in, a short touch or tap on any metal part of the lamp will turn it on and off, while a longer touch will brighten or dim it. For extra lighting control, you can also get a touchpad that will let you control the light from up to 10 feet away. Romantic lighting at the touch of a finger —ooh la la!

Jane Tip:
FOR STEP 5
If after you connect all of the wires some bare copper wire is still visible, wrap black electrical tape around it to cover it up.

A Family Room For Everyone to Enjoy

Remember those moments of your childhood when your family was all together? All was well with the world as you shared time with your parents and siblings. You might have played a board game or watched TV. There was a sense of warmth and security you looked forward to experiencing and now cherish the memories of. Moments like these were typically created in a family room—a room designed for the sole purpose of gathering together and sharing special times.

Is your family room such a place?

How do you go about making a family room a place where everyone *wants* to gather? A big television shouldn't be the only enticement. What if you were able to transform your family room into a place where your friends and your family and your family's friends all loved to spend time simply because it is an enjoyable place to be?

Well, it can be done. First off, think what would attract you to a room like that. Clearly, the room should be aesthetically pleasing and show you and your family in your best light. The room should also be functional.

"It's so nice to have a room where all of us can kick back together. I find we're doing a lot better as a family."

Ina M.
San Diego,
California
Age 59

Ultimately, a family room is a gathering place, so functionality here is less about working fixtures and faucets and the like and more about how the room functions as a whole. You want everything—seating, storage, recreational activities, and ability to accommodate guests—to be multifunctional and appropriate.

Finally, the style of the room, the mood it portrays, even a mantelpiece covered with pictures of your family at the best times of their lives should be shared with all those who enter.

A family room can be and should be the warmest room in the house—because it's the heart of what makes your house your home.

Jane Profile

Whatever you do, don't give up or give in to someone telling you to let a man fix it—unless he's really hunky.

Arlene "Jane" Hoffman

Age: 59

From: Austin, Texas

Favorite tool: My favorite tool would probably have to be a reciprocating saw. I haven't used it much, but I like what I've seen. I also like my set of drill bits/screwdriver bits that pop in and out of my drill so I don't have to keep screwing in and out the pieces.

Projects accomplished: A home is a living classroom. I've learned there are no small jobs. With each one, my knowledge and skills increase. When I bought my house, the bathroom in the master bedroom was very small and was papered very dark, so I wanted to change it. I thought, a small room, replacing wallpaper, no problem! Then I found out that the dark paper had been put on over the original wallpaper, which had been put directly on the drywall without a primer under it.

I quickly learned about drywall, plaster, mud, tape, and patching a big hole hidden under the wallpaper. My "easy" project took me weeks rather than days, but I came out of it with so much knowledge I was ready to take on anything. This was pure "girl power," and I didn't have to have someone tell me how great I was and what a good job I'd done!

Inspiration for starting home improvement: I bought my house in 1991. It's a great house and needs mostly cosmetic things done, but it is a work in progress.

Owning my own home and not being able to hire someone—or hiring someone who did a poor job—that would have to be my inspiration. Besides, I really wanted to learn how to do this myself anyway.

Fears about home improvement: Even to this day I procrastinate over that first cut. Getting started, making that first cut, or doing wiring—I say to myself over and over, "I know I can do this." It's the initial commitment to starting any project, punching that first hole in the wall, knowing all along that once you start, you've got to finish it.

How has doing home improvement affected your life? I never thought much about housework (the Be Jane kind) other than as something that had to be done. Now that I have learned so much, I am aware of things that need to be done to my house and have an idea how to repair them. Thanks to Be Jane, I have a source to go to with questions without the intimidation I feel at home stores.

How has doing home improvement affected others in your life? My sister has become interested in the things I have done and decided that if I can do it, then she can do it. My brother is a handyman, and I always call him four or five times during a project to get advice. I also have a girlfriend who decided that if I could do it, she could do it, too. So we went shopping together so she could have the same kind of tools I have. She's done some refinishing of her cabinets and changing things like that. I haven't done any projects like that just yet, but I feel if she can do it, then I can do it.

Advice for others just getting started in home improvement: Get yourself a good home improvement book, or several, and don't hesitate to go at a project. Maybe start small with fixing cracks—not just covering them up but really fixing them. Whatever you do, don't give up or give in to someone telling you to let a man fix it—unless he's really hunky. Then *I'd* like to apprentice!

Making Your Family Room Aesthetically Pleasing

This should be the one room in your house that reflects everyone's tastes. It's a gathering place, so it's important that your family members feel they are a part of the room as a whole. If they have no personal connection to the aesthetics of the room, they will be less likely to want to spend time in there.

Ultimately, you want to portray a uniformity of design and functionality.

But you also want each member of your family to take pride in this room and be glad to show it off to guests.

The aesthetics aren't just about the way the room looks; you want to be sure there are family moments you share together.

Make your family room as appealing and comfortable as possible so the time you all spend together in it is true quality time.

Project: Remove a Popcorn/Acoustic Ceiling

Jane Quotient: ① ② ❸ ④ ⑤
Estimated Time: 3 to 5 hours

When you were a kid, popcorn was such a joy. Now that you own your home and have it on every ceiling in the house, though, you're not so crazy about it. These acoustical ceilings, which resemble popcorn (and cottage cheese), once served the purpose of toning down the echo in a room. With most modern insulations, the need for this type of ceiling has faded. Popcorn ceilings tend to look tired, old, and desperately in need of a face-lift. They are a common sign of older construction.

If you're ready to update your family room and take down that cottage cheese dust-containing mess above your head, don't stop here. The job is messy, but it's really not difficult to change the appearance of the ceiling or remove it all together.

MATERIALS

Tools
- Ladder
- Spray bottle
- Paint scraper or putty knife (or tile scraper)

Supplies
- Plastic drop cloths
- Protective eyewear
- Mask
- Hat
- Coveralls or clothing you don't mind getting dirty

Option 1: Remove It Altogether

The ideal, of course, is to get rid of the ceiling completely, but if the ceiling has been painted it will be more difficult to remove because the removal process is just wetting it down and scraping it off. If the ceiling has been painted, the water won't penetrate the paint. Unfortunately, you might need to have the job done professionally.

> "When my three-year-old son asked me why we put cottage cheese on his ceiling, I knew it was time to get rid of it."
>
> Arlene X.
> New York,
> New York
> Age 34

⌒ Safety Check

Does your acoustical ceiling material contain asbestos? Home builders once thought that asbestos was as good as sliced white bread and added it to everything, including acoustical ceilings. If your home was built prior to 1900, the safest bet is to scrape a small sample into a plastic ziplock bag and take it to an asbestos processing lab. You can find these businesses in the Yellow Pages under "Asbestos Testing." Some online companies process results through the mail. One such is www.asbestostesting.com.

This may seem like overkill, but trust us, it's important. Results are usually available in 24 hours. The testing costs between $40 and $60 and is worth *every penny* because if your ceiling does contain asbestos, you must hire someone to remove it.

Asbestos can cause serious respiratory problems when inhaled. Some people think if they cover themselves well enough they're fully protected, but even the dust that falls onto your furniture or carpeting can be harmful. Leave this job to a pro.

Note: Heads up! If you take on this project yourself, you will use muscles you never realized you had. Throughout the project you will have your hands over your head. This can become increasingly difficult as the project goes on.

We suggest you contact friends for help. Don't be a hero! Pizza and beer works every time. Just make sure you've got masks and protective eyewear for everyone. Even when your ceiling doesn't contain asbestos, you don't want to breathe in this stuff if you can help it.

1 Cover everything below the surfaces you'll be working on with plastic. Sheets and canvas tarps are not as good as plastic because you will be wetting down the ceiling and anything that falls on the sheets or canvas could soak through.

2 Put on your gloves, mask, protective eyewear, some type of head covering, and coveralls or very old clothes. We can't stress enough the importance of protecting your eyes while doing this project. Think of it this way: Stuff is coming off the ceiling while you're looking up. Got it? Good.

3 Get your ceiling wet—not dripping, but wet enough so the material becomes mushy. The fastest and most efficient way to do this is to get a handheld pressurized garden sprayer, fill it with warm water, and start spraying your ceiling. We suggest you start in patches of around 5 square feet. If the room is pretty small, a regular spray bottle filled with warm water should do the trick.

Give the water a few minutes to soak in—15 to 20 minutes should do.

4 Use a 3- to 4-inch paint scraper or putty knife to scrape off the moistened popcorn. Discard the mess. We find a bucket on the ladder is the easiest place to store the goop once you've scraped it off. While scraping,

take care not to gouge the wallboard underneath with the pointed corners of the putty knife, as you'll have to repair that damage later.

Note: Although removing the stuff is easy, once it's gone you'll need to prime and paint

STEP 4 Once you've sprayed the warm water on the ceiling and let it sit for 15 to 20 minutes, begin scraping with a 3- to 4-inch putty knife. Make sure you are wearing gloves, a dust mask, and goggles.

(or otherwise cover) all of the exposed surface area as soon as possible—otherwise, it may warp. Depending on the climate in which you live, you should have up to 72 hours to do this. However, another key point to remember is that once you've primed a surface, it must be covered in paint within 48 hours or the primer will break down and lose its adhesive traits.

Note: Once you remove the popcorn, the drywall tape may show through. You can try to spackle and blend this together, but for the best results, consider a skip trough, a ceiling covering made of drywall mud, fine white sand, and a splash of water. It is applied with a skip trowel in a nonuniform manner, giving the ceiling a textured look.

Jane Tip:

FOR STEP 4
Instead of a typical putty knife, consider purchasing a tile scraper with a long handle (like that of a rake or a shovel). This will allow you to work from the ground rather than have to constantly climb and move a ladder.

Option 2: It Can Be Saved!

If you like the look of it, or if removing your popcorn ceiling isn't an option, then painting over it is your best bet. This is not difficult, but it can be tricky if not approached correctly.

Quite often, popcorn ceilings are first covered with alkyd paint (a synthetic resin called alkyd and a mix of mineral spirits as a solvent) so they can be repainted with water-based paint. If you know your ceilings were previously treated, go right ahead and apply any water-based paint you wish.

If you don't know whether your ceiling was treated, we suggest you prepare it with a premium, no-spatter alkyd paint designed for use over stucco popcorn and plaster ceilings.

As for the paint itself, a matte finish is ideal for hiding surface irregularities and reducing glare, but we prefer an eggshell so the ceiling doesn't end up looking chalky.

The painting portion is pretty straightfor-

Jane Tip:

FOR OPTION 2

Use a paint roller with a long handle so you can work while standing safely on the floor. Your back, shoulders, and neck will also thank you!

ward. Just remember the following guidelines as you paint:

- Always wear protective eyewear.
- Cover your hair.
- Stop periodically to stretch your neck and back. Painting ceilings puts a great deal of strain on your body; make sure you give it what it needs in order to let you finish the project.
- Try to use a roller with a large nap, and get yourself a paint roller that allows you to draw the paint directly into the handle. That way you won't have to constantly be bending down to put more paint on the roller. It also allows for better control of the amount of paint on the roller at any one time, leading to less splatter.

This project will reward you for years to come. It is quite time-consuming, so take one room at a time when you can and don't try to paint or scrape all of your ceilings in a weekend unless you're completely crazy.

Project: Update an Old Brick Fireplace

Jane Quotient: ① ② ❸ ④ ⑤
Estimated Time: 6 to 8 hours
Drying Time: 2 weeks

For centuries, the hearth was the most important place in one's home. The mere fact of it being lit could be the difference between life and death. All the meals were cooked in it, and it was the brightest and warmest place in the house. We no longer depend on our fireplaces for survival, but the many years we did created strong emotional ties that remain today.

A lit fireplace tends to pull everyone in to seek warmth of body and spirit. A television is often no match for a lit fire. A lit fireplace is often a conversation starter; a fire helps inspire quality time with those you love.

If your fireplace is hardly a place for gathering, it may be time to update it. You might have an old brick fireplace that feels outdated and stale. Tiling it over with beautiful slate or travertine is an easy way to add years of joy and will bring your fireplace back into your family's routine.

MATERIALS

Tools
- Electric palm sander
- Hammer
- Chisel
- Scoring tool
- Notched trowel
- Tape measure
- Electric tile saw or tile cutter
- Chalk line
- Level
- Rubber mallet
- Grout float

Supplies
- Mask
- Protective eyewear
- Latex or vinyl gloves
- Course sandpaper
- Hardibacker board
- 1 1/2-inch concrete screws
- Seam tape
- Latex fortified Thinset adhesive
- Tile/slate/travertine (whichever you choose)
- Tile spacers
- Blue painter's tape
- Grout
- Water-based sealer

Jane Tip:

FOR STEP 1
If the surface of your fireplace has a few random bricks that stick out farther than the others, use a hammer and chisel to chip off the high spots. You'll want a more uniformed surface to tile over.

Note: Before getting started, fully clean the inside of your fireplace, as ashes can affect the adhesion of the stone or tile.

1 If your fireplace isn't painted, go on to step 2. If it is painted, roughen up the surface as much as possible with very coarse sandpaper and an electric palm sander. Remove as much of the slick surface as possible. Make sure to wear gloves, a mask, and protective eyewear during this process, as the dust you create isn't something you want to inhale or get in your eyes. Proper ventilation is also important.

Clean the surface of your fireplace, getting rid of all grease, dust particles, and residue to ensure proper adhesion.

2 Prepare the surface in one of these two ways:

■ Apply a layer of latex modified Thinset to fill in the surface variations.

This approach offers a better chance of proper adhesion, though it entails more work.

Figure out the measurements of your fireplace, then score the board with a scoring tool (such as a utility knife) and snap the board to fit. Coat the backside (the side going up against the fireplace) of the board with latex modified Thinset mortar and attach it with concrete screws. We recommend using Hardibacker board, as it shows you where you will need to attach it.

Apply seam tape along all of the seams where the two pieces of mortarboard abut. Cover the tape with a thin coat of Thinset. Once it dries, you are ready to set your tile. Make sure the backer board is plumb on the face of the fireplace and level on the hearth. Otherwise, it will be difficult to get the tiles level and even.

■ Even out the surface of the brick, and apply a coat of latex modified Thinset, between $1/4$ and $3/8$ inch thick. Any thicker and it will dry unevenly, as it tends to shrink and crack. Apply this with the straight edge of a trowel, fill in the gaps between the bricks, then let it dry. We recommend applying two thin coats rather than one thick one. Once the coats are dry, you are ready to set your tile.

3 To set the stone tile, lay out your pattern with tile spacers first. Be creative; remember, your fireplace is the largest

Jane Tip:

FOR STEP 2

Cutting the mortarboard to fit the fireplace is easy. Just score the board and then apply pressure away from the score. The board will snap right where you wanted it to. If you use a metal square when you score it, you should end up with a perfectly straight edge.

Jane Tip:

FOR STEP 3

The best way to accurately lay out your pattern is to buy a roll of kraft paper and cut out a piece the same size and shape of the surface you are tiling. Lay out the pattern on it the same way you envision it—stone tile, spacers, and all (skip the mastic).

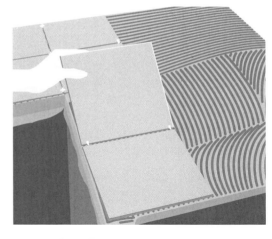

STEP 3 **Before adhering the stone, lay out the pattern with the spacers. Mark any cuts on the tiles, and make all necessary cuts before you begin setting the tiles into the Thinset.**

accessory in this room. Make it a place you and your whole family will love to sit near.

In laying out your design, you will need either a tile cutter (which cuts porcelain) or a wet saw (which is made for stone but cuts it all). A wet saw uses what's known as a diamond blade metal grinder. It's not necessary to buy one unless you plan on laying a great deal of tile. You can rent one for $50 to $100 per day.

If you aren't able to lay the tile right away or have to move your template and tiles, keep them in order by numbering them on the back. Each row should start with a different letter. Only mark on the back, as the mark might not come off later.

4 You can purchase premixed Thinset or save money by mixing it yourself. This job is not rocket science, but it can get messy and tiring. Apply the Thinset with a notched trowel to the prepared surface, spreading it as if it were peanut butter. The notched trowel ensures both even distribution and increased suction when you place the tiles.

While placing the tiles, periodically check them with your level. Even if they look parallel to the ground, check them anyway.

You can move the tiles around until the Thinset sets. If it sets too much, pull off the tile and scrape off the Thinset below it (discard it in the trash). Apply new adhesive and try again.

If you're having trouble getting the tile to stay attached to the wall, gently tap it in place with a rubber mallet. This increases the suction between the tile and the Thinset. If that doesn't work, use blue painter's tape to hold the tile in place. Once the adhesive is dry, remove the tape.

Jane Tip:

FOR STEP 4
Spread only as much Thinset as you can cover with tile in 10 minutes.

Jane Tip:

FOR STEP 5
If you've used a highly polished stone or spacers $1/8$ inch wide, we suggest using a nonsanded grout. Any spaces larger than $1/8$ inch should be filled with a sanded grout. If the surface of the stone you used is well polished, be careful when using a sanded grout, which can easily scratch.

STEP 4 After applying the Thinset with a notched trowel, set your tiles in it, using spacers to guarantee proper spacing. Lay them out the way you did before.

5 Once all the tiles are up, leave them alone overnight to dry. The next day, remove all of the spacers and mix up the grout according to the manufacturer's instructions.

To apply the grout, load the rubber grout float with grout and hold it at a 45-degree

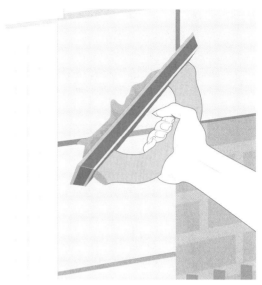

STEP 5 After mixing up the grout, apply it to the stone's surface. Hold the grout float at a 45-degree angle to get the best retention in the grooves.

STEP 5 Once you've applied your grout, quickly remove any excess on the stone surface before it fully dries. Do this with a slightly damp sponge. If you wait too long, the grout will dry on the surface and ruin your beautiful new stone fireplace.

angle against the tile. Then, pushing the tile into the openings, move the float diagonally across the tile face. Apply the grout to the tile until the spaces are full.

With a clean, damp sponge, wipe off excess grout on the tiles before it gets a chance to dry.

It will probably take several passes to remove it all. Rinse out the sponge with clean water between passes. Wipe off the haze on the tile once it's dried a bit more.

6 Let the grout dry for 72 to 96 hours.

7 Stone can be susceptible to stains, and considering you are looking forward to using this fireplace, make sure to seal it. Most sealers require that you wait 7 to 10 days after you've grouted before applying. Even though you're dying to use your new fireplace, wait until it is sealed before doing so.

Once the fireplace is sealed according to the manufacturer's instructions, you will have created a hearth that family and friends will love to congregate around. Now all you need to do is invite everyone you love over for a game of Scrabble.

Jane Tip:

FOR STEP 6
To prevent cracking, especially with larger grout lines, spray the grout with water from a spray bottle twice a day for the first three days. This way, the outside layer won't dry before the bottom layer does.

Jane Tip:

FOR STEP 7
To avoid any unsightly stains or streaks from typical household cleaners, be sure to use cleaners that are made specifically for stone and granite.

STEP 7 Apply a water-based sealer to the fireplace with a lint-free rag or paintbrush and gloves. This will help protect it and allow you to enjoy it for years to come.

Project: Apply a Tuscan Wall Treatment

Jane Quotient: ① ② ❸ ④ ⑤
Estimated Time: 5 to 8 hours (longer if you are covering a large surface area)

The walls that surround you in your family room can play a part in how you are affected by the room as a whole. Walls with bland or muted tones tend to be lost and forgotten.

You might try to give your walls a little life above and beyond simply painting them. A number of wall treatments are fun and simple projects that can give your family room some real pizzazz—and possibly give you something to do as a family. One of the most popular is a Tuscan wall treatment. If you've ever been lucky enough to travel to the Italian countryside, you've seen how beautiful the villas are. They radiate a sense of warmth and history unlike any other buildings in the world. The aging look of this Italian wall technique offers a warm, welcoming feeling that when duplicated, translates perfectly to any family gathering area.

MATERIALS

Tools
- Large trowel
- Paint roller

Supplies
- Gloves
- Protective eyewear
- Plastic and cloth tarps
- Taping mud (joint compound)
- Latex paint
- Oil-based stain (1 or more colors)
- Lint-free rags

Note: The idea of a treatment like this can be scary because you aren't just changing the color of your walls, you are also changing the texture. If you're afraid you'll screw up your walls permanently, you're not alone. We have had thousands of women write to us that they have been dying to try something out in their homes but are afraid of making a potentially

Jane Tip:

FOR STEP 1
When you are purchasing your joint compound, you might see another product called topping compound. It's a bit thinner than joint compound, and some contractors recommend it as an alternative for this project.

devastating mistake. We think of this fear as keeping you from creating the life you want and deserve to live, so acknowledge it and get past it! What's the worst thing that could happen? You won't like it. Your house wouldn't be worthless. Your life won't be ruined. All you would have to do is to paint over it. And in the end your walls will look like they were done with an old plaster technique. Or imagine this: You might end up with a room that you and your family love! Anything you do can be fixed, altered, or changed—but the biggest change when you accomplish a task of this magnitude will be the change you'll see in *you*.

1 Cover your furniture and floor with tarps. Don't forget your gloves and protective eyewear. Apply taping mud, also called *joint compound*. This is a substance you already have

STEP 1 Apply the joint compound on the wall using a trowel. Don't worry about doing this perfectly because the texture adds to the effect you are creating.

on your walls in a thinner and more even coat; it helps get rid of the seams between pieces of drywall. Apply it with a large trowel, which is a big rectangular metal tool with a handle.

The great part about this project is that the less perfect it is, the more beautiful it turns out. Therefore, try to apply the mud in a way that creates many variations in height and texture. Start by throwing five or six handfuls of the joint compound randomly on the wall within arm's reach, and then use the large trowel to spread it. Remember, don't try to be perfect and create a smooth surface, or the end product won't be right. Rough it up a little. Wipe off the trowel and then "knock down," or flatten, the top part of the texture you've just created, leaving slight indentations. Create either small patterns or large patterns, whichever you prefer.

Remember, the more uniform the surface is, the less Tuscan it will look. Note that the entire wall will not necessarily have joint compound on it. The variations will add more dimensions to your wall and make it look more aged.

2 Let the surface dry completely. Look at the label to see how long it needs to dry. We suggest waiting at least overnight, though

Jane Tip:

FOR STEP 3
The sheen of the paint is totally up to you, but be aware that each will create a different look. We suggest a satin finish, as a semi-gloss or high-gloss paint will create less depth and have more sheen. Flat paints tend to absorb more of the darker color, creating fewer differences between the textured areas and the flat ones. Satin sheen is just right.

Jane Tip:

FOR STEP 4
Wait at least 6 hours after painting before applying the oil stain, or you'll wind up with a different look. When applying the stain, make sure not to stop in the middle of a wall with the intention of finishing it later. We've found this causes a variation in the color and will make the wall look uneven. We can't stress enough the importance of starting and finishing a wall in one session.

if it still feels damp to the touch, then wait until it is completely dry, because you'll want to knock down or sand some of the texture to remove any sharp or jagged edges.

3 Apply a coat of lightly colored latex paint with a regular paint roller, but don't press down too hard. When you're done, there should be paint on the flat surfaces but very little or none in the indented areas. You want both painted and unpainted surfaces. Just let the roller choose for you.

4 With a lint-free rag, rub on an oil-based stain such as one normally used on furniture. Apply it heavily with one rag and wipe it off with a second, clean one. Apply stain as far as you can reach and then wipe it off and move on to the next area. You will find

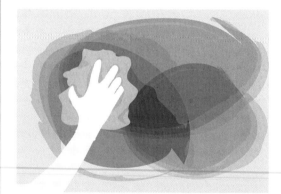

STEP 4 First, apply the oil-based stain to your painted wall with a lint-free rag. Work in areas no larger than 3 feet x 3 feet. With a clean, lint-free rag, remove the stain you just applied. Repeat this process until you've finished the entire wall.

that any areas left unpainted absorb more stain and create a variation of colors.

To add even more depth to your wall, add a second color stain over the first. One beautiful example we've seen is first applying a cherry stain and then a walnut stain on top of it. This creates a warm caramel color.

5 You can always come back and add extra color around the corners and perimeter for a halo effect that is especially Tuscan in feel.

Now your family room has the ambiance you've always desired. Pick up an English/ Italian dictionary because it might not be long before you want to compare your handiwork to the real thing!

Jane Tip:

FOR STEP 5
Experiment before choosing the finished look. Take a piece of Sheetrock, add the mud, and then paint three different colors of paint on it. Apply the stain and possibly even try a second color of stain to see if you like it. You'll get three different finishes to choose from, and you can practice without worrying you didn't choose the right color!

Jane Profile

Just do it. It's fun and satisfying.

Peg "Jane" Achterman

Age: 45

From: Seattle, Washington

Favorite Tool: I love my reciprocating saw—I've had to do a lot of demo on lathe and plaster, and this is the best. I had a major mishap when I was learning how to use it (pulled down about four feet of plaster from my bedroom ceiling when I meant to just open a little hole for an electrical junction box—oops). But I don't know what I'd do without it.

Projects accomplished: The first one was a sixty-foot fence to replace a mass of blackberries. Second, I relocated my washer/dryer outlets in order to move a wall. Then I gutted my kitchen and did the electrical and plumbing. Most recently I designed and built my deck, using recycled bleacher lumber for the decking.

Inspiration for starting home improvement: The Seattle housing market was very expensive, so I had to buy something that needed work in order to live in a particular neighborhood. Buying a fixer house was how I could get there. Also, I like doing things with my hands, and I don't trust contractors as much as I would like to. I may not do the best job, but I know that it's done the way I want and I don't have to watch over someone else's shoulder.

Fears about home improvement: I'm what I like to call a plunger. I just plunge into things without fear and then turn around and say, "What did I get myself into?!" What I've found works best for me is to call my "house coaches" for words of encouragement to tell me it will be okay.

My other fears are around the types of projects that seem like they went great, but you find out weeks, months, or even years later that you didn't do it right, like plumbing or reroofing your house. Plumbing can come back and bite you later. The in-the-walls kind of plumbing is intimidating. I tackled soldering copper once, but I was always wondering, how is it going to bite me later?

How has doing home improvement affected others in your life? Many of my good friends now ask me for help and advice. My friends know they can come to me for help, and I have many friends who have done much of the work themselves. A few have told me that I was their inspiration to work alongside their husbands. I love being able to encourage them to do home projects. I was able to help one of the hairdressers at a local salon by convincing her she didn't need a plumber, just a new toilet mechanism. She went and bought the stuff and did it—she was so proud!

I have girlfriends that call me and say, "Can you come help me?" or call and ask how to do things. I also find it's a great starting point with some guys who are not chatty. If you kind of talk the talk of tools, it's an easy thing to chat about.

Advice for others just getting started in home improvement: Just do it. It's fun and satisfying. Ask questions. Don't worry about being taken advantage of. If you have even a little vocabulary and you ask questions of smaller, specialty stores like good plumbing shops, electrical shops, or good lumber yards, and you show you're fairly serious about it, you'll find it's like having a hundred big brothers. It's nice that as a woman you don't have the whole thing about having to be prideful that men typically do. We can ask for help and advice.

Creating a Functional Family Room

Your family room is your place of gathering, so it must be set up for that purpose. This means having seating to accommodate all of your guests, maintaining a comfortable temperature, and having enough storage for toys, magazines, games, and everything else.

Also, your family room is a room that showcases your family. So you want to make it a place where your family is shown in their best light.

Trophies, pictures, accomplishments—they should all be proudly displayed for all who enter to see.

It's a fact that children who are recognized early for their talents, abilities, and

> "Our family room is the neighborhood clubhouse."
>
> Kelly B.
> San Antonio,
> Texas
> Age 37

achievements lead more confident and fulfilling lives. Kids aside, you want this to be a room that showcases you as a family unit—even if your family is you and your cat. Photos of family trips, dear friends, games you love to play, pieces of your family history—this is the room where these things should live.

Be proud of who your kids are. Be proud of who your friends are. Be proud of who you are. A family room must be functional on multiple levels, as it serves your guests as well as your family. You want your friends and family to want to come in, stay a while, and one day return.

Project: Install a Programmable Thermostat

Jane Quotient: ① ❷ ③ ④ ⑤
Estimated Time: 20 to 30 minutes

When you think of spending time in your family room, of course you expect it to be a comfortable temperature. But you're not always in your family room. With energy prices soaring out of control, this is one area of the house you'd like to heat and cool as you need to.

One easy way to accomplish this is by putting in a programmable thermostat. Most of these thermostats allow you to program changes in temperature for settings such as home, away, day, and night. If your family has a routine, you can program your thermostat to cool and heat as needed.

A programmable thermostat is a great way to start being more energy efficient.

MATERIALS

Tools
- Screwdriver
- Level
- Wire stripper

Supplies
- Programmable thermostat

Note: If you have a heating pump, you should check with a heating contractor before installing a programmable thermostat, as it can actually wind up giving you a higher heating bill.

Note: When buying your thermostat, make sure to get one that is compatible with your current system's electric current. Most systems use 15- to 30-volt wires; don't try to connect one to a 120-volt system.

Jane Tip:

FOR STEP 3
Tape the wires up against the wall while you are working with the new thermostat so they don't fall into the wall.

1 Shut off your furnace (turn the knob to the pilot position) and the electricity coming to the thermostat (turn off the breaker).

2 Remove your old thermostat. To do this, you have to unscrew it from the wall. Most thermostats have a facing that must be pulled off to reveal the screws holding them in place. Once you find them, remove them and pull the thermostat off the wall.

3 The thermostat should now be connected to the wall only by the wires attached at the back. Release them with a flat head screwdriver and remove the old thermostat.

4 Pull the wires through the new base plate. Place the plate up against the wall and use a level make sure that it is level. Attach the plate to the wall using mounting screws, leaving them slightly loose. Check the level again before tightening the screws to the wall.

5 Attach the wires to the appropriate terminals. Typically, the wires are color coded and follow the color coding on your thermostat. Use your wire strippers to expose the copper wire and attach them by creating a hook to fit under the screw terminals and tighten them in place. Push the excess wire back through the hole in the wall.

Jane Tip:

FOR STEP 6

When shopping for your programmable thermostat, you may want to consider purchasing a model that is compatible with your home computer system. This will give you the ability to control the temperature of your home no matter where you are!

6 Put the faceplate on the base; it should just snap in. It should turn on quickly. Now all you need to do is program it to fit your needs. Review the manufacturer's instructions on how to do this. Over the next few weeks, adapt the temperature and settings until you don't notice the variations in temperature.

It may seem a small factor in creating a warm and inviting home, but a continuously comfortable temperature will make a big difference for both your home and your wallet.

Being Creative with Family Photos

Many of us spend a great deal of money for artwork when we actually already have pictures we like looking at. One simple project you can do is to cover a wall with pictures of family and friends. That picture of you with knobby knees and braces is far more interesting than a print that matches your couch. Think of it as a visual way of telling the stories of your life to your friends and family. And forget about the days when pictures had to be hung a certain way. Get a few frames you love and create groupings with the help of a laser level like the Ryobi MultiTASKit. Place your pictures diagonally or vertically, or blow up one of your favorites and create a frame collage with lots of different-sized frames around it. It may not be a Gauguin or a Picasso, but the artwork on this wall will draw everyone's attention while adding a comfortable and familiar feeling to your family room.

Project: Build a Window Seat with Storage

Jane Quotient: ① ② ③ ❹ ⑤
Estimated Time: 5 to 6 hours

One way to dramatically increase the functionality of your family room is to supply it with enough seating and storage. Window seats are a great way to do both! Window seats are practical, beautiful, and, if planned out properly, multifunctional.

Building a window seat from scratch can be quite intensive. So for this project, we'll use pre-manufactured wall cabinets to create a "built-in" window seat that beautifies your window while providing that extra storage space every family needs!

MATERIALS

Tools
- Tape measure
- Prybar
- 4 to 6 pieces 2 x 4-inch lumber
- Screwdriver
- Clamps
- Level
- Cordless drill
- Jigsaw or circular saw
- Caulk gun
- Nail set
- Putty knife (if necessary)

Supplies
- Premanufactured wall cabinet set
- Safety glasses
- 2-inch wood screws
- Adhesive caulk
- #6 finish nails
- Caulk or wood putty

Jane Tip:

FOR STEP 2
Consider also purchasing a bit of molding that matches your cabinets. This will help you to finish off the base and sides of the cabinets to give you that professional look.

1 The first thing you'll want to do is determine the measurements for height, width, and depth in the area you plan adding a window seat. You'll want to be certain to complete this before selecting your cabinets. Make sure the depth of the seat is at least 20 inches (otherwise, you'll feel like you're constantly slipping off), but not so deep that you lose any back support you might get from the partial wall.

2 It's time to shop! By visiting a kitchen supply store or major home improvement store, using your measurements, you should be able to find appropriate-sized cabinets for your needs. There are often dozens of potential selections. Just make sure you choose cabinets that satisfy your storage needs and can support the weight of one of two people (it is still a "window seat" after all!).

3 You'll need to prep the area first by removing any baseboard molding from the sitting area. Otherwise it may impede the new cabinet from going flush against the wall. Use a pry bar with a piece of scrap wood (a shim) between the pry bar and your wall to protect the drywall.

4 Create a wooden frame pedestal out of the lumber. It's important that your frame be the same width as the window seat area but approximately 3 inches less than the depth of your window seats. This will help the overall support of the unit. For even greater stability, add a center support board. Once your frame is built, lay it inside the seat area. If it fits, go ahead and screw both the back boards and the side boards to the wall.

5 You're now ready to place your cabinets onto the frame. To keep your fingers safe and to lighten the load, first remove the doors from the cabinets. Be sure to keep any hardware you remove in a safe place.

6 If you're using two sets of cabinets, clamp them together to make sure they are flush on top. You'll also want to be sure to check along the front. Use a level across the seam where the two pieces meet.

7 Once you've determined that they're level, use a drill bit that is narrower than the screws and drill pilot holes in the side frames of each cabinet. Then, using wood screws, screw the units together.

8 To give your window seat that professional look, make sure to properly center the cabinets between the two side walls. You will have space on either side of the cabinets at this point, but not to worry—we're going to fill those in during a later step.

Jane Tip:

FOR STEP 5

If you intend to paint your cabinets, consider doing this before you install them onto the frame. It will be easier to touch them up than to paint or stain them after you've installed them.

Jane Tip:

FOR STEP 9

To make sure you screw into the wood, mark where the base meets the underside of the cabinets. As the base is recessed, it's easy to potentially miss this.

9 Now you'll want to screw the cabinets into the base pedestal. Be sure to drill pilot holes first to make this easier.

10 You will most likely have a space between the cabinets and the wall. Then measure the width of this space. Measure the height by measuring from the top of the cabinets to just above the baseboard molding. You'll use these measurements to cut a filler piece with a circular saw or a jigsaw. Remember, the filler piece should be as high as the face of the cabinets. You may need to use your jigsaw to shape the bottom of the filler piece of you need it to go around your baseboard molding so that it will be flush against the wall.

11 Attach the filler pieces to the sides of the cabinet with wood screws. You'll want to be sure to keep the pieces flush with the cabinets as you work.

12 To complete the seat top, you'll want to first find some shelving material that closely matches the cabinets both in material and style. Take measurements of both the cabinet face and the depth of the cabinets. Keep in mind that your seat can slightly overlap the front of the cabinets. Cut your piece according to your measurements and check the fit. If all is well, remove the piece and run a bead of adhesive caulk along the cabinet edges. Press the seat back in place.

13 If you would like to upholster the seat top, it's a great way to add a bit of decorative flair. If not, go ahead and skip this step. You don't have to paint or stain the seat, just start by cutting a piece of fabric that fits the dimensions. You'll also need a piece of 1½- to 2-inch foam cut to the size of the seat top. Lay the fabric facedown on the floor, then lay the batting on top of it, with the cut foam evenly spaced on the batting. Place the seat top facedown exactly on top of the foam.

Wrap the fabric and batting around the edge to the underneath of the top. Use a staple gun (preferably electric) and staple the fabric to the seat in the gap between the edge of the seat before the cleat. Staple the fabric all the way around, wrapping the corners like presents and stapling them down. Trim off any excess fabric and batting, then place the top on your window seat.

Jane Tip:

FOR STEP 13

An easy and effective way to cut the foam is with an electric carving knife. Just mark and cut, being careful to know where your fingers are at all times.

14 Use your jigsaw to cut a piece of cabinet trim the same length as the face of the cabinets. You'll want to install this on the face of the seat piece by using finishing nails. Use a nail set to countersink the heads of the nails.

15 Replace your cabinet doors and fill in any noticeable crevices with caulk or wood putty. If you have large gaps between the seat and the wall, consider using trim pieces to disguise them.

Extra-large Pillows Make Great Chairs in a Pinch

If you need additional seating space for kids, friends, or family, consider making a few oversized throw pillows for the floor. They're not only an inexpensive alternative to new furniture, but you can make them in an afternoon! These are especially great for children, who can sit with their friends or be comfortable while playing on the floor.

Purchase the largest pillow forms you can find—no smaller than 22 inches square. Most fabric stores carry them, as do numerous websites. Keep in mind that both padding and durability count, as people will be placing their entire body weight on the pillow. Whenever possible, buy high-quality pillow forms that use down feathers rather than fiberfill or other man-made materials. Alternatively, if you're looking for something bigger or longer than a square pillow form, consider high-density foam. This material forms a square or rectangular box shape instead of a soft square like a pillow, but it provides more room to stretch out on. You can purchase 4-inch-thick foam at most fabric stores, and they often will cut it to size for you. Again—be sure to buy the highest-quality foam for the most comfort and durability.

Your next step is to find fabric that matches your taste and current décor. Keep in mind that these pillows will be used as seating, so be sure to choose fabric that's durable and easy to clean. Additionally, when creating these "pillow cases," consider sewing in a zipper so you can clean them regularly.

Project: Build an End or Coffee Table with Storage

Jane Quotient: ① ② ③ ❹ ⑤
Estimated Time: 3 to 4 hours

First and foremost, your family room should be a place that makes you feel comfortable. It shouldn't be a place where clutter comes to die. All too often, this room seems to attract everything that won't fit in the rest of the house.

Many family rooms don't have enough room for storage, especially in homes with children and their many toys. Relaxing in a room full of clutter can be a challenge. The trick is multifunctional furniture, such as end tables that double as storage units.

They're easy to make and fun, too!

MATERIALS

Tools
- Tape measure
- C-clamp
- Jigsaw or circular saw
- Drill
- Drill bits
- Screwdriver bit
- Countersetter
- Miter box
- Hammer

Supplies
- Protective eyewear
- Pencil
- $1/2$-inch birch plywood
- 1 x 2-inch inexpensive wood boards
- $1^{1}/_{16}$-inch wood screws
- Wood glue
- 1-inch wood screws
- $1^{1}/_{4}$-inch wood screws
- 1 x 4-inch poplar or pine boards
- Sandpaper
- 1-inch brad nails
- Spackle (for painting) or wood putty (for staining)
- Decorative molding
- Pine laminate board (optional)
- Primer
- Paint or stain

"Having a coffee table that can double as a toy chest is awesome!"

Tanya T.
Oklahoma City, Oklahoma
Age 39

1 The dimensions of the box you're making are 20 x 20 inches. Cut the 4 sides and the bottom. For the bottom piece, mark a 20 x 20-inch square on the birch plywood. For the sides, measure the thickness of the plywood (it should be $1/2$ inch). You'll want to take this thickness into account when cutting the other sides of the box. Subtract the thickness of the bottom piece from the length of the side pieces to ensure you get a 20 x 20-inch box.

(The reason for the variance is to create a true square. You must take into account the amount each of the sides will overlap onto the other. Once they are attached, they will create a 20-inch square.) Once you've marked everything out, clamp your birch plywood down, put on your protective eyewear, and cut out all 5 pieces using a jigsaw or circular saw.

2 Attach the 4 sides of your box together, using the 1 x 2-inch pieces of wood as cleats. Cleats form a larger surface area to use in attaching the sides to each other. Cut 4 pieces that are 19 inches long. Then, with your tape measure and a pencil, mark a line ½ inch going vertically along the left of the 19-inch side—that is, off ½ inch from the one that is 19½ inches. Attach 1 cleat to each of the 4 pieces to the right of the line you've drawn, with one edge lined up on the bottom.

Attach the cleat with 1 1/16-inch wood screws and wood glue, screwing through the cleats into the wood below. Have the wider side of the cleat flat on the board. If you've measured the right amount of room, when you place the board to attach it, the edges should be flush.

3 Lay one of the side pieces on a work surface with the cleat facing up and toward you. Place wood glue on the ½-inch area between the cleat and the edge, then stand a second side piece up where you've put the glue. Proper placement will have the cleat of the second piece on the opposite side of the plywood facing away from you and toward the inside of the box. While holding the second side in place, predrill with a small drill bit to prevent splitting. Attach the second piece by screwing in three or four 1-inch wood screws with your drill through the side and into the cleat.

Attach the other 2 pieces to finish the sides of your cube.

4 Attach the bottom of the box to the sides using wood glue and two or three 1¼-inch wood screws per side. For better surface area, attach the screws through the cleats, which should all butt up against the bottom.

5 Add a bit of pizzazz to your cube. Using 1 x 4-inch boards, cut pieces with your miter box to go around the edges of each side. You don't need to miter these edges; just butt them up together. Make sure to sand down the

Jane Tip:

FOR STEP 3

Try to counterset all of the screws, which will make it easier to add trim later. Once all 4 sides are attached, you will be able to get better leverage with your drill. Insert the screwdriver bit into the screw, push down, and activate the drill.

Jane Tip:

FOR STEP 5

To know what size pieces you'll need, cut 2 at 20 inches and attach them to the vertical sides, up against the edges. Measure the distance between the 2 attached pieces, cut 2 pieces of that length, and attach them the same way. If you are using 1 x 4-inch pieces, they will probably end up 12 inches in length.

cut edges with fine to very fine sandpaper before attaching. Attach them with wood glue and 1-inch brad nails. Counterset the nails so that all that is left behind is a hole. Fill the holes with spackle if you plan to paint the box or wood putty if you plan to stain it. Do this on all four of the sides.

6 To trim your box, add ½-inch decorative molding to the corners of the sides by cutting 20-inch pieces. Attach the pieces with wood glue and counterset brad nails.

Cut 8 pieces of the ½-inch molding to go around the top and bottom of the box, but this time at 45-degree angles. When cutting them, hold the molding vertically against the miter box to get the correct angle.

To make your panels look more detailed without using a router, cut 4 pieces of the same molding for each side. Place these in the center of the panel against the 1 x 4-inch molding you already attached. Cut these at a 45-degree angle, but lay the molding flat on the miter box when cutting.

7 Once all of these pieces are attached, it's time to cut the top. Cut a 24-inch square from pine laminate board, and then cut four 1 x 2-inch cleats to fit into the center of the box. Attach them to the top using brad nails and wood glue to keep the top from sliding around. Then cut 4 more pieces of the ½-inch decorative molding. Add them to the edge of the top using brad nails.

8 Fill in any holes left behind with either spackle or wood putty. To paint the box, start with a layer of primer, both inside and out, and then paint 2 coats of satin-finish paint. If you plan to stain and urethane, apply a coat of wood conditioner before staining and sealing.

Project: Install Childproof Outlets

Jane Quotient: ① ② ❸ ④ ⑤
Estimated Time: **Less than 1 hour per outlet**

If you have young children, one constant worry is what they might do with an electrical outlet when you're not looking. Electrical accidents take just a fraction of a second.

Most new homes are built with protective measures in place, but if yours isn't, consider changing out the outlets in your family room for childproof safety outlets. These are fairly simple units that won't supply any power unless both prongs of a plug are inserted. So if your child experiments with a fork and an outlet, there is much less chance of an injury.

This project has a double benefit in that you'll also update the look of your old outlets.

MATERIALS
Tools
- Phillips head screwdriver
- Needlenose pliers
- Lineman's pliers
- Wire strippers
- Penlight electrical tester or similar electrical tester

Supplies
- New outlet
- Wire caps/nuts
- New faceplate (optional)

👓 **Safety Check!**
If you think your outlet is seriously deteriorated, call an electrician. It could be a fire hazard, or you could harm yourself by trying to remove it.

Note: Your outlet and receptacle consist of wiring, a mounting bracket, and a faceplate. For the most part, older homes have two-holed outlets—one hole is hot and the other one neutral—while in newer homes the outlets have three holes: still one hot and one neutral, plus

Jane Tip:
For those outlets that are near a water source, consider installing GFCI outlets instead for added security. (see "Install a GFCI Outlet," on page 85) These outlets, though a little more expensive, are specifically designed to break the flow of electricity should a surge occur.

A three-pronged outlet (left) is grounded for added safety. This two-pronged outlet (right) is not.

a smaller bottom hole (the grounding connection), which serves as a safety feature.

Be sure to match the color of your new outlet terminal to your faceplates as best you can. Outlets are inexpensive and easy to change out, and new, fresh-looking outlets give a room a professional-quality look.

👓 **Safety Tip!**
Be sure to purchase the same type of outlet you have now. *Do not* try to upgrade an outlet from an older two-hole outlet to a three-hole outlet, as this can be very unsafe. To make this upgrade, call an electrician.

1 Turn off the power to the work area by tripping the correct circuit breaker. Verify it is off by using an electrical or voltage tester on the outlet you plan to change out. If it is still hot—meaning electricity is flowing to it—the tester will make a noise or illuminate. If it does, go back to the electrical panel and consider shutting off all power coming to your home to be safe. If, after this step, you test it again and it is *still* hot, call a professional. **Do not proceed if you are not 100 percent certain the power is off.** If, however, you test the outlet and the power *is* off—you're good to go!

👓 Safety Tip!

In a damaged outlet (receptacle), the wires may be hot even though no power was evident when the outlet was tested. If you think the receptacle is damaged, remove the faceplate and, using a voltage tester, touch the top pair of terminals with the probes and then the bottom two terminals to be sure it's safe to work on.

2 Unscrew and remove the faceplate. Be sure to save the tiny screws for later, especially if you plan to use the same faceplate.

3 Unscrew the 2 mounting screws holding the outlet in place. Without moving any wires yet, gently pull out the old outlet. You may need to wiggle it a bit if it's been in there a while. The stiffness you feel is normal; it's simply the tension of the copper wiring.

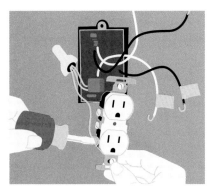

STEP 3 Unscrew the 2 mounting screws holding the wires in place on your old outlet.

Jane Tip:

You can find outlets in standard white, off-white, and almond. You can also find them in stainless steel and some other colors, usually by special order through your home improvement center.

Jane Tip:

FOR STEP 3

Before you remove the old outlet, hold the new outlet next to the old one. Note where the wires on the new outlet will go and line them up. This will make it easier when you install it.

Jane Tip:

FOR STEP 4

Mark where each wire is attached to the old outlet with a different colored pen. This way, you know exactly which wire is connected where, and you can duplicate the order on the new outlet. Be sure to make note of which pen color represents which wire.

4 Detach the wiring. If you need to check for the eleventh time, use your penlight tester again. That's okay; we like to be sure, too.

Note: Note either 3 or 5 wires coming out of the wall. If you have 5 wires, it means the outlet is in the middle of a run, which is one line that feeds numerous switches or receptacles. One wire is wrapped around a screw—this is the grounding wire—and the remaining wires attach to holes in the back of the outlet. If you have 3 wires, the outlet is at the end of a run and you can attach the wires as indicated.

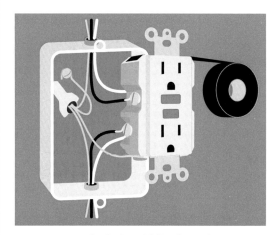

STEP 4 Receptacles in the middle of a run have 5 wires: 2 white, 2 black, and 1 ground.

STEP 4 Receptacles at the end of a run have 3 wires: 1 white, 1 black, and 1 ground.

5 One by one, loosen the terminal screws that hold each wire in place. Be sure the wires coming from the wall have enough bare wire to allow attachment to the new outlet wires. If there is too much insulation around the wire tips, use wire strippers to pull off some of the insulation. Make sure the bare wires are completely encased in the wire nut.

6 Now that the old outlet is free from your wall, attach the wires to the new childproof outlet in the same places as the old outlet.

7 Once all the wires are attached, gently push the outlet back into the box and tighten the mounting screws. Be sure the outlet is sitting straight; you may have trouble putting on the faceplate if it is not.

8 Before you replace the faceplate, make sure the job was done right. Go back to your electrical panel and restore power. Return to your new outlet and test it again using your electrical tester. Assuming you get a signal and your outlet is functioning, replace the faceplate and you're done!

Note: If the outlet is not working after you've turned the power back on, check the wires. You may not have inserted them correctly, or they are not quite tight enough. Often the problem is just one loose wire. *Be sure to turn the power back off* before you mess with the wires again!

Jane Tip:

FOR STEP 8
If you have young children who get their fingers into everything, you can protect them by easily inserting inexpensive electrical outlet caps. These are thin plastic disks that insert directly into the holes and cover the outlet so kids can't get into trouble.

Other Safety Issues

Many family rooms are the children's play area. Knowing this made us think about how you can protect your child from some of the seemingly innocuous but dangerous things in there. A good example is the cords hanging from horizontal blinds. Your child can get dangerously entangled in these! To prevent this, purchase inexpensive cord wind-ups. These devices retract extra cord and hold it out of your child's way.

You can put outlet protectors into any electrical outlets within reach of small children if you don't have time to change them out for childproof units. If you have toddlers, cover the edges of your coffee table with a protective bumper. These are just a few of the ways you can protect your family from avoidable household accidents.

Jane Profile

I look at what I've done in my home and say, "I did that! That's really cool!"

Sandra "Jane" Johnson

Age: 51

From: Orlando, Florida

Favorite tool: Table saw.

Projects accomplished: My kitchen. I turned my old, dark kitchen cabinets into antique white cabinets that have a sage green faux finish on the fronts. I installed antique silverware. The walls are brick red, and I installed new countertops that match my new white appliances, and I put in a great-looking light fixture too!

I used joint compound in the master bathroom and troweled it on the walls, let it completely dry, then painted. I also removed the ceramic toilet paper holder. I replaced the old baseboards with new ones and even glued a matching piece along the bottom of the bathtub. I had pulled off the old existing vinyl piece and found that part of the tub had rusted away. I didn't want to tackle replacing the tub, so I just put a matching baseboard piece along the bottom of the tub and painted it to match the others. I faux-finished some shelves, a cute little wooden table, and a window frame with glass in which I placed a piece of art I painted to make it look like a window facing a garden.

I also fauxed some picture frames and bought Victorian-style figurines to fill the shelves. All the faux finishes are done in the shabby chic technique.

Inspiration for starting home improvement: It needed to be done and no one else wanted to do it but me. So I said, "Why not?" Besides, I like to do stuff like that anyway.

Fears about home improvement: My biggest fear was, "Am I going to mess it up?!" I was afraid I'd get started and ruin everything and in the end have to buy new cabinets.

How has doing home improvement affected your life? The most obvious way it affects me is that it makes my house look better—though on a deeper level it makes me proud of my home and of myself. I look at what I've done in my home and say, "I did that! That's really cool!"

Advice for others just getting started in home improvement: I'd have to say to definitely do a lot of research before you start doing anything. The research will save you a ton of time and sometimes money, too.

Project: Update Your Mantelpiece

Jane Quotient: ① ② ❸ ④ ⑤
Estimated Time: 3 to 5 hours

Picture a relaxing evening spent reclining by the fireplace, enjoying its warm, crackling, magical flames. You're all cuddled up, snug as a bug, when all of a sudden you realize something's amiss. There are no photos of your family, no antique knickknacks sharing shelf space—no mantelpiece at all!

Updating or adding a mantelpiece can quickly turn your fireplace into a hot item—and not just because of the flames!

It might be that your mantelpiece simply needs a face-lift. In less than an afternoon you can change the face of your fireplace by framing the heat of the fire in the warmth of your heart.

MATERIALS

Tools

- Tape measure
- Level
- Stud finder
- Drill with screwdriver bits and masonry bits
- Hammer
- Screws

Supplies

- Piece of wood at least 36 x 2 x 8 inches (These measurements are a minimum. Be sure the wood is long enough to extend past your fireplace by at least 2 inches on each side.)
- Pencil
- Wall anchors
- Masonry anchors (should your wall be made of brick or cement)
- 2 to 4 mounting brackets with predrilled holes (corbels)

"Our son's achievements have turned our fireplace into a trophy case."

Sophie K.
Montreal, Quebec
Age 47

1 Get familiar with your work area and your tools. Look at the space above your fireplace where you will place the mantelpiece. Is it made of brick, cement, or drywall?

👓 **Safety Check!**
If you have tile above your fireplace, you will need to place the shelf above it. Do not install a shelf into decorative tile, as tile does not have the strength to hold it securely.

Note: The type of tools and fasteners you use to anchor your shelf depends on the material above your fireplace. If you have cement or brick above your fireplace, use the masonry bits and masonry anchors. If it is drywall and studs, anchors may not be necessary.

2 Decide how high your mantelpiece should sit. Hold it above your fireplace until you are visually happy with its location, leaving at least an 18-inch clearance from the fireplace opening. (You need this minimum height so you don't burn your gorgeous home improvement project—or the rest of your house!)

3 With your pencil and level in hand, make a straight horizontal line above your fireplace. Remember to stay a minimum of 18 inches above the opening. Be sure the line extends past the fireplace at least 2 inches to both left and right.

4 Use a stud finder to find the wall studs. Hold the stud finder in one hand and move it along the straight line you drew. In your other hand, hold the pencil and mark the studs as you go. Mark the beginning point and ending point of the stud (studs are usually 2 inches wide). The easiest way to find these edges is by marking the spot where the stud finder first goes off and then marking the spot where the beeping stops. This will help you locate the center of the studs. Otherwise, by

STEP 4 Using a pencil and a stud finder, mark the studs in the wall.

Jane Tip:

FOR STEP 6
We know it's redundant for us to say, but use only masonry bits for cement and brick. Drywall bits may break apart.

drilling willy-nilly into a stud, you may hit the edge, which would negate the purpose of drilling into the stud.

5 Continue marking all of the studs along the straight line you drew. Because your fireplace is at least 36 inches wide and studs are placed every 16 inches, there should be at least two studs but more likely three.

6 With your drill and your drill bits (masonry bits for cement and brick, regular drill bits for drywall), create pilot holes in the center of the studs. The size of the drill bit depends on the material you are drilling into. If it is brick or masonry, use the same size as the anchor you are placing in the wall. If you are drilling into a stud, use a drill bit about 2 sizes smaller than the size of the screw. The purpose of drilling a pilot hole is to make screwing into wood easier.

7 If you are using anchors, push one into a hole until you feel a little resistance, then use your hammer to tap it the rest of the way in. Do this for the remaining holes.

8 Screw the predrilled corbels (decorative mounting brackets) into the wall. If you are drilling into brick or cement, use masonry screws for this step. If you are drilling into a stud, use wood screws. Place a corbel onto the wall, lining up the predrilled hole in the corbel to the predrilled anchor/hole in the wall. Attach the corbel by screwing through the corbel. Repeat this step for the remaining corbels.

9 Place the shelf on the corbels. Because you already leveled the line and used it as your reference point, the shelf should be level as long as the tops of the corbels line up with your line. Place a level on the shelf to be certain. If the air bubble in the level is nowhere near the center, remove at least one of the corbels and drill another anchor hole.

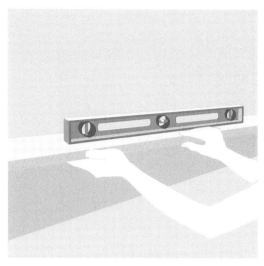

STEP 9 **Place the shelf on the mounting brackets and then place the level on the shelf to be certain it isn't tilting.**

10 Drill the shelf onto the corbels—first through the corbel and up into the shelf, not down through the shelf into the corbel. If your shelf and corbel together are only 3 inches thick, be sure not to use screws 4 inches long, as they will stick up through the shelf. Instead, use screws about $1/2$ inch shorter than the total thickness of the wood. Try to hold the drill as close to true vertical as possible. Continue this until you have attached all corbels to the shelf.

Making a Spa-licious Bathroom

Your bathroom is one of the first things you see each day. It's usually your first stop after getting out of bed. You brush your teeth, you wash your face, you shower, you do your hair and makeup, and you get started with your day.

You do this *every single day*.

What you might not realize is that if your bathroom doesn't convey a feeling of luxury, comfort, and relaxation, it might very well subconsciously affect the attitude you carry with you for the rest of your day.

Your bathroom should be your own personal spa. It should be a retreat—a place for you to relax, replenish, and rejuvenate.

But your bathroom may be drawing your energy from you rather than providing you with the atmosphere of pampering and care you deserve.

If you could give your bathroom a spa makeover, what would you do? Spas that make you feel like a queen for a day are clean and comfortable. They don't have chipped porcelain sinks or rusting faucets. In fact, everything functions perfectly. The toilets, faucets, and showerheads work as if they were brand-new.

To really make your bathroom seem like a spa, it would also have to have a feeling of relaxation and luxury. High-end tile counter-tops, beautiful mirrors, and fluffy towels on elegant towel racks can make you feel like using them is a guilty pleasure.

Now that's the kind of spa you'd love to wake up to every day. The good news is that with just a little effort, you can.

> "I am a single mom who doesn't want to always have to wait for someone to come and do something for me. I needed a bathroom makeover and couldn't afford to have it done, so I have attempted to do it myself."
>
> Lynn F.
> Clawson,
> Michigan
> Age 45

Jane Profile

Don't be afraid of making mistakes.

Brooke "Jane" Coe

Age: 35

From: Redondo Beach, California

Favorite tool: Reciprocating spindle sander—because it smoothes the curves in my wood projects just right, and I have lots of curves in my furniture designs.

Projects accomplished: I've done a bit of everything! At my first home in Atlanta, we had a backyard that was a mess. The door from the master bedroom had two concrete steps that went down to a patch of weeks and cotton. We liked to entertain and needed a place to do it. Since our house had only two bedrooms and one bath, we decided to extend the party outdoors. With this in mind, I designed a deck that was multilevel and had integrated seating, lighting, and custom copper sunburst railing detail. It was almost 25 x 20 feet and was amazing.

I've also redone kitchens, bathrooms, bedrooms, dining rooms, and living rooms in houses of friends and mine, as well.

Inspiration for starting home Improvement: I purchased a 1947 bungalow in Atlanta, Georgia. The bones of the house were pretty good, but the flow and the cosmetics were awful. The one really funky thing was that the kitchen had a window looking into a "storage area," which used to be an exterior porch. When previous owners remodeled and turned the porch into an additional room, they left the window so you would look out it into another room of your house—odd. It was either do it myself or live with it.

Fears about home improvement: I think the biggest fear for anyone when starting home improvements is a fear of messing up. Trust me, I've messed up *many* times, but I've always been able to fix the situation. When I opened up my first wall to inset a medicine cabinet, I was afraid that I'd cut into wiring or plumbing—basically, it was a fear of the unknown. But it turned out perfect, and I've since moved entire walls with no issues.

How has doing home improvement affected your life? It's made me want to challenge myself more. The more I learn, the more I realize that there's so much I don't know. But instead of being afraid of the unknown, I now want to tackle it and learn it. It's driven me drive to continuously improve my knowledge and myself.

How has doing home improvement affected others in your life? I love it when men come into my home and are blown away by all I have done. At first, they're intimidated and play the macho card, but then they loosen up and start asking me for advice on their projects. The truly funny thing is the reaction of my two boys (ages four and six) whenever they hear people talking about doing something to their homes. They say, "Why don't you just do it? My mommy does stuff like that all the time!" I love that they don't know any different—it's empowering to them to have a role model, and it gives me a feeling of fulfillment knowing that they don't see any boundaries or male/female roles.

Advice for others just getting started in home improvement: Don't be afraid of making mistakes. Actually, by making mistakes, you really get to learn and understand the process. The biggest obstacle to home improvement is just getting started. Pick up a tool, do your research, and try. You might not get it right the first time, so try again. It's okay. Good luck!

Creating a Clean and Comfortable Bathroom

The first thing you want to feel when you walk into your bathroom is that you have just entered your own personal retreat. It should immediately evoke a sense of relaxation and calm, both mentally and physically. Unfortunately, having a dirty sink or countertop will quickly pull you out of this Zen-like state and into a feeling of needing to clean.

But sometimes, no matter how much you clean, your bathroom is in need of more than just a good scrub. Maybe the grout is stained. Maybe the tiles are broken. Maybe the toilet is old. Maybe you don't have a sense of true privacy. All of these can negatively affect your comfort level.

Let's start with one of the bigger problem areas in most bathrooms: the tile. It might be broken, stained, chipped, or simply outdated, or you might love your tile, but you're disgusted by the grout. Or maybe just one or two tiles are broken.

The good news is that just like many do-it-yourself bathroom projects, this is easy to fix. These simple projects will make a world of difference in helping you create that spa-licious feeling!

> "Ever since we redid the bathroom, we've called it the 'room for a bath.'"
>
> Meaghan M.
> Sioux Falls,
> Nebraska
> Age 29

Project: Replace a Broken Tile

Jane Quotient: ① ❷ ③ ④ ⑤
Estimated Time: 2 to 3 hours

When you want to relax, you don't want to be distracted by anything—so replace the problem tile! Luckily, this is easy to do. The hardest parts of the following projects are finding a tile that matches what you've got and making sure the new tile grout matches the old.

MATERIALS

Tools
- ▨ 5-in-1 putty knife
- ▨ Hammer
- ▨ Flat head screwdriver
- ▨ Rotary tool with grout-cutting blade
- ▨ Grout float

Supplies
- ▨ Safety glasses
- ▨ Mastic
- ▨ Grout in your choice of color
- ▨ Sponge
- ▨ Grout sealant

Note: Try using the 5-in-1 putty knife first to see if you can scrape away the grout on your own. If you find that it is too difficult (or time-consuming), move up the grout saw. But the easiest way is with a little power. A rotary tool (like a Dremel) often has a grout-cutting blade as a separate attachment. This terrific tool will dramatically speed the process.

👓 **Safety Check!**
Make sure you're wearing your safety glasses for this project. Small pieces of tile or grout might fly up at you, and you should be protected.

Jane Tip:
Rotary tools are a perfect addition to any tool collection and are extremely affordable!

1 Before you can get to the broken tile, you need to remove the grout that surrounds it. If you try to remove the tile without removing the old grout first, you run the risk of breaking additional tiles. Using a rotary tool with a grout-cutting blade, cut away the old grout by working the tool back and forth between the tiles. Sweep up the debris to get it out of your way once this step is complete.

STEP 1 Using a rotary tool with a grout-cutting blade, remove the old grout.

2 With the grout gone from around the damaged tile, see if you can lift some of the broken pieces of the tile itself. Depending on where the tile is broken, you might be able to use the 5-in-1 putty knife or the hammer and flat head screwdriver to lift it up and off. If these techniques don't work, place a rag on the broken tile and hit it with the hammer. You want the rag there to keep pieces from flying up at you. Hit the tile hard enough to break it into a number of pieces that you can now easily remove. Don't forget to wear your safety glasses!

3 Using the flat head screwdriver, lift out the broken pieces of tile. Use your hammer to chip away at stubborn pieces, being careful not to damage the surrounding tile. Use the 5-in-1 putty knife to scrape away the old mastic. The goal is to create a smooth, clean surface for the new tile to stick to.

4 Brush away any debris to make sure the area is clean. Apply mastic to the new piece of tile by spreading it on the back as if you were buttering toast. Then run your trowel with the ¼-inch notches through the

"I can finally prove to everyone and anyone—well, specifically a man I know as Dad—that I can do the fix-its that he would have casually taken over or hired out to someone who "knows what they're doing."

Ashley B.
Winston-Salem,
North Carolina
Age 25

mastic, which will leave ridges, allowing the tile to be set. Set the tile in place, leaving the appropriate amount of space for grout. Let it dry completely before continuing.

5 If you need just a little grout, consider buying the smaller, premixed package. If the tiles you're working on are relatively small (such as shower tiles), you can work in the grout with a damp sponge. For much larger tiles, like floor tiles, use a grout float to work the grout into the tile joints. Wipe away any excess and let dry according to the manufacturer's instructions. A haze will remain on the tiles that you can wipe away with a damp sponge.

6 Don't skip this step! One of the easiest things to forget is that *grout should be sealed.* Sealing your grout ensures that it will last a lifetime. The color, quality, and durability will hold up for years to come. Make sure the grout you used has cured long enough (10–30 days) according to the manufacturer's instructions. Apply the grout sealant to the affected areas and let dry.

Project: Recolor Grout

Jane Quotient: ❶ ② ③ ④ ⑤
Estimated Time: 2 to 10 hours depending on the size of the area

We know that grout is one of those little things you probably never think about. But there it is, staring at you every morning as you brush your teeth, pour your morning coffee—all the cracks, stains, and discolored spots crying out, "Please help me!"

If removing the grout is too time-consuming, or if your grout is simply discolored, there's an easy way to restore the grout to its original splendor. By coloring it, you can dramatically enhance your tile, often making it look like new! This technique is great for your spa-licious bathroom but can also be used on kitchen counters and any other tiled area.

To restore grout to an attractive, uniform color, apply an epoxy grout colorant, also known as *grout paint*. It's available in typical grout colors such as white, beige, and gray as well as many premixed colors and even custom blends. Today's colorants are easy to apply, can last up to fifteen years, and, best of all, they actually look good. You can even use them to brighten the appearance of an entire floor.

MATERIALS

Tools
- Paintbrushes

Supplies
- Grout colorant (your choice of color)
- Ceramic tile cleaner
- Heavy-duty rubber gloves
- Safety glasses
- Knee pads or thick towel
- Light-duty scouring pad

Note: Because this project is detail-orientated, it calls for both time and patience. If you're working on a floor, you could be kneeling for hours! Be sure to purchase high-quality knee pads before you start!

> "I thought I'd have to retile my whole floor until I discovered grout colorant. It was tedious but worth it!"
>
> Sharon B.
> Montreal, Quebec
> Age 28

1 Each grout colorant brand has somewhat different instructions, so choose your colorant brand first. Brands vary in drying time, waiting time between coats, and application methods. For example, some brands call for finishing the application and cleaning up (more on this later) within 1 hour. Thus, for large jobs, you must stop painting and clean up what you've done before the project is completely done.

You'll want to be sure of the color as well. Paint in general may dry slightly differently than the container indicates. Consider starting your project in an inconspicuous area such as behind an appliance or on the edge of a countertop. When the test area is done, check the color to be sure you're happy with it.

2 Inspect and repair any broken tiles and cracked grout. Now is the time to make repairs to deteriorating grout or to replace broken tiles (refer to "Replace a Broken Tile" on page 150). We promise you that if you don't, once you apply the colorant, you'll wish you had made the effort!

3 Clean the surface area. The grout must be properly prepared so the colorant will stick. Any old food, oils, soap residue, or grout sealers may cause the colorant to fail or even bead on surface.

Clean the tile with a special ceramic tile cleaner. These cleaners are harsh (so gloves and eye protection are required) and take off almost anything, including aged grout sealer. Some colorant manufacturers have their own branded cleaning product but choosing to use it is up to you. Whatever product you use, rinse carefully with hot water to remove chemical residue.

Allow the area to dry thoroughly before continuing. A large floor fan will speed drying if you're working on a tile floor.

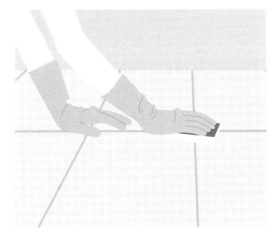

STEP 3 **Clean the tile with a special ceramic tile cleaner to remove old grout sealers. Make sure to wear gloves and protective eyewear, as the cleaner can be caustic.**

Jane Tip:
FOR STEP 2
A special caution if you have unglazed tile such as terrazzo, natural stone, or any raw clay variant: This type of tile must be sealed prior to colorant application because the colorant may permanently stain it. Because fresh sealant will keep the colorant from sticking to the grout, any tile resealing must be done carefully and painstakingly, one tile at a time, to avoid sealing the grout. Patience is key here.

Jane Tip:
FOR STEP 4
Depending on the width of the grout line, you can trim the brush with scissors so it is stiffer and more controlled. Have two or three brushes handy in case you make a mistake when cutting the first. Experiment to find the right brush and brushing style for you.

4 Apply the colorant. If you're working on a floor, be sure to get out your knee pads or a thick towel. Trust us; you're knees will thank you later.

■ **CHOOSE A BRUSH.** We've tried various types of brushes, including the cheap, throwaway hog bristle brushes that come with some colorant application kits. Keep in mind that you want to give the grout a thin, even coat of colorant with minimal overlapping onto the tile. We prefer to use small, cheap artist brushes, found in most hardware or paint stores. Purchase a size that will easily run down the grout line in one stroke when used with the flat part of the brush parallel to the grout.

Some manufacturer's instructions suggest using a toothbrush to apply the colorant. This does scrub the colorant nicely into the grout, but the short bristles tend to flick, spreading droplets everywhere. We recommend you stick to a brush.

Run your fingers through the bristles to remove as many loose hairs as possible. This helps avoid the possibility of their ending up in your paint later.

■ **DON'T APPLY COLORANT DIRECTLY FROM THE CONTAINER.** Always pour out a small amount of colorant into another container. Clean tuna or cat food cans are great because they are shallow and broad. Don't fill the can, as a little grout colorant goes a long way.

Put a small amount of colorant on the brush and apply to the grout in long strokes, smoothing it with a back-and-forth motion into all the nooks and crannies. Grout can be rough, so you want to get a thin, even, and complete coat. If the colorant pools or puddles, you are applying too much.

■ **DON'T POUR USED COLORANT BACK INTO THE BOTTLE.** Throw unused colorant away. If you poured out a small amount into your container as we suggested, there shouldn't be much left. Wipe out the excess from the

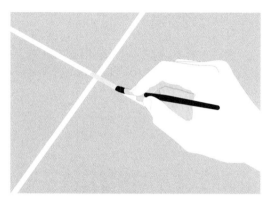

STEP 4 Apply the colorant with a small brush in long strokes back and forth to get into all of the indentations of the grout. Put on a thin, even, complete coat, being careful not to apply so much that the colorant begins to pool. If this happens, you are applying too much.

Jane Tip:

FOR STEP 4
Depending on the brand you choose, you may have to remove excess grout colorant from the tiles before applying a second coat. Make sure you closely read the instructions.

container with a paper towel and allow it to dry. Wash the brushes with soap and water to reuse for subsequent coats.

Should you overlap colorant onto tiles? If your tile is ceramic, go for it! This will assure that the colorant covers all the grout. This is similar to painting wood windows, where you want to overlap slightly onto the glass to assure a paint seal between the glass and the wood. Similarly, you want colorant on all the grout. Slight overlapping assures a good seal.

How many coats should you apply?
That's up to you. In our experience, except in the case of dark colorant over dark grout or white over white, you will probably need two coats and even a third touch-up coat in ornery areas. Even though you can get good coverage with one coat, our opinion is that at least two coats should be applied for greater long-term durability, just like regular wall or trim paint.

Depending on the brand, you may have to remove excess grout colorant from the tiles

before applying a second coat. Again, make sure to read the instructions!!

How do you remove excess grout colorant from the tiles? This is the second most laborious part of the job, though much easier than the original cleaning. Check the manufacturer's instructions for the appropriate drying time. With some products, you must wait at least 1 hour before cleaning the tiles.

Spray the tiled area lightly with water, wait a few minutes, and then scrub with a light-duty plastic scouring pad. "Light-duty" means just that. Read the label on the pad; it should say "safe for plastic shower enclosures and ceramic tile."

Clean a small bit at a time, rinse the pad in a bucket of cool water, and continue until the entire area is done.

■ **APPLY MOST OF YOUR FORCE TO THE TILES.** Though the colorant is fairly hard, you can scrub it off if you apply too much force directly on the grout line. Using a circular motion is safest, but you will probably have to do a little scrubbing along the grout lines, so take it easy.

By the way, the purpose of the water is *not* to soften the grout colorant (it is waterproof once dry). The water acts as a lubricant to protect the tile from abrasion and make it a little harder to rub the colorant from the grout, where it adheres more firmly than to the tiles.

What if you find some dried colorant on the tiles a few weeks after applying it? No problem. Although the colorant is firmly attached to the grout, it can be removed from the tiles with a sharp single-edged razor blade. Dull, used blades have edge defects that can leave scratches in the tile.

Project: Replace a Toilet Seat and Lid

Jane Quotient: ❶ ② ③ ④ ⑤
Estimated Time: 30 minutes

Can we get a bit personal?

Sometimes you have just one intention when you enter your spa-licious bathroom. You don't want to bathe, you don't need to brush your teeth, you don't need to put on makeup, you simply need to use the facilities. Nothing to be embarrassed about; we're all human, so we all do it.

The fact is that many toilets are simply not what they should be. Yes—the toilet should be the most comfortable seat in the house.

If your toilet seat is cracked, chipped, or missing a screw, making going to the bathroom like a trip to an amusement park, it's time to replace it!

Replacing a toilet seat and lid is a quick and easy job. Toilet seats are often inexpensive and come in an array of styles and colors. You can stay with the standard white or ivory smooth-top seat or opt for a more decorative look.

MATERIALS

Tools
- Tape measure
- Standard screwdrivers
- Adjustable wrench
- Hacksaw (optional)
- Groove joint pliers (if necessary)

Supplies
- Toilet seat with mounting bolt hardware
- Rubber gloves
- Penetrating oil (like 3M lubricant or WD-40, optional)
- Masking tape (optional)
- Soft-scrub sponge
- Cleanser

"Twenty bucks and ten minutes and I had a toilet I loved again."

Brooke D.
San Diego,
Texas
Age 58

1 Make sure the toilet seat and lid you buy are the correct size and shape for your toilet. Measure the length, width, and height of your current seat. You can also snap a picture and take it with you. If you're still unsure,

STEP 1 Before purchasing your new toilet seat, measure the length, width, and height of your current one. This will help you pick out the perfect new toilet seat on your first try.

you can always unscrew your existing seat according to the instructions below, clean it, and take that with you.

2 Put on rubber gloves. Close the old seat and lid to access the bolts at the back that fasten the seat to the toilet bowl. If necessary, pop off the plastic caps that cover and protect the bolts. You can use a standard screwdriver to lift these plastic caps off the toilet (don't worry about breaking them, as you're getting rid of that seat anyway).

3 If you turn the bolt using your screw-driver, the nut on the bottom side of the

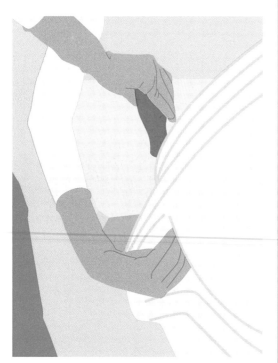

STEP 3 **To remove the bolts that hold your toilet seat in, use a screwdriver to unscrew them while you steady the nuts underneath.**

Jane Tip:

FOR STEP 3
Sometimes bolts refuse to turn due to rust—the result of years of moisture accumulation. If this is the case, apply penetrating oil or lubricant (like WD-40 or 3-in-1 oil) directly on the bolts and nuts. Wait a few minutes and then try unscrewing the bolts again, this time using a wrench to hold each nut still.

"I have recently replaced a toilet, the water line and the shutoff valve to it, and the floater valve. I have also recently replaced all of the under-sink pipes, valves, lines, faucet, and the sink plunger pipe for the bathroom sink."

Myra V.
Arkansas Pass,
Arkansas
Age 43

toilet will also turn. To prevent this from happening and to loosen each bolt, hold the nut on the underside of the toilet in place with either your hand or with a pair of groove joint pliers while you turn the bolt on the top of your toilet to the left with your screwdriver.

Don't be concerned about applying too much pressure to the bolt. If it snaps and breaks, that's fine because you'll be using new bolts. If you absolutely cannot unscrew a bolt, however, you will need to saw it off with a hacksaw. To prevent scratching the toilet, apply masking tape to the rim around the bolt, and then—carefully—cut off the bolt.

4 Lift off the old toilet seat and lid from the bowl and throw them away or recycle them (if possible). Before installing the new unit, clean and sanitize the rim of the toilet bowl.

Align the holes on the new seat and lid unit with the mounting holes in the toilet. Drop the seat into place and the new bolts through the holes of the seat and toilet bowl. Screw the nuts onto the bolts on the underside of the toilet. Turn the nuts with your fingers until they are tight, and then give the nuts no more than half a turn with your wrench. Be careful not to overtighten the screws, or you could crack your porcelain toilet!

Raise and lower the seat and lid a few times to make sure they move freely. If the unit seems loose or has some play in it, give the nuts another quarter-turn.

Fit the plastic caps over the bolts and enjoy the best seat in the house!

Project: Replace a Toilet

Jane Quotient: ① ② ❸ ④ ⑤
Estimated Time: 2 to 3 hours

In recent years there have been many efforts to conserve water. Regular toilets use an average of 4 to 7 gallons of water every time you flush! That may not seem like a great deal of water at first, but most homes use more water to flush their toilets than for any other use. Most new toilets manage to decrease that to just $1^1/_2$ gallons per flush. That's less than half the amount of water. Install one, and you'll help the environment *and* see a big difference in your water bill.

As if you would need any more incentive, many cities give generous rebates for installing low-flow toilets. Check to see if your municipality is one of them. Home improvement centers that carry toilets know what rebates are available in your area.

MATERIALS

Tools

- Pliers
- Screwdriver
- Utility knife
- 3-inch stiff putty knife
- Crescent or box wrench
- Level
- Caulking gun

Supplies

- Heavy tarp
- Penetrating oil (like 3M lubricant or WD-40, optional)
- Gloves
- Old rag that can be thrown away
- New low-flow toilet
- Plumber's putty
- Clean towel
- Shims
- Silicone caulk
- Spud washer (if not already included with your new toilet)
- Plumber's tape

Jane Tip:

Low-flow toilets are now required by the Environmental Protection Agency. Toilet manufacturers have found that for a family of four, changing out toilets can reduce water usage by 22,000 gallons per year.

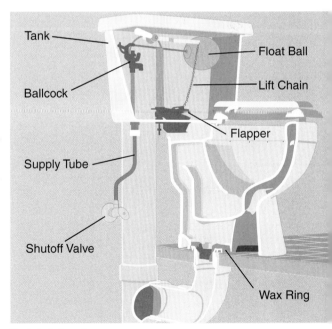

Basic toilet anatomy

Tank — Float Ball — Lift Chain — Ballcock — Flapper — Supply Tube — Shutoff Valve — Wax Ring

1 Remove your old toilet. Start by finding and tarping with heavy plastic an area where you'll place your old toilet once you've removed it. You won't want to put it just anywhere; we suggest finding a spot preferably outside of your home. Don't forget to wear gloves from the very beginning of this project.

2 Turn off the water supply to the toilet by turning the water valve until it is closed. The valve should be located on the wall behind your toilet.

STEP 2 **Turn off the flow of water to the toilet by turning the valve behind it clockwise. Once you've done this, flush the toilet to make sure the water is completely off.**

3 Once you are able to shut off the water, flush the toilet to empty the tank. Then remove the tank lid to make sure all of the water is gone. If a little bit is left in the tank, just hold down the handle to drain it. Absorb any remaining water with a sponge.

4 Remove the water supply hose from the tank. Some units unscrew from the outside, while others must be disconnected from the inside of the tank. Move the hose out of your way.

5 If you need to remove the tank, hold the bolts in place with the pliers on the bottom/outside while you unscrew the screws

Jane Tip:

FOR STEP 2
If your valve won't turn and seems locked in place, try using a lubricant like WD-40 or 3-in-1 oil.

Jane Tip:

FOR STEP 3
If there's quite a bit of water in the tank, use a wet/dry vac to remove it.

from within the tank. Remove the tank from the bowl and place it on the tarp.

STEP 5 **Remove the toilet tank by holding the bolt underneath in place while unscrewing the screw within the tank. Do this to both screws.**

6 Check the bowl to make sure it is empty. If it's not, use the sponge to absorb any water. Now remove the toilet bowl itself. Believe it or not, all that holds your toilet bowl in place is the caulk around the edge and 2 bolts, one on each side. Pull the coverings off the bolts and unscrew them with a crescent or box wrench. If the coverings have plumber's putty in them, you may have to remove it before taking out the bolts.

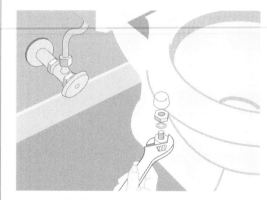

STEP 6 **Pull off the coverings over the bolts on the base of your toilet. Remove the plumber's putty, if any is there. Unscrew the bolts using a crescent or box wrench.**

7 Using a utility knife, cut into the caulk sealing the bottom of the toilet. Be careful not to cut the floor when doing this. Rock the bowl back and forth, breaking the seal between the toilet and the floor. Once you've done this, pick up the bowl and carry it to the tarp. Make sure not to set it down anywhere else, not only because of the bacteria but also because the wax ring at the bottom will leave a mess.

8 Right after you put down the toilet, quickly place a rag in the opening to stop any gases from escaping into your home. This is a very important step, as these gases can be harmful.

STEP 8 **After you've removed your toilet, quickly place a rag in the opening to stop any gases from escaping. Scrape around the flange with a putty knife to release the plumber's putty holding it in place.**

9 Remove the flange, which is the ring left on the floor around the opening, by sliding out the screws holding it in. Remove the flange and the bolts from the floor with your putty knife. Scrape up any plumber's putty that is left behind.

10 Put on the new toilet. The procedure is the same in reverse, plus a few extra steps. Apply a small amount of plumber's putty to where the flange was earlier to hold the bolts in place. Put down the flange and screw it into the floor around the drainpipe.

Jane Tip:

FOR STEP 7

If you have any animals that might get curious, confine them away from both your old toilet and where it used to be. Pets can be very curious, and the last thing you want is for them to track raw sewage through your house.

Jane Tip:

FOR STEP 9

Most flanges are either cast iron or ABS and are screwed into the floor. The toilet flange bolts attach to the flange, so the flange must be screwed into the subfloor before the new toilet is installed.

11 Get the new toilet ready for installation by turning it upside down on a clean towel. This will help you apply the new wax ring you'll need to seal it. Place the ring on the circle on the bottom, which is called the base horn. Push it with enough force so that it will stay on when you turn it over. That's all you'll need to do to prepare your new toilet for installation if the tank and bowl are attached.

STEP 11 **Turn your new toilet upside down and, with both hands, push the wax ring onto the base horn. If the toilet is new, you won't have to worry about using gloves.**

12 To install the new toilet, remove the rag from the pipe and immediately place it in a plastic garbage bag to throw it away. Pick up the toilet bowl and place it on top of the drainpipe, allowing the bolts to pop through the openings on either side. This is not difficult, but you will definitely want someone to guide you when placing the toilet.

13 Push down hard on the toilet and rock it back and forth to enable the wax ring to seal against the floor. Place a level across the top of the bowl to make sure it is level. If it's not, apply pressure along the rim until it's level. If necessary, add shims to the underside of the toilet until it's even.

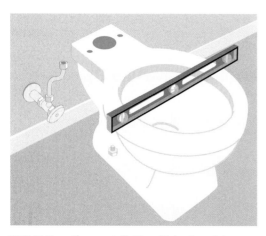

STEP 13 **Once the new toilet bowl is in place, take a level and put it across the bowl. If it isn't level, apply pressure along the rim of the toilet bowl until it is. If necessary, add a shim to make it even.**

14 Place the metal washers and bolts that came with your new toilet on the screws. Tighten the bolts slowly, going back and forth from side to side; if you tighten one side too much, you might crack your new toilet. Place the covers that came with the toilet over the bolts. Some attach on their own, others need to be filled with plumber's putty and placed on.

15 It's common for the toilet not to be flush to the floor, as the wax ring might keep it from touching. Sealing this area will prevent moisture from escaping. To achieve this, put down a bead of silicone caulk all around the toilet base. Right after placing the bead, go over it with your finger to remove

Jane Tip:

FOR STEP 14
If the bolts are too long to be covered, get a mini-hacksaw and saw them down. This will take elbow grease, but at least you'll be able to cover them up.

Jane Tip:

FOR STEP 17
Wrap plumber's tape once around the threads of the supply hose for a better seal.

STEP 16 **Place the spud washer on the inlet valve at the bottom of the tank.**

any extra caulk and to make sure the edges are properly sealed.

16 Put the tank on the bowl. Replace the screws and bolts in the way they were on the old tank (bolts on the outside, screws on the inside). Place what's called a spud washer (usually included but may need to be purchased separately) into the large hole at the bottom of the tank. This is the inlet valve.

17 Reattach the water supply hose to the bottom of the tank and the water source.

18 Attach the new toilet seat (see "Replace a Toilet Seat and Lid," page 155).

Jane Profile

I feel like I can do anything.

Tania "Jane" Tremaglio

Age: 35

From: Meriden, Connecticut

Favorite tool: An electric drill/screwdriver. If I had used a regular screwdriver to take down all those kitchen cabinets, I would have been there for hours. I also like the handheld electric sander. It made sanding the cabinets so easy.

Projects accomplished: We recently moved into a new home, though before we moved in I discovered BeJane.com and absolutely loved it! I was so impressed with all of the information and great ideas that I couldn't wait to move in and get started. The one part of the house I was the most disappointed with was the kitchen cabinets. They were old, brown, and just plain ugly. I read all the information on refinishing cabinets and how to sand and paint them. A few days later, I had a brand-new kitchen. I painted the cabinets white with black knobs and painted the walls a red-wood color. It looks beautiful, and my husband and I love it.

Inspiration for starting home improvement: I would have to say my true inspiration for starting home improvement was the Be Jane website. I found it just before we moved into our new house. Even when I rented, I always looked around and wanted to do projects, but I never knew how. So when I came across the site I knew I could do so much more. Besides, my husband is *not* handy. I started with painting, spackling over the holes and priming first. I just kept reading and have been going crazy ever since. I've painted the entire house, and we've only lived here three months.

Fears about home improvement: I was afraid that I was going to make the biggest mistake and it was going to be worse than what I had started with. Which, by the way, I have done, but I learned from it what to do and what not to do. Even though what I was afraid of came true, I learned so that the next time I would know how not to make the same mistake again.

How has doing home improvement affected your life? It's affected my life in a positive way, and I am so happy to be working on my home. I feel like I can do anything. It has made me much more patient and confident. It has also built my confidence in being a homeowner, which I was really unsure of. I really enjoy working on different projects, and it is such a great feeling knowing I did it myself.

How has doing home improvement affected others in your life? It has inspired them. I was supposed to go over and paint my mother-in-law's house and now, after seeing all that I've done, she wants to do it herself. She's ready to take on the sanding and painting. Then there's my dad. He's very impressed with all that I am doing. It's so funny because normally he would be the one to do all that I'm doing; now he just sits back and smiles. I've even empowered my friends to take on projects of their own.

Then there's my husband. He thinks I am the greatest. He even looks at me in a different way now. He's impressed that I can take the initiative to start a project and complete it. He thinks it's wonderful. He even buys me tools for gifts on Mother's Day. I recently told him I wanted a palm sander and a toolbox for Christmas.

Advice for others just getting started in home improvement: Go to Be Jane's website; take your time and read through everything. Be patient, be positive, and know that it just comes with time.

Creating a Functional Bathroom

One of the relaxing things about going to a spa is that you don't have to wonder if the toilet is going to overflow, if the faucets are going to work, or if there will be enough hot water to make it through a long shower. Your expectation is that everything will be in good working order.

The same thing should apply to your spa-away-from-the-spa. Everything should

"All I want is a shower I can relax in."

Anna K.
Portland, Oregon
Age 40

not only function the way it is supposed to, it should also have a look that is pleasing to the eye and mind.

There are three facets to a functional bathroom: (1) fixtures that work; (2) contents that are appealing to look at and use; and (3) adequate storage.

If any of these are problems in your bathroom, the time has come to fix them for good.

Project: Install a New Sink

Jane Quotient: ① ② ❸ ④ ⑤
Estimated time: 2¹/₂ to 3 hours

If the sink at the local gas station bathroom looks and functions better than yours, it's time to consider a change. Your sink is hardly going to provide you with a spa-licious feeling if every time you look at it you consider taking a sledgehammer to it.

You can choose from a wide variety of sink types depending on your budget, available space, and décor preferences. The trick is to find the style that best suits your needs. Remember, with pedestal and bowl sinks your counter space will be limited.

Installing a sink is easier than you think. No matter which style you decide on, the technique is similar.

MATERIALS

Tools
- Work light
- Utility knife
- Pipe wrench
- Flat head screwdriver
- Razor
- Jigsaw
- Caulking gun

Supplies
- Bucket
- Marker
- New sink
- Protective eyewear
- Caulk

Note: Not all sinks and faucets are created equal. When you buy your new faucet, make sure it fits the holes in your new sink. What we mean by this is that the hot and cold handles with the spigot can come attached on a single bar (4-inch spacing), or they can be separate (8-inch spacing). This is key to completing this task.

"I am a single mom who doesn't want to wait for someone to come and do things for me. I needed a bathroom makeover and couldn't afford to have it done, so I attempted to do it myself."

Lynn F.
Clawson,
Michigan
Age 46

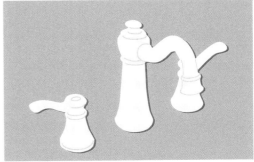

In picking out the proper sink, decide whether you want a single-bar 4-inch faucet (top) or an individual 8-inch faucet (bottom), and choose the proper faucet to match.

1 Jump ahead to "Change Out a Faucet" (page 166) to see how to remove your current faucet. You'll need to do this before you can remove your sink. Remember, you'll need a work light to see clearly under the sink.

Note: Most people think their sink is glued to the countertop. If it's what's called an *undermount* sink, this is correct. The sink sits directly below the countertop, which overhangs the sink slightly. If the lip of the sink goes on top of the counter, it is being held in with caulk and sometimes clamps underneath the sink.

2 With a utility knife, cut away the seal made by the caulk bead placed around the sink.

3 Place a bucket below the U-joint under the sink and, using a pipe wrench, unscrew the fittings that hold it in place. You'll want the bucket to catch the water in the trap.

STEP 3 Using a pipe wrench, unscrew the fittings that hold the U-joint in place. Make sure to place a bucket underneath to catch any water trapped in the joint.

Jane Tip:

FOR STEP 3
If you have trouble unscrewing the fitting of the U-joint, try lubricating the seam with WD-40 or 3-in-1 oil.

4 Remove the drainpipe from the bottom of the sink by unscrewing it at the fittings.

5 Apply force from the bottom of the sink and, as the sink shifts, place a screwdriver in the gap. This will give you enough access to the rim of the sink to pull it up and out of the hole in the countertop. If the sink is still attached by the caulk, move the edge of the screwdriver around to break the seal.

6 Once the sink is out, you can see the mineral buildup on the countertop, which develops over time. Start by going over the buildup and any leftover caulk with a straight razor. Don't be surprised if you change your mind and decide the countertop needs to go, too!

7 If you are comfortable with reusing your countertop, wipe it down thoroughly to get rid of any leftover caulk or dirt you couldn't get to with the sink still in. Check to see if your new sink will fit into the same hole your old sink fit into. If the hole is too large, you'll need either a bigger sink or a new countertop. If it's too small, this is an easy fix.

Most new sinks come with a paper template that will help you determine the proper size and shape of the hole needed. To use it, place it over the old opening so it evenly covers the

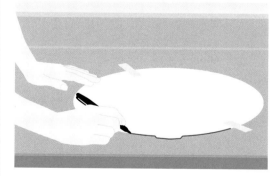

STEP 7 Tape the paper template to the countertop and draw a line around the edge of the template with an indelible marker.

hole. Draw a line around the template to give yourself an idea of where to cut.

8 If the new sink is bigger than your current opening, you'll need to make the hole larger with a jigsaw. (Don't forget your protective eyewear.) Follow the lines you made from your template as a cutting guide. Cut all the way around until the hole is the right size. Don't worry if it isn't exact; the lip of the new sink will cover up any mistakes. Keep in mind, you can only use this technique with a formica top.

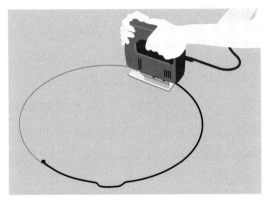

STEP 8 Cut out the opening for the sink using a jigsaw. Start by drilling a hole with a $^1/_2$-inch drill bit. This is the point at which to insert the jigsaw blade and begin cutting.

9 Put a bead of silicone caulking underneath the lip and place the sink into the hole you've just created. Reattach the drain pipe, U-joint, and faucet.

10 Caulk around the edges of the new sink where it meets the countertop so no water gets trapped underneath.

Allow at least 24 hours before you use your new sink.

Jane Tip
FOR STEP 8
If you are cutting the hole in a new countertop, you first must decide where to place the sink. This choice is based on both looks and where you can attach the water/drainage pipes. Once this is decided and the pattern is drawn (Sharpies are best for this), drill a $^1/_2$-inch hole into the center. This will allow you to insert the blade of the jigsaw so you can start cutting.

A Chip off the Ol' Sink

You might slip out of your relaxation mode in your spa-licious bathroom when you see those little nicks and chips in your porcelain tub or sink. There's a ton of products on the market that will make this one of the easiest repairs you'll ever do.

For a professional, long-lasting porcelain chip repair job, invest in a professional-grade bonder and refinisher. Make sure your porcelain or tile resurfacing and repair kit contains everything you need to perform professional-quality porcelain and tile chip or crack repair, including a high-gloss refinishing top coat to match your existing color.

You can repair chips or cracks and restore missing pieces of tile in any porcelain or high-gloss tile surface quickly and easily. Although most kits are touch-up kits for cracks and chips less than 5 inches long, there are also full restoration kits that allow you to spray or paint on a full coat of porcelain bonder and then spray or paint on the refinish coating. They're great for resurfacing sinks, vanities, showers, and more. Remember, though, that the fumes from these products are often highly toxic, so make sure you protect yourself by allowing proper ventilation. If this is impossible, consider using a respirator and safety glasses to avoid mishaps.

Project: Change Out a Faucet

Jane Quotient: ① ② ❸ ④ ⑤
Estimated time: 1¹/₂ to 2 hours

You may still love your sink, but maybe it's time to change out the faucet. Maybe it doesn't work, or drips like a fountain, or you have recently discovered that even after you cleaned through the layers of lime or corrosion it was way past its prime.

A fully functioning faucet is a must in the spa-licious bathroom. In addition to simple functionality, faucets are an easy way to add a more luxurious feel as well as instantly updating the look of the bathroom as a whole. You don't have to spend a fortune to find something beautiful, as prices begin as low as $25—although they do go up to thousands for those gold and diamond-encrusted faucets. (Yes, they actually exist.)

But even though you're not Ivana Trump, if you do happen to fall in love with a faucet that costs a bit more than you planned to spend, remember you'll be saving yourself a nice little chunk by installing it yourself. So splurge a little. The enjoyment you'll get by doing so will last for years.

MATERIALS

Tools
- Work light
- Water pump pliers
- Basin wrench
- Screwdriver
- Putty knife

Supplies
- 3-in-1 oil
- New faucet
- Plumber's putty

Note: Check the spacing of your existing faucet before buying a new one. Remember, if you're not replacing your sink, you can replace your faucet only with one that has the same spacing you are taking out. Your sink/countertop has holes that determine the

"Hey, my new faucet doesn't drip anymore!"
Carolyn T.
Ashland, Oregon
Age 46

spacing you can use, and changing that will be a second and possibly third project. Although bathroom sink faucets are sold in standard 4- and 8-inch configurations, additions such as stopper mechanisms and shower cover plates can vary from model to model. You can, however, install flat metal disks (known as escutcheons) to hide any leftover holes if necessary.

You need to also decide which type of faucet you are putting in. Faucets come in three basic types:

■ **SINGLE-HANDLE FAUCETS.** Common in both bathrooms and kitchens, where the hot and cold are controlled by one lever or knob that's often part of the spout.

■ **WIDESPREAD FAUCET.** Usually in bathrooms, where the hot-water valve, cold-water valve, and spout are all mounted separately.

■ **TWO-HANDLE-CENTER SET.** Also common in bathrooms and kitchens, where the spout and both turn valves are combined on a single base unit.

Removing the Old Faucet

1 Turn off the water. There are two ways you can turn off the water. The first is to close the two valves immediately under the faucet you are replacing. Then, turn on both the hot and cold water to allow it to drain and to release any pressure. The second way is to turn off the water supply at the main water supply valve. Be aware, though, that this will turn off the water to your entire house. Be sure to turn on both the hot and cold water to drain the pipe of any excess water and pressure.

STEP 1 **Turn off the water valve underneath and behind the sink before getting started. Remember, "lefty loosey, righty tighty."**

2 Once you've emptied the line, disconnect the water supply lines. Turn on your work light and you'll see the two tubes that

Jane Tip:

FOR STEP 1

If the valves are frozen in place due to corrosion and lack of use, spray some WD-40 on the threads. If you still can't get them closed, you will have to shut off the main water valve.

Jane Tip:

FOR STEP 1

Turning off a main water valve can be difficult if you live in a complex that doesn't have individual ones for each unit. If this is your situation, it may be worth the cost of having one put in; otherwise, you'll have to turn off water to the whole building any time you want to work on your plumbing.

connect your faucet to the two water valves under the sink. If your water lines look new and aren't leaking or dripping, there is no need to replace them. In this case, disconnect them on the faucet side only.

Otherwise, disconnect the lines from the shutoff valve as well as from the faucet. It's hard to know the right time to change these out; we feel, though, that because changing out a faucet happens so rarely, you might as well change out the water supply lines at the same time. Think of it as saving you from a second trip under the sink later.

3 Faucets are mounted in one of two ways. Bottom-mount (widespread or separate hot/cold/spout fixtures) faucets are removed from above. In order to do this, remove the screws that hold the handles in place. Then you will be able to remove the nuts that hold up the faucet.

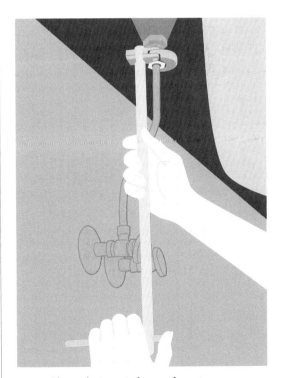

STEP 3 **The easiest way to loosen the nuts on a top-mount sink is with a basin wrench. This is a tool designed for use in tight spaces such as under the sink.**

Top-mount (center-set or all on a single bar) faucets are held in place by nuts located underneath the sink, which is where they must be removed using a basin wrench.

If you are working on a newer top-mount/center-set faucet, the basin nuts may be simple to remove with your bare hands. Faucet manufacturers realized that having to buy a tool to install their product makes it harder to do, so fewer people will do it. If the nuts on your sink are flat against the sink and have 2 flanges that you can push on to turn, you won't need a basin wrench, just your hand.

4 Pull out the faucet. Much to your dismay, you will probably find a fairly nasty buildup left behind on the sink where the faucet plate or escutcheons were attached. Don't take it as a reflection on your cleaning abilities; this is normal. The best way to remove this residue is with a 50-50 solution of vinegar and water. You can also scrape it away with a razor blade and/or scouring pad.

Now that the messy part is over, putting in the new faucet will be a pleasure.

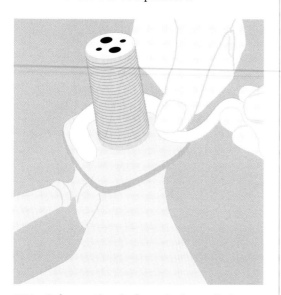

STEP 1 **Before putting the faucet in place, roll a long, thin snakelike piece of plumber's putty and place it around the faucet base. After you place the faucet, wipe away any excess that squeezes out.**

Jane Tip:

FOR STEP 3
If the sink is old and the nuts are rusted or corroded in place, apply lubricating oil and allow it to work into the threads before trying to remove the nuts.

Installing the New Faucet

How to do this depends on the type of faucet you are putting in.

CENTER-SET/TOP-MOUNTED FAUCET

1 Apply a bead of plumber's putty or silicone caulk around the faucet base. Here's where all that time spent playing with Play-Doh will come in handy. To make a bead of plumber's putty, roll a long, thin snake-like piece of it. Some faucets have rubber or plastic gaskets for the base and do not require this step. Check the directions that came with the faucet to know for sure.

2 Gently set the faucet in place, pressing against the putty to assure a good seal. Do not, however, apply *too* much force when you are doing this, as you can press out too much. The tailpieces should fit perfectly into the hole spacing on the sink.

3 Go back under the sink to install the washers and mounting nuts on the tailpieces (these are pipes that stick out under the faucet on either side). Tighten the nuts by hand.

STEP 3 **Install the washers and mounting nuts onto the tailpieces (the pipes that stick out underneath the counter). You will be able to do this by hand.**

4 Straighten the faucet to make it parallel with the back of the sink. Tighten the mounting nuts with an adjustable wrench or a basin wrench. When you come back up, you will probably notice excess putty or caulk around the faucet. Wipe away any excess.

WIDESPREAD/BOTTOM-MOUNTED FAUCET

1 Line the faucet with plumber's putty and then place it in the center hole. Gently press the putty against the base, setting the spout in place. Go under the sink to hand-tighten the washers and mounting nuts just enough to hold the faucet in place. Don't overtighten, or you won't be able to center the spout on the sink later.

2 Run a bead of plumber's putty along the base of the escutcheons or the base plate of the handles and screw them in place. Align the faucet with the back of the sink and tighten the mounting nuts with water pump pliers or a basin wrench.

3 Install the faucet handles over the escutcheons. The one marked *hot* should go on the left (this is standard in the United States). Wipe away excess putty from around the bases.

Jane Tip:

Most faucets come with the drain stop assembly. You may need to tie this into the drain. Check the manufacturer's instructions for how your particular drain stop connects with your new faucet.

Note: Many faucets already come with their handles installed.

If you aren't going to replace your supply lines, just hook them back up and turn on the water. If you're going for the whole enchilada, it's not much more difficult than that.

Note that different types of supply lines are available. Chromed copper lines are the most difficult to replace; you have to buy the right length and then bend them to fit. They may be the most attractive, but unless you have a pedestal sink or the lines are exposed, they're not necessary. You're better off going with the flexible lines, which are inexpensive, can be cut to size with a knife, and are very easy to use. Braided metal supply lines are also available and tend to be long lasting.

There are also copper supply tubes, which have a rounded end that fits into the seat of the faucet's water inlets. But again, the flexible lines are most often all you'll need.

You did it! Trust us when we say small things like brushing your teeth and washing your hands will have a different feel now. Every time you splash water on your face, you can take pride that your effort made it possible.

Project: Update a Bathroom Utility Cabinet

Jane Quotient: ① ② ❸ ④ ⑤
Estimated Time: Working time: 6 hours; drying time: 36 hours

More often than not, the bathroom cabinets are neglected. Unless they were bought custom, they rarely serve as beautiful accents. Usually they just hold extra toilet paper.

You will be surprised at how easy it is to turn an outdated bathroom cabinet into a spa-licious one.

If you don't have a cabinet to reface, consider purchasing a small wall-mounted cabinet to go over the toilet and creating your own special spa storage space. These are inexpensive and easy to change to match your bathroom. Besides, they are the perfect place to keep special bath salts, bubble baths, and body lotions especially meant to treat you and only you. Every time you look at it, it will remind you to pamper yourself.

The materials and equipment you'll need are pretty much the same for most cabinet styles, although a plasticized laminate surface like Formica needs a special blade for even cutting. If your cabinet is covered with a Formica-like substance, ask at your local home improvement center which drill bit and jigsaw blade are right for the task.

MATERIALS

Tools
- Screwdrivers (Phillips and flat head)
- Drill
- Jigsaw
- Drill bit assortment (including $\frac{1}{2}$-inch drill bit)
- C-clamp
- Paintbrushes and rollers
- Scissors
- Staple gun or electric staple gun with staples

Supplies
- Cabinet
- Plastic ziplock bag
- Protective eyewear
- Glove or towel
- Fine-grit sandpaper or sanding sponge
- Primer
- Paint (satin finish)
- Plastic tarp
- 8 small nails
- Tape measure
- Pull doorknobs
- Wire mesh
- White (or a color to match) duct or tacky tape

"My husband was blown away by how I converted our bathroom."

Stephanie B.
Paris, Texas
Age 26

Note: We did this project with a common type of bathroom cabinet with two single-paneled doors. The directions may vary slightly if the size or type of cabinet you have is different, but they should be applicable to most.

1 Remove the hanging cabinet from the wall. This will allow you to get around it easily and obtain proper ventilation while painting. If your cabinet won't or can't come off the wall, start with step 2.

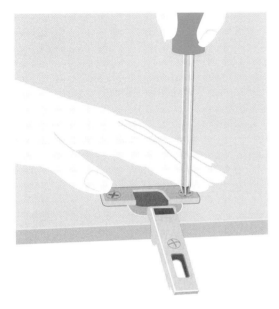

STEP 2 Once you've taken the door off of the cabinet, remove the hinges from the back of the cabinet door.

2 Remove the doors and hinges from the cabinet using a screwdriver or a cordless drill. Put all hinges and screws in a ziplock bag for safekeeping.

3 Cut out the panel in the door with a jigsaw. This tool is easy to operate, but in order to cut out the inside of your panel with it, you must first drill a hole to insert the blade into—that is, a starting point to cut from. Drill two holes, one on each opposing corner. This will help you get into those 90-degree angles. Pay attention so that you don't drill into the frame/edge of the cabinet, as you'll want that to stay intact.

👓 **Safety Check!**
Wearing protective eyewear is important while cutting, as the jigsaw will generate a lot of sawdust.

Jane Tip:
FOR STEP 2
When removing hardware such as hinges, place everything you remove in a plastic ziplock bag, including the hinges and the screws. This way you won't have to worry what you did with the pieces when you go to put it all back together.

Jane Tip:
FOR STEP 4
When using the C-clamp, place either a ruler or a straight piece of wood under it to help you create a straight cut, and place a piece of fabric in between the clamp teeth and the door to prevent marring the surface. A leather glove works well.

Jane Tip:
FOR STEP 5
While sandpaper is a tried-and-true method of sanding, because of the many curved and rounded areas of most cabinet doors, we think using a sanding sponge makes the process much easier.

Using a ½-inch drill bit, drill a hole in the center of the panel, keeping away from the edge where you will be cutting. This is the place all your cuts will begin.

4 Cut out the panels. Do this part of the project in a place that can get messy, as it will generate a great deal of sawdust (if you have one, use your garage). Place the door on a surface on which you can steady it with a C-clamp. The saw can shake things around a great deal. While you're using the jigsaw, keep your fingers where you can see them and do not hold the cabinet anywhere near where you are cutting.

Begin your cut from the hole you drilled in the door, sawing toward the edge and turning the blade parallel to the cut you would like to make. Make sure you never lift the saw with the blade still moving. Once you've finished your cuts, the panels should be free to be removed from the cabinet door. These wood pieces are now scraps.

STEP 4 Using a jigsaw, cut out the panels in the door. Use a C-clamp to keep your work steady.

5 Now that the cabinet door is cut, the hardest part of the project is done and you are close to halfway finished. Sand down the rough edges you created by cutting out the panels. Sand down the entire cabinet, inside and out, using a medium- to fine-grit sand-

STEP 5 Use a fine-grit sanding sponge to get rid of the shiny surface on your cabinet. This will allow the paint to adhere properly.

paper. If any of your cabinet is covered with laminate, sand down the smooth finish on it or else the primer will bead up like oil in water.

6 Prime and paint the surfaces of the cabinet (see "Paint Your Cabinets," page 50). Lay down a plastic tarp to protect your floor.

7 If you plan to install new door pulls, now is the time to do so. Measure where you want them and then mark and drill the hole.

8 Before putting the doorknobs on, fill in the new openings in your cabinet doors. The choices are endless: fabric, hammered steel, glass, and so on. We chose wire mesh for an open feeling and so you can glimpse the spa-licious contents without even opening the doors.

Jane Tip:

FOR STEP 7
To help find the right size drill bit for this job, place the threaded end of the screw against the barrel of the drill bit and compare the diameters. In this case, you want the drill bit to be slightly larger than the screw.

To install wire mesh, cut a piece slightly larger than the opening in your cabinet. Add an extra 1 inch to both measurements, which allows ½ inch overlap to attach it with. Be careful to cut the mesh in a place where you can easily clean up shards, as you do not want them under your bare feet. Fold ½ inch of tacky tape over all the edges of the mesh.

9 Staple the mesh to the doors using either a staple gun or an electric staple gun. We prefer an electric staple gun because it makes the process quicker and less fatiguing. Make sure to place staples every ½ inch to 1 inch.

STEP 9 Attach the mesh to the back of the cabinet door by stapling it in place with a staple gun.

10 Reassemble the cabinet. Reattach the hinges and the doorknobs. Put the cabinet back up on the wall (that is, of course, if you took it down). If you're installing it on the wall for the first time, be sure to attach it directly to the wall studs. Because of its weight, we don't recommend mounting it directly into the drywall even with the use of a wall anchor.

Project: Install a New Bathroom Vanity

Jane Quotient: ① ② ❸ ④ ⑤
Estimated Time: 5 to 6 Hours

It's ironic that the one bath furnishing that's named for looks, the vanity, is usually the worst-looking thing in the bathroom. Yours might need nothing more than a coat of paint or a little molding on the cabinet doors to brighten it up. But if you have a vanity that is clearly beyond repair, the time has come to change it. The good news is that there are many to choose from now in almost every style and color. If your vanity feels like it belongs more in a gym than a spa, this is one project you'll definitely want to consider.

We recommend that if you're going to replace the vanity, you might as well replace the sink and countertop as well. Nothing ruins the effect of a new vanity faster than an old sink and countertop.

MATERIALS

Tools

- Adjustable wrench
- 5-in-1 putty knife
- Drill
- Screwdriver
- Tape measure
- Stud finder
- Caulk gun
- Level
- Hammer
- Chisel
- Keyhole saw

Supplies

- Safety glasses
- Bucket
- Towel
- New vanity
- Wood shims
- 3-inch wood screws
- Tub and tile caulk
- Latex caulk
- Pipe tape
- Quarter-round moulding

Jane Tip:

If you like the size of your existing vanity but hate the way it looks, consider buying a new vanity that is the same size. More than likely, you will have quite a few choices in the size you want.

1 Turn off the two water valves located at the base of the sink. If you don't have these or you can't locate them, be sure to turn off the water at the main valve.

2 Turn on the faucet to check that the water is indeed off. Use an adjustable wrench to remove the supply lines that lead to the faucet. Also disconnect the P-trap (the

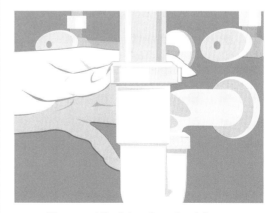

STEP 2 Disconnect the P-trap from the sink.

U-shaped pipe underneath the sink). Use a bucket to catch any water that might still be in there.

3 Use a putty knife to break the caulk seal between the vanity and the wall. Be careful not to damage the wallboard. You may have to go from the top of the vanity all the way down to the floor.

4 Using the edge of your 5-in-1 putty knife, cut away the caulk seal between the sink and the countertop. If you plan to reuse the sink, lift it out and set it upside down on an old towel to protect the porcelain. Remove any excess caulk. If you're going to reuse both the sink and the countertop, leave the sink in the countertop and remove the screws on the underside of the countertop that secure it to the cabinet. If your countertop doesn't have screws holding it in place, you may need to use a pry bar to remove the countertop from the vanity once the caulk seal is broken. Depending on the size of the countertop, you may need help lifting it off.

5 Loosen the screws that hold the vanity in place against the wall. Be careful if you're using a drill to remove the screws. They can strip quite easily, so try a regular screwdriver first. You should now be able to pull the vanity away from the wall. Move slowly so as not to damage the wall or the floor underneath.

6 Measure the height of the new vanity and make a corresponding mark on the wall. Use a stud finder to locate the studs in the wall. Make your marks just above the height of the new vanity. Remove all of the doors and drawers of the new vanity to prevent damage as you work. Install your new vanity, making certain it is flush against the wall. Use your carpenter's level to make sure

Jane Tip:

FOR STEP 6

Install the faucet before you put on the countertop. This will save you from spending the rest of the afternoon under the sink.

Jane Tip:

FOR STEP 8

Consider changing out your old steel P-trap with one made of Teflon. Teflon seals are less prone to leakage and will never rust.

Jane Tip:

FOR STEP 9

When applying caulk, consider lining the area just to the side of it with blue painter's tape. Push the caulk into place and then remove the tape; you'll have a beautifully straight line and a professional-quality caulk job.

there are no gaps between the floor and the wall. Use wood shims on the underside of the vanity until you are 100 percent sure it's flush against the wall and level. Attach the vanity to the wall with 3-inch wood screws. Check again, and correct as needed.

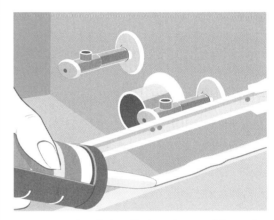

STEP 7 Run a bead of caulk along the top of the vanity before attaching the countertop.

7 Run a bead of tub and tile caulk along the top of the vanity and put the countertop in place.

8 Reconnect the plumbing, making sure the supply lines and the P-trap are securely fastened. Use a thin layer of pipe tape on the supply line connections to help prevent leaks.

9 Apply latex caulk all along the vanity where it meets the wall and the floor. Be meticulous here, because this line of caulk is fully visible.

10 If you used wood shims, trim the excess by using a hammer and a chisel. Be careful not to damage your floors. If the shims are still noticeable, consider adding a bit of molding to the base of the vanity to hide them.

One way to make your new vanity even more special is to install a new towel bar and toilet paper holder. It's like putting jewelry on your bathroom.

Towel racks and toilet paper holders come in many sizes, shapes, and colors, so you'll always find a style you love. Your local home improvement store should have plenty of well-priced options. Want a modern style? Opt for a brushed nickel with smooth lines. Feelin' a little bit country? Try a polished chrome with white porcelain accents. You can also search the Internet, as there are now dozens if not hundreds of stores that offer their catalogs online.

Jane Tip:

FOR STEP 10
Consider installing rolling shelves in your vanity to make your makeup and other spa items more accessible.

Happiness Is a Warm Towel

There's nothing better on a cold morning than stepping out of the shower and wrapping yourself in a soft, cuddly, *warm* towel. Now, you can have this spa-licious luxury any time you want it!

A number of heated towel rack models are now available. They work either by means of a hot water pipe extension or by adding a small heating element to the bar itself. For just a few dollars, you can have warm towels waiting for you each and every day.

Project: Replace a Ceiling/Vent Fan

Jane Quotient: ① ② ❸ ④ ⑤
Estimated Time: 1 to 2 hours

The last thing you want is to be in a relaxing bubble bath and stuck listening to the loud hum of a dying exhaust fan. Over time, exhaust fans collect dust and grime, and they get louder and louder with each passing year until they finally burn out.

Replacing the fan with a quieter and more powerful one is not only the way to reduce noise but also to reduce the amount of moisture left in the room following a shower or bath; this prevents the buildup of mildew on the walls and ceilings. Black mildew spots on your ceiling wreck an otherwise spa-licious bathroom experience. In addition, have you looked inside your exhaust fan lately? You may be appalled to see how much muck has built up.

These units are both inexpensive to replace and easier than you think to install.

MATERIALS

Tools
- Electrical voltage tester
- Stepladder
- Screwdriver
- Cordless drill
- Utility knife
- Tape measure

Supplies
- Bathroom exhaust fan kit
- Reciprocating saw or hand saw

Note: There are two terms to understand before you shop for a new fan. The first is the *CFM*; the second is the *sone rating*.

CFM stands for "cubic feet per minute" and reflects the volume of air the fan moves per minute. There is a way to calculate the minimum CRM you need, although, generally, the higher the better:

1. Determine the volume of your bathroom by taking its measurements.
   volume = length x width x height
2. Determine the CFM by dividing the volume number by 7.5.
3. The result is the absolute minimum CFM you should have for your bathroom.

For example:
Our bathroom is 12' W x 10' L x 9' H = 1080'
CFM = 1080 / 7.5 = 144

So, we would purchase a fan that has a CFM no less than 144. But buy the best you can! This is not something you are likely to replace often, so buy an exhaust fan with the highest CFM you can find.

The sone rating refers to the noise level of the fan. You should purchase the quietest fan your budget can buy. Usually, the quieter the fan, the more costly it is. Sones range from a

> "It was hard, but nowhere near as scary as I thought it would be."
>
> Donna K.
> El Cajon,
> California
> Age 39

very high 4.0 (way too high for a bathroom exhaust fan) to less than 1.0, equivalent to a gentle whooshing sound. Aim to buy a fan with less than 1 sone.

1 Because your fan runs on electricity, turn off the power going to it from your circuit breaker. Use an electrical tester to be sure no electrical current is running to the unit.

2 Put on your protective eyewear, and then remove the cover of your existing exhaust fan. You may have the type that has small screws holding it in place, or you may have the kind held in with small metal springs so you can simply pull it off. If the cover is stuck to the ceiling, you may have to use a utility knife.

3 Remove the old unit. It may be wedged in place and held in with a few screws, or it may be nailed into the ceiling joists. After removing any screws, gently wiggle and pull out the unit. Unplug any cords or detach the wires. Disconnect the ducting from the unit, making sure not to damage the ducting vent, which you will be connecting to the new unit.

4 Before purchasing the new fan, measure the width, length, and height of the existing unit, or make note of its model number and research the same manufacturer for the same size units. Make sure the new unit uses the same size and type of ducting. When in doubt, take a picture of the old unit, or even bring it with you to the store! Be certain there is enough space for your new unit, or you'll be cutting into the ceiling and the wood joists above it.

5 Before installing the new unit, hold up the provided template or the unit itself to your ceiling to be sure the opening is the

Jane Tip:

FOR STEP 2

If your fan cover is stuck to the ceiling, it was more than likely attached while the ceiling paint was still wet and thus adhered to the paint. Use a utility knife to make a light cut around the edge of the fan cover, which should make it easier to remove.

You will now see the exposed fan unit, which is more than likely covered in dust.

Jane Tip:

FOR STEP 3

If the unit is nailed into the ceiling joists, it may be a bit more difficult to remove. Be sure to cut any power to the unit before proceeding.

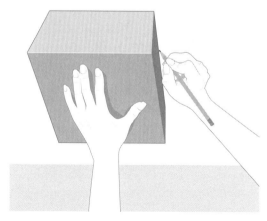

STEP 5 Trace the size of the new unit on the ceiling and make sure there is enough room.

same. If it's slightly larger, you can use a reciprocating saw or a utility knife to cut into the drywall to increase the size of the opening.

6 Once you are sure the new unit fits, it's time to install it. An extra pair of hands is useful at this point so you can have someone hold the fan while you make the connections, but it is possible to do this alone if you have good balance and multitasking skills. Attach the duct vent to the new unit, and then place the unit up into the space. Secure the unit using any fasteners provided.

STEP 6 Reattach the ducting and place the unit inside your ceiling.

7 Reconnect the electrical wiring by matching the colors of the fan wires to the same colors coming from the ceiling (known as the switch wires) and according to the manufacturer's directions. Be sure to secure the wire connections well using the supplied wire connectors.

8 Push the unit into place and secure it using any provided screws. Attach the front grille.

9 Return to the circuit breaker, restore power, then test out your new, quieter, super-air-sucker fan!

Jane Tip:

FOR STEP 7

Your unit's wiring may need to be done in the junction box of the unit, which will have to be done before the fan is pushed up into the ceiling.

Jane Tip:

FOR STEP 9

If you restore power but find that the fan won't turn on, it could be that you did not attach the wiring correctly or that one or all of the wires are loose. Turn off the power again, reopen the fan grille, and improve the wire connections.

Painting Your Bathroom Walls with Mildew- and Mold-Inhibiting Paint

As you can well imagine, the bathroom is prone to mold and mildew, but you can add mold and mildew inhibitors to your paint. These specialized additives can be purchased online or in most home improvement retailers. Some paints are specifically made to inhibit mold and mildew growth, but they may not come in the color you want. Remember that if you already have mold or mildew on your wall, putting on a mold and mildew inhibitor paint will *not* solve the problem. You must first remove the mold and spores with a solution of water and bleach. If the problem is serious, call a professional.

Second, considering you're making your bathroom a spa-licious retreat, paint the walls a color that you enjoy. A color that is soothing and calming rather than blaring will go a long way in making you comfortable in your slice of paradise.

Last, a flat latex paint is not a good choice for the high humidity level of most bathrooms. Choose paint with a slightly higher sheen and take great care to properly prep your walls before painting them. Your paint job will better stand the test of time if you do.

Jane Profile

It's not as hard as you think.

Marie "Jane" Gaudiello

Age: 62

From: Huntington, New York

Favorite tool: I would have to say my compressor and brad nailer.

Projects accomplished: I replaced all the wood-work around my entire house, I faux-painted several rooms, sand-painted my ceilings with a pattern, and changed all of the old locks to new decorative locks. I found that I can even use power tools. Of course, my son initially had to show me what to do and what not to do, but now I can use them on my own.

Inspiration for starting home improvement: I would have to say my biggest inspiration was my late husband. He was a professional building con-tractor and a great carpenter. If I wanted anything done around the house, I'd tell him, and then I'd turn around and it would be done. In 1990 he was diagnosed with lung cancer, and in 1998 he passed away. A few months after his passing an opportunity arose for me to buy a home that was being repossessed. I had always admired the things my husband could do around the house. Since he had passed away, I had no one to help me fix my new home. Hiring contractors was out of my price range. One day, my son turned to me and said, "Why don't you try it?" I figured I had my husband's old tools and said, "What the heck? I will!" Once I got started, I found that I not only liked doing home improvement, I also found it consoling, as I still miss my husband very much. Working on these projects makes me feel close to him.

Fears about home improvement: I was afraid it would look horrible and it wouldn't come out right. Sometimes I was afraid of the equipment I had to use. I was definitely leery of the compound miter saw, but my son got me over that. Some of the equipment looks kind of scary, but I just do it.

Things I was afraid of I've gotten past. It's amazing how comfortable I've become with my tools. I can even fix my lawnmower!

How has doing home improvement affected your life? I never would have thought I could do some of the things I've done. I have much more confidence now. If there's something I want to do, in the house or out, I say, "Why not? I'll try it!" I would have to say it's because I've done things I never thought I could do.

I would also say it's affected me by allowing me to create my home in a way that makes me happy. I am very affected by the atmosphere of where I live. If it's not aesthetically the way I like it, it has an effect on me that makes me unhappy. I've taken everything out of my house that was dark and made it bright and cheerful. How things look affects my feelings, and all the work I've done in my home makes me happy.

How has doing home improvement affected others in your life? Everyone is amazed at how different my house looks compared to other houses on the block. My coworkers think it's great I do the things that I do, but they think I'm crazy. I think I inspired my oldest daughter to faux-paint her home.

Advice for others just getting started in home improvement: Don't be afraid to try certain projects. If it doesn't come out right, you can always start over or hire a professional. Usually, it all works out. You just have to start small and gain confidence. Start with something simple, like refinishing a piece of furniture. It's not as hard as you think; just think it through and get some information before you start. None of these projects is as hard as you think it's going to be.

Luxury in the Spa-licious Bathroom

The reason most of us love going to a spa is that we feel like we are being spoiled. The towels and robes are plush and the shampoos and body lotions are made from exotic oils, making it all seem luxurious.

You can bring that same sense of luxury to your own home. You can add small touches to your own bathroom that will give you the spa experience each and every day for less than you think.

Sometimes, of course, it's okay to splurge. You know the expression "Work to live, don't live to work." Sometimes you need a little "me" time. Make your "me" time *quality* "me" time. Spending an hour passively watching TV is fine, but spending an hour reenergizing in a hot bubble bath with essential oils and your favorite music playing softly in the background—now doesn't that sound a little more like the kind of "me" time you'd like to have?

How was your shower this morning? Did it spoil you? Or did it spoil your morning?

You have waited way too long to get rid of

"If I had a masseuse living in my bathroom, it'd be the perfect room."

Star L.
Fort Wayne,
Indiana
Age 52

your old showerhead. An aging showerhead tends to be corroded and filled with lime and calcium deposits, giving you a subpar shower. A spa-quality showerhead is one of those affordable luxuries every person should have in her home.

Showerheads are available in every style and every budget, but the quality of shower you get from each varies dramatically. If you like to conserve water, you might lean toward the purchase of a low-flow showerhead that, over its lifetime, will pay for itself many times over. Nothing memorable, but a fine shower nonetheless.

However, you might be looking to bring home a truly spalike experience. At almost any home improvement center you can find a wide range of showerheads that provide a plethora of amazing shower encounters—full-size rain makers, massagers, swirl motion, double showerheads, and many, many more. Your choices seem endless. There's no excuse for suffering with a spitting showerhead any longer.

Project: Replace Your Old Showerhead

Jane Quotient: ❶ ② ③ ④ ⑤
Estimated Time: 20 to 30 minutes

If you've never installed a showerhead before, this project will be one of those things you wish you had done a long time ago—if only you had known it was that easy! It's a perfect launching pad for those of you looking for your first home improvement project.

MATERIALS

Tools
- Adjustable wrench
- Channel lock pliers
- Slot head screwdriver

Supplies
- Pipe joint compound or pipe tape
- New, luxurious showerhead
- Male or female adapters (depending on your faucet)

1 Unscrew the old showerhead. You will probably need to use a wrench. Often there is a corrosive buildup that causes the showerhead to get stuck.

Place the wrench around the flat part of the showerhead where it attaches to the water

Jane Tip:

FOR STEP 1
Place a small rag or a piece of tape between the teeth of the pipe wrench and the channel lock pliers and your pipes. This will help you avoid damaging your showerhead with unsightly teeth marks.

pipe. Once it loosens, unscrew the showerhead. Make sure to wipe off any corrosion on the pipe so the threads will grab the new showerhead easily. If you need to, go over it with a rag and white vinegar or a decalcifier such as CLR.

2 Apply pipe joint compound or pipe tape around the screw threads of the water pipe. If you are using pipe tape, make sure to wrap it around the pipe only 1 or 2 times. More than this will get in the way, make it difficult to put on the new head, and not allow proper sealing—and then the showerhead will drip.

3 Screw the new showerhead onto the pipe and tighten it with the wrench. Run water through the showerhead to make sure it has no leaks, and tighten it more if necessary.

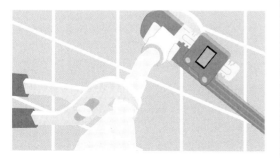

STEP 1 If your showerhead doesn't unscrew easily, use a wrench and channel lock pliers to loosen it.

Project: Install a Pedestal Sink

Jane Quotient: ① ② ③ ❹ ⑤
Estimated Time: **4 to 6 hours**

We mentioned earlier that you have several types of sink to choose from. If you're looking for a way to add elegance to your bathroom and make it look more spacious, a pedestal sink may be the way to go. You can even add his-and-her pedestal sinks if it's a high-traffic bathroom. Just be sure, no matter what you choose, that you'll still have enough storage in the rest of your bathroom for all those under-sink bottles that tend to collect. Now there's a good reason to get organized.

Pedestal sinks come in a variety of shapes and widths and range from classic styles to ultramodern silhouettes. Although they are primarily made of vitreous china (least expensive) or enameled cast iron (most expensive), they can also be mixed with a wood base or even a glass top. Do your research and get creative!

MATERIALS

Tools

- Bucket
- Fixed wrench or ratchet wrench
- Screwdriver
- Utility knife
- Tape measure
- Level
- Caulking gun
- Stud finder

Supplies

- Pedestal sink
- Mounting brackets
- Toggle bolts
- Faucet (be sure it matches the pedestal sink for width and number of holes)
- Plumber's putty
- Pencil
- Screws
- Silicone caulk (the kind made for bathrooms)
- Flexible supply tubes (optional, but a good idea to replace while you're changing everything else)
- Pop-up drain assembly (optional)

"I started tackling home projects because it seemed like it would be fun. My philosophy has always been, 'What's the worst thing that will happen?' If it doesn't work, I can always call someone."

Yvonka H.
Boynton Beach,
Florida
Age 43

Note: If an existing vanity must be removed, the wall behind it may need minor drywall repairs. You may also find it needs to be painted to match the rest of your bathroom, in which case it's a good idea to repaint the entire bathroom to be sure the color matches exactly. Have a friend or two over to help, as it can be difficult to hold the sink in place while you're measuring and installing it. Have a party!

1 Before removing the old sink or vanity, turn off the water by hand by closing the hot and cold water valves located against the wall at the back of your sink. Use a wrench or slip-joint pliers to remove the water supply tubes connected to the valves.

Before disconnecting the supply hoses altogether so you can remove the faucet, place a bucket underneath them so you can drain any remaining water. Do this by placing the ends of the hoses in the bucket, and then open the faucet until no more water runs out. Remove the existing faucet, if necessary, using a basin wrench and unscrewing the nuts from the underside of the faucet. If they're stuck, use a penetrating oil or spray like WD-40, and be sure you're twisting them the right way ("righty-tighty, lefty-loosey").

2 The next part to disconnect is the P-trap, which is the metal U-shaped pipe underneath the sink. There will be some water in it, so be sure to place the bucket underneath. Remove the slip nuts at each end of the pipe. When the P-trap is off, you can then remove the pop-up drain link.

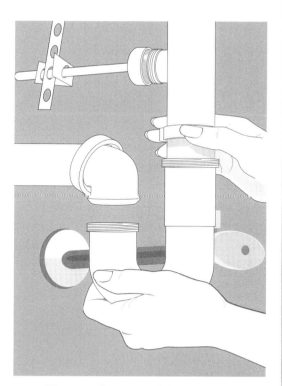

STEP 2 **Disconnect the P-trap and the pop-up drain link.**

Jane Tip:

FOR STEP 1

If you are reusing the faucet for your new pedestal sink, be sure to store all the parts in a bag for safekeeping so you have everything necessary to reinstall them.

Jane Tip:

FOR STEP 1

If any sink pipe pieces are rusty or well worn, now is the time to replace them.

3 Now your existing sink and vanity should be ready to remove. If there is caulking between the sink and the wall, or along any edges, slice through it with a utility knife. We'll warn you now: If your vanity was built in or has been there a while, you may need to do some work to get it off! Try combining a pry bar and brute force to remove the sink/countertop and vanity. There may also be screws to remove, which you can do with your drill. Do your best not to damage the surrounding wall area! If it's a large vanity, you may need a few friends to help carry it out, too.

4 With the vanity out of the way, fix drywall holes or nicks as needed.

5 Position the new sink against the wall, making sure the top piece is seated and correctly aligned with the bottom pedestal. Use two 2 x 4s to hold the sink in place as you do this. Use a pencil to mark the holes where the screws will be inserted.

STEP 5 **Using 2 x 4s to support the pedestal sink, mark the screw locations on the floor and the wall.**

6 Your pedestal sink will be secured to the wall by a mounting bracket and bolts that should be included with your sink. The bracket will be installed first by securing it to a wall stud and/or blocking (a piece of wood inserted horizontally between the studs to which the previous sink may have been secured). Using a stud finder, determine if there is wood you can drill in to.

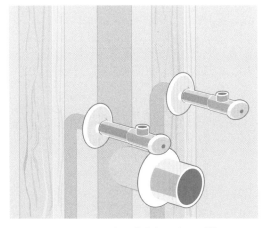

STEP 6 Secure your pedestal sink to the wall by attaching it to a stud or blocking.

7 Assemble the sink and faucet before attaching them to the wall. Apply a small amount of plumber's putty to the faucet hole on the sink. Insert the faucet and secure it in place from underneath using the hardware provided. Attach the hot and cold water hoses

Jane Tip:

FOR STEP 10
Once you've determined that your new sink has no leaks, run the faucet for a few minutes to make sure any sediment or debris from the installation flows though.

to the appropriate sides. (For details, see "Change Out a Faucet," page 166.)

8 Once the sink is assembled, secure it to the wall. Start by placing the complete pedestal sink in line with the holes you made. Insert the supplied screws and attach them to the wall through the blocking or wall studs you located earlier. Next, insert the lag screws to fasten the pedestal to the floor. Be sure not to overtighten, as you could crack the base.

9 Reconnect the water supply lines from the faucet to the hot and cold water valves on the wall, and then replace the P-trap and slip nuts to reconnect the drain arm and tailpiece.

10 Once everything is hooked up, slowly turn on the water valves again. Open the hot and cold water faucet one side at a time, checking for leaks and allowing any air in the lines to bubble out. It's also a good idea to check for leaks by filling the sink with water and allowing it to drain.

11 Once you are sure everything is in order, complete the project by using a caulking gun to run a bead of silicone caulk along the back of the sink against the wall to prevent moisture from collecting.

Project: Jazz Up a Boring Bathroom Mirror

Jane Quotient: ① ② ❸ ④ ⑤
Estimated Time: 4 hours
Drying Time: 24 hours

Usually the first thing you look at in the morning is your reflection in the mirror. But what if you hate the mirror? Unfortunately, no matter how good your reflection is, if the mirror itself is hard to look at, it will start to reflect on how you feel about yourself.

While many of us have large mirrors in our bathrooms, they typically don't shout luxury and are frequently frameless and glued directly to the wall. Your mirror is the largest accessory in your bathroom. With a little time and a few dollars, you can give that centerpiece a complete overhaul.

MATERIALS

Tools

- Tape measure
- C-clamp
- Jigsaw
- Cordless drill
- $1/2$-inch drill bit
- Paintbrush and roller
- Razor blade or utility knife
- Caulking gun
- Miter box with hand saw or electric miter saw
- Electric staple gun with staples

Supplies

- Mirror that fits your bathroom size (the ideal one is plain and glued or attached to your wall)
- $1/8$-inch piece of plywood large enough to cover your mirror
- Protective eyewear
- Mask
- Primer
- Glass tiles
- Clear adhesive (such as Liquid Nails)
- Wood, MDF, or polystyrene (foam) molding
- Silver or gold spray paint
- Q-tips
- Spackle
- Blue painter's tape
- Wood screws or drywall screws (necessary only if you can't get the frame to adhere to the mirror in the last step)

Note: This is one of those projects you can do the way we suggest or change a bit to match your tastes and style. We hope our suggestions will help you create your very own mirror masterpiece.

1 Make the backing for your frame. Start by figuring out how wide of a frame you want around your mirror. Mark the corresponding size on the $1/8$-inch plywood and cut off any excess from the edges.

To make cutting the board easier, use a C-clamp to hold the plywood in place while using your electric jigsaw. Remember, the jigsaw tends to kick up a great deal of sawdust so make absolutely sure to wear protective eyewear and a sanding mask for this step.

2 Now cut out the middle of the backing to create the edges of the frame. While cutting an outside edge with your jigsaw can be easy, cutting out the center of the backing requires an extra step. Drill a hole in the middle of the board with a $1/2$-inch drill bit to make a starting point for the blade of the jigsaw. Make your cuts starting in the middle of the board rather than an edge. (To guarantee the integrity of the frame, it must be made as one solid piece.) Drilling one hole will be enough to get all of your cuts done, but you can make more if it is more comfortable for you.

Place the blade of the jigsaw in the hole you drilled and begin cutting. Use the jigsaw to cut toward the lines that indicate the inner edge of your frame, and then cut them out by tracing them with the jigsaw. When you come to a corner, don't try to make a 90-degree angle in just one cut. Instead come at the angle from each direction separately to get a cleanly cut corner.

3 Coat the backing with primer. Raw plywood doesn't like anything sticking to it unless it's primed first. Apply a coat of good-quality primer on both sides to increase adherence and to prevent warping from steam or condensation on or around the mirror.

In the next step, you will be applying glass tiles to the backing. To keep the backing looking bright, a coat of solid white paint is needed. (You can then apply two to three coats of primer if you prefer.) If you plan to paint

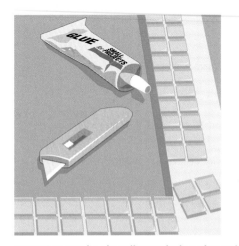

STEP 3 Lay out the glass tiles on the board to make sure they fit the way you want them. Glue them in place. You may need a razor to cut the plastic film on the tiles or the mesh below them.

Jane Tip:

FOR STEP 1

If you want to make your mirror appear larger and more luxurious, create a frame that extends beyond the mirror itself. Start by purchasing a board bigger than the mirror, and then cut the edges so that the inside of the frame touches the mirror and the outside extends past it. Make sure to leave enough wall space between the edges of the frame and any light fixtures or sink backsplash that could get in the way.

Jane Tip:

FOR STEP 2

If you have chosen to create an over-sized frame, make sure its inside edge will cover the outside edge of the mirror. The opening of the frame should be 2 to 4 inches smaller than your mirror in both width and height. This will allow 1 to 2 inches of the frame to touch the mirror directly. You will want at least 1 to 1 1/2 inches on each side to ensure stability and staying power when you glue your frame on the mirror.

the backing a different color, apply one coat of primer and then two coats of the finished color.

4 Once the paint or primer is dry, apply the glass tiles. Before gluing the tiles down, lay them on the board to check the placement and to find the look you want. If you don't want to do this freehand, many smaller tiles come attached in sheets to allow for even placement. To create the frame we chose, you'll need only two rows of tiles along the inside edge of the frame. You may need a razor blade or a utility knife to cut the material holding the rows in place. Be sure to keep the tiles attached to one another for easier placement.

Firmly attach the tiles with an adhesive. For glass tiles, a clear adhesive such as Liquid Nails is a good choice because it won't show through the tiles. Once you've attached the tiles, lay the frame flat to dry.

5 While the adhesive dries, prepare the molding for your frame. You can choose solid wood, MDF, or polystyrene foam molding. We chose polystyrene molding for its light weight and ease of cutting.

If you want a gilded look, lightly spray the molding with a silver or gold spray paint. For a slightly uneven effect to soften the look of the frame, spray it from a distance. This technique is often seen on expensive frames. Let the paint dry for at least 4 hours or as stated on the label of the can.

6 Measure the outside edge of the tiles adhered to the backing. These measurements will dictate your cuts for the framing material, especially if you want the molding to butt up against the tiles. Using a miter box and back saw or an electric miter saw, cut the molding. We suggest using a miter box for MDF, as it is too soft for an electric saw.

Cut the edges at 45-degree angles on each end

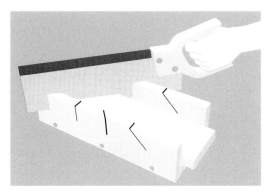

STEP 6 If you choose to use foam or polystyrene molding, use the miter box and back saw to cut the corners.

of the molding so that when put together they will form the 90-degree corners of the frame.

7 To attach the molding, turn it upside down and put all of the pieces together in a rectangle. Do this over a towel to protect the fresh paint.

Apply a small amount of the clear adhesive to the two sides of a corner. The easiest way to do this is to remove the cotton from the end of a Q-tip and use the now bare stick to apply the glue. (Place a paper towel underneath to protect your towel from getting glue on it.) Try to keep any excess glue away from the paint, as it will remove it.

Hold the glued pieces together to make a perfect 90-degree angle with one hand, and with the other use an electric staple gun to place three to four staples on the back. This will help hold the corners together while the glue dries. Repeat this step with the rest of the corners. Carefully turn over the molding and place it on a flat surface to dry.

8 After the glue dries, apply spackle to any openings or gaps to fill them in. If you have chosen a detailed molding, make sure to remove any spackle that gets stuck in the detailed areas. Use a damp rag to remove any excess before it dries, as sanding will remove the paint you've just applied and can quickly abrade the foam molding. Touch up with the spray paint as needed and let dry.

9 To apply the molding to the wood backing, place the wood backing on a plastic tarp to protect the surface you are working on. Apply a wavy line of the adhesive on the base around all four sides. Place the molding on the backing and press down. Let it dry for the amount of time stated on the adhesive label.

10 Once everything is dry, apply a thick, wavy line of a quick-drying construction adhesive like Liquid Nails along the four edges of the mirror. Press the frame up against the mirror and then pull it away for 30 seconds to a minute. (This will help the adhesive to become tackier [stickier], helping the frame hold to the mirror better.) Place the frame back on the mirror. To keep it in place while the adhesive is drying, use blue painter's tape to hold the frame tight against the mirror.

Don't forget, this is about creating your very own spa-licious bathroom. Think about the colors or things that would do that for you. Maybe you'd prefer shells instead of glass tiles to go with your Nantucket Beach spa bathroom. Get creative and find out what you like.

Project: Replace an Old Countertop with Stone or Tile

Jane Quotient: ① ❷ ③ ④ ⑤
Estimated Time: 4 to 7 hours (longer if you are covering a large surface)

Is it time to change out that old, worn countertop? After all, the brown faux-marble laminate-coated countertop you have now, complete with a collection of toothpaste stains, doesn't exactly say "luxury." To change the feel of your bathroom, that countertop has got to go.

What material should you to replace it with to add luxury to your bathroom? Tile? It's certainly a traditional option and an excellent choice, but we want something that screams luxury. Corian? That would be wonderful—it's beautiful—but it's definitely not for those of us on a budget. Okay, what about Formica? That hasn't been luxurious since 1976. There's one more material left, and one that might not readily come to mind: stone.

You may well ask, "But isn't stone too heavy and too expensive, and don't you need a pro to install it?"

The answers are no, no, and no, because what we're referring to is stone tile—an affordable alternative to stone made from real stone aggregate suspended in a polymer binder. This project is fun and easy and will bring your bathroom closer to spa-liciousness.

MATERIALS

Tools
- Tape measure
- Jigsaw
- Safety goggles
- Cordless drill
- Notched trowel
- Scoring tool
- Chalk line
- Tile cutter
- Level
- Mallet
- Grout float

Supplies
- ⁵/₈-inch plywood
- Pencil
- Wood glue
- 1¹/₂-inch flat-top screws
- Mortar-based backer board
- Thinset (adhesive for stone)
- ¹/₂-inch galvanized screws
- Stone tiles
- Tile spacers
- Grout
- Sponge
- Grout sealant

"Every time I do a home improvement project I keep asking myself, why'd I wait so long!"

Linda T.
Miami, Florida
Age 46

👓 **Safety Check!**
Wear safety goggles for this project.

1 Get rid of your old countertop by using a combination of crowbar, screwdriver, and hammer. (This is the best way to get out your aggressions!) Be careful not to scar the cabinet it's sitting on.

2 Cut the plywood to fit the counter. Place it over the countertop surface, and if any of the edges touch a wall, decrease that measurement by ¼ inch to allow for expansion. If you want the finished counter to have a bullnose or lip (also called an apron) edge, add 1 inch to the outside edges. Mark out your counter area on the plywood and cut it with a jigsaw. Remember to wear safety goggles.

STEP 2 **After marking the shape of your countertop on your plywood, cut along the markings with a jigsaw. Pay attention to where you place your hands and the cord while cutting.**

3 Attach the wood by putting wood glue on the cabinet edges, laying the wood on top, and screwing in 1½-inch flat-top screws every 4 to 6 inches where the cabinet edges and plywood meet. Make sure the screws are flush.

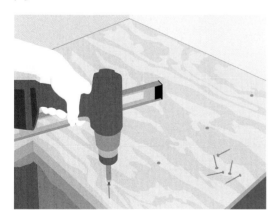

STEP 3 **Once you've applied the wood glue to the edges of the cabinet, put the plywood in place and screw it into the top of the cabinets with 1½-inch flat-top screws and your cordless drill. Set a screw every 4 to 6 inches. Make sure to countersink them.**

Jane Tip:

FOR STEP 2

If you need to cut from the middle of the plywood, drill a hole in an area that will be scrap. This hole is where you will insert the blade to start cutting.

Jane Tip:

FOR STEP 4

Backer board is the easiest to cut. All you do is score and snap. Cut it to cover the plywood you've just installed. If the surface isn't solid and you need more than one piece to cover, place mesh tape over the seams where the backer board and plywood meet. The tape will keep the tiles from cracking. Make sure to put some Thinset adhesive in the area when you apply it and smooth it out to before drying. Let it dry before applying the stone.

4 To install the ¼-inch mortar-based backer board (Hardi Backer is our favorite), apply a coat of Thinset on top of the plywood with a notched trowel. Then place the backer board faceup (there are dots to indicate the up side). Put in ½-inch galvanized nails or screws (galvanized to prevent from rusting) anywhere you see a dot. Make sure the nails are flush with the board, or they will interfere when you go to set the stone.

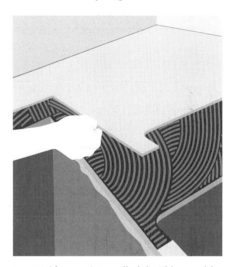

STEP 4 **After you've applied the Thinset with a notched trowel to the plywood, lay down the backer board (dots side up), which you've already cut to fit the surface. Once it's in place, gently push down on the surface to make sure that the Thinset properly adheres to the board.**

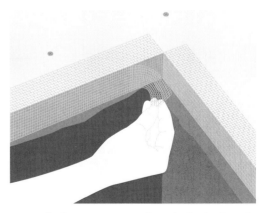

STEP 4 **Apply seam tape anywhere the backer board has seams. It typically has a sticky texture, but go ahead and apply a thin coat of Thinset over the tape with a putty knife.**

5 Lay out the pattern you want the tile in. Start by finding the exact middle point and move out from there. The easiest way to do this is with a tape measure and a chalk line. Mark the center on the top and bottom and snap a chalk line; then do the same thing from right to left.

Make sure to use spacers no wider than 1/8 inch between each tile. Anything larger will need a sanded grout, and if the surface is well polished it can get scratched when you place the grout.

At the edges, be sure to leave enough room for the bullnose or edging that will hang over the lip. Once you've finished your design, remove the entire puzzle one piece at a time. Using a pencil, number each tile on the back and draw an arrow pointing to the top.

Jane Tip:

FOR STEP 7
Spread only as much adhesive as you can cover with tile in 10 minutes. If you have precut the entire surface, start from a corner; otherwise, start from the middle. Don't forget to use spacers when putting your puzzle together.

6 Check that the counter is level by placing a level on it. If it's not, adjust it when you lay the tile.

7 The adhesive you're going to use, Thinset, is made for laying stone. It's easiest to buy this premixed, but of course that costs more than if you mix it yourself. Apply it with a notched trowel to ensure even distribution and increased suction when you place the tiles.

If you plan to add a bullnose to the edge of the countertop, get this ready at the same time as you prepare your tiles for the counter. When laying the nosing pieces, you can either apply the Thinset to the counter

STEP 5 Before adhering the stone to the counter, lay out the pattern with the spacers. Mark any cuts on the tiles, and make all necessary cuts before you begin setting the tiles into the Thinset.

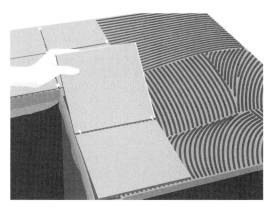

STEP 7 After applying the Thinset with a notched trowel, set the tiles in it, using spacers to guarantee proper spacing. Lay them out the same way you did before.

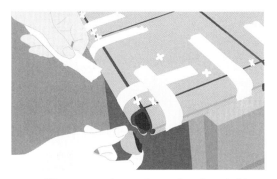

STEP 7 When you apply a nosing to the edges, hold the pieces in place with tape until they dry so they stay straight during the drying process. Once they're dry, remove the tape.

edges or to the nosing pieces themselves. Once you've positioned them properly, apply masking tape to hold them in place while they dry.

If your counter wasn't level when you checked it, now is the time to address the problem. Use a beating block or a rubber mallet to level out the individual pieces. Make sure to use your level to check this.

8 Leave your countertop alone for 24 hours (don't put anything or anyone on top of it).

9 Remove all of the spacers. Mix the grout according to the instructions on the bag. Hold the rubber grout float at a 45-degree angle and move it diagonally across the tile face. This will force the grout between the tiles. Apply the grout all over the tile until all of the spaces are full.

Using a clean, damp sponge, wipe off any excess grout. This may take several passes. Rinse out the sponge between passes.

The grout needs 72 to 96 hours to dry all of the way through.

Jane Tip:

FOR STEP 9
To prevent cracking, especially with larger grout lines, spray the grout with water in a spray bottle twice a day for the first 3 days. This way the top won't dry fully before the rest does.

STEP 9 Once you've applied the grout, make sure to quickly remove any excess from the stone surface before it fully dries. Do this with a slightly damp sponge. If you wait too long, the grout will dry all over the surface, ruining your beautiful new stone countertop.

10 Stone can be susceptible to stains. Considering stains were one of the reasons you changed the countertop in the first place, make sure to seal the new one. Most sealers require that you wait 7 to 10 days after you've grouted before applying the sealer.

Apply the sealer according to the instructions on the can. Voila! Not only did you save a fistful of dollars, you just added pure luxury to your bathroom.

STEP 9 After mixing up the grout, apply it to the countertop's surface. Hold the grout float at a 45-degree angle to get the best retention in the grooves.

STEP 10 Apply sealer to the entire countertop with a lint-free rag or a paintbrush and gloves. This will help protect your countertop and allow you to enjoy it for years to come.

A Dining Room That Makes Every Day a Special Occasion

Do you remember when you were a child and the dining room was considered off limits? It was a special room that was used only for *special* occasions.

Even if you were never told directly, you learned from watching that the only dishes, glasses, and silverware used in it were the "good" ones. And of course, this was the room where guests ate; it wasn't a room for everyday meals. Many of us have taken the same approach in our own dining rooms.

It might be time to ask yourself, "Is this a tradition I *want* to carry on?"

Why is it that we reserve the good dishes for special days? Isn't the first time your child gets an *A* on a report card, or when you and your spouse get home from a busy week at work, enough of a reason to celebrate? Or do you have to wait for a date in the calendar that comes with a card? Birthdays, Thanksgiving, Christmas, Kwanzaa, Hanukkah, Ramadan, and so on are all holidays that warrant celebration, but so do the rest of the days of the year.

If your dining room were more comfortable and inviting, would you be more inclined to use it on an every day basis? If it could better accommodate your guests, would you have

"Every Thanksgiving I can't help but show off my dining room. I did it, after all, so why not?"

Rene V.
Dayton, Ohio
Age 46

them over more often? If it were more aesthetically pleasing, would you consider spending more time there with your own family?

By the way, who says you have to *eat* in a dining room? Just because it's called a *dining room* need not limit your activities to dining. A dining room can be used any time, any day, and in any way you choose.

Even if you don't have an actual dining room, take a look at where you eat most of your meals—whether by yourself or with your family, guests, or that special someone. You are affected on multiple sensory levels in the place you eat. If you enhance *one* of your senses, you enhance them all. If the space you eat in looks good, smells good, and feels good, then whatever you're eating will taste better and you'll enjoy it more. It's important to remember to feed all your senses, because those things you don't put into your mouth are often food for the soul.

Break out the good china and make *today* a day to celebrate.

Jane Profile

Don't be afraid to use a power tool.

Danielle "Jane" Halliday

Age: 27

From: Forked River, New Jersey

Favorite tool: It is a toss-up between my new nail gun and my Dremel. Either way, I have more tools than my husband!

Projects accomplished: I stripped every room of wallpaper and redid it with new paint and faux finish. I refinished several flea market finds such as an antique hutch, my end tables, my cabinets, and several decorative items.

Inspiration for starting home improvement: My mom was a huge inspiration. She's the one who taught me how to use power tools. The other inspiration was when I moved in with my husband before we were married. I had moved into a house that could only be described as a genuine bachelor pad. So I started redecorating the house. When I started, he was afraid of color, but before he knew it, it was a whole new house. Room by room, I took over.

Fears about home improvement: The unexpected. Whenever I took on a room, I found it had its own underlying project. I was and still am always afraid of what problems will pop up in each room I start. Each room seems to have its own issues. However, it's always good because it's a great learning experience, and now I know I can handle almost anything.

How has doing home improvement affected your life? It helped me find what I wanted to do with my life. I didn't know I wanted to be a decorator until I started working on our home. When I refinished our cabinets, my husband turned to me and said, "You really know what you're doing. You should do this for a living!" So we signed me up for an interior decorating course. People have since told me my house looks like a picture out of a magazine.

How has doing home improvement affected others in your life? I think I was the inspiration for many friends to get over their fear of using color. I was so happy when my husband (who initially had to have nothing but white walls) fell in love with all of our colored walls. I even had a next-door neighbor try out bright color on her walls, and she loved it!

Advice for others just getting started in home improvement: Painting is the cheapest way to redecorate a room. Don't be afraid of color. Research everything about what you're doing before you do it. Oh, and when male store clerks try to sell you the dinky little power tools, say, "No, I want the biggest, most powerful one you've got!" Don't be afraid to use a power tool, and never wait around for men to do things.

Making Your Dining Space Aesthetically Pleasing

To be able to spend quality time in any room of the house, you must enjoy being in that space. Whether it's the furniture, wall accents, the floor, or the ceiling, there should be something about each room that makes you feel good.

As we mentioned earlier, when you nourish your body, it's important not to forget to nourish your other senses as well. As the

"Home improvement is hard but ever so satisfying."

Mikala D.
New York,
New York
Age Unknown

body becomes satisfied with food, the mind becomes satisfied with the aesthetics of the room.

To get the most out of your dining area, give the aesthetics of the room or space the same attention you give making a dinner for a group of friends. Make it a room you are proud to show off and a space you'll enjoy being in.

Project: Refinish a Dining Room Table and Hutch

Jane Quotient: ① ② ❸ ④ ⑤
Time Estimate: 4 to 6 hours

If your dining room table—which is, of course, the focal point of the room—looks more like a beat-up slab of wood than a sparkling smooth table fit for a feast, the time has come to refinish it. Refinishing is the process of removing an existing finish, preparing the surface, and then painting or staining it with the new finish. You can refinish most table surfaces, including paint, varnish, and even lacquer, inexpensively and with just a little effort.

If you don't like the style of your current table and want to get rid of it altogether, instead of buying a new one, consider finding a slightly used wood table at a garage sale, county fair, in your local newspaper, or even on eBay for half the cost of a new one. In the course of a weekend you can transform nearly any table into the one you have been dreaming of.

MATERIALS

Tools
- Paint scraper
- Electric palm sander (optional)
- Paintbrushes

Supplies
- Fine-grit sandpaper
- Coarse sandpaper
- Paint stripper (optional)
- Protective eyewear
- Protective gloves (latex)
- Face mask
- Disposable paintbrushes
- Apron or old clothes
- Small bucket
- Clean rag
- Tack cloth
- Paint or stain

Jane Tip:

FOR STEP 1
You should use 100-grit, then 150-grit, and a final 220-grit sanding on refinishing projects. Each rise in grit tightens the grain, allowing for a smoother finish.

1 The old paint or varnish must be removed, or stripped. Choose between these two methods:

■ **SCRAPE-AND-SAND METHOD.** If the paint on the table is flaking off and there's not much left, you can scrape and sand it off. This can be done using a paint scraper to literally scrape off as many paint flakes as you can, followed by a thorough sanding of the entire surface to remove the remaining paint. You can use either fine-grit sandpaper or—to get the job done faster—an electric palm sander. Go easy with the palm sander, though; you don't want to press too hard and damage the wood. Even with an electric sander, you will probably still need to use regular sandpaper by hand for any corners or grooves. Overall, the scrape-and-sand method requires elbow grease and time, but it can be a good option

STEP 1 After the paint stripper has soaked in, start scraping it away to remove old coats of paint.

Jane Tip:

FOR STEP 2

There are a number of "green" paint strippers on the market. Check online for the variety that works best for you.

Redefining the Family Heirloom

It's wonderful to inherit furniture from family members. You might consider some of these pieces heirlooms, passed down for each new generation to cherish and enjoy. Heirlooms hold a special place for many of us simply because we are given the opportunity to continue building on the history and tradition the object represents. Such pieces hold a significance above and beyond their retail value.

What happens when you are next in line for the family furniture . . . but you hate it? Well, we have some good news. It's *yours* now, and you can change it. A few minor changes to an existing piece might make a huge difference and turn it into something you love.

Of course, you must consider a couple of issues before moving forward: (1) You might upset some members of the family; and (2) some antiques might lose significant value if they're altered in any way. But if you don't plan on selling it, your family can't wait to see the changes you come up with, or the antique factor doesn't apply, then make the piece your own by changing it!

Refinish it, change out the drawer pulls and handles, add rolling shelves— heck, paint it blue with pink polka dots! It's completely up to you. The point is, don't live with something you hate out of obligation. It's your life, it's your home. Make it the best it can be by doing what makes you happy.

on a solid wood table with little paint remaining. Remember: Always wear protective eyewear and a sanding mask! You don't know what type of residue might come off an antique table. It's safe to assume you don't want it in your lungs or your eyes.

■ **STRIPPING METHOD.** The alternative to scraping and sanding is using what's called a **stripper.** Paint stripper, also called wood stripper, is a chemical solution that dissolves old paint or varnish. There are two primary kinds of stripper: the stronger—and faster working— which is more chemically toxic, and an environmentally friendly paint stripper, which although kinder to you and Mother Earth, takes longer to get the job done. It's up to you which one to use. In either case, you'll need protective eyewear, gloves, a face mask, disposable paintbrushes, an apron to protect your clothes (or wear old clothes), and a small bucket and a rag. Make certain you have proper ventilation as well, as these chemicals can emit toxic fumes.

Always start by reading the manufacturer's directions on the label. Pour the stripper into a small bucket or can, and then use a paintbrush to apply a thick coat to the table. Allow the stripper to soak in for several hours, based on the product instructions.

After several hours, you can apply a thin second coat. You can then begin to scrape off the existing paint or varnish with a paint scraper or a putty knife.

2 Once you have removed all the old paint via either method described above, allow the table to dry completely. This can take anywhere from a few hours to overnight. Next, sand the surface using a fine-grit sandpaper with either a sanding block or a palm sander. Wipe down the table with a tack cloth to remove remaining sawdust and other debris.

3 As a final step before repainting or staining, you may want to use mineral spirits or a cleansing paint-removal wash. This will help remove all final grease and dust and show you the true surface of the wood.

4 Your wood table should now look smooth and ready for the final finish. You can choose to paint the table with oil-based paint, high-gloss latex paint, or wood stain. Apply the finish according to the manufacturer's instructions for the product you choose.

Show off your accomplishment by celebrating with a big dinner with all your friends and family!

Jane Tip:

FOR STEP 3
There are also a number of environmentally friendly paint-removal washes available. Check online or with your local home improvement center.

STEP 3 Remove any paint stripper residue with a mineral spirits wash.

STEP 4 Apply the paint or stain color of your choice to the prepared wood.

Project: Install Crown Molding

Jane Quotient: ① ② ③ ❹ ⑤
Estimated Time: 4 to 10 hours

Crown molding is one of those additions that can change the look and feel of a room. It brings together a sense of sophistication and elegance while creating a warmth and grace that makes the room more inviting.

Crown molding artfully conceals where a wall and ceiling join, yet often can make a room look bigger and taller. You might find it adds that perfect dose of something special to your dining room.

It used to be that installing crown molding was considered one of the more difficult home improvement projects, but with today's tools and prefabricated materials, it's not that hard. That doesn't mean that once you've completed this project you won't want to brag!

MATERIALS

Tools

- 2 ladders of medium height
- Tape measure
- Stud finder
- Angled sash paintbrush
- Compound miter saw
- Coping saw
- Rasp (metal file) or palm sander
- Pneumatic finishing nail gun (compressor or gas canister)
- Hammer
- Caulking gun
- Countersetter

Supplies

- Pencil/pen
- Paper
- Crown molding
- Primer
- Semigloss paint
- Work gloves
- Protective eyewear
- Finishing nails
- Spackle
- Fine- to medium-grit sandpaper
- Painter's caulk
- Shop towels

"I want to do my own moldings. I figure if men can do it, it can't be that hard. I don't say that to be a wiseguy; it's just that women are more detail oriented. I really think I can do it with some instructions."

Rita D.
Medford,
New York
Age 58

Note: Not one corner in your house is perfectly square (90 degrees). The corners may *look* square to the naked eye, but you will soon find out that they can range from 87 to 93 degrees. (By the way, most of your walls and ceilings aren't really flat either.) The reason this is important to know is so that you won't be surprised when you measure your walls and start to see how off they are. But don't think your house is poorly made; it's actually a normal and expected occurrence. As you'll see later in this project, with a little patience, you can correct for and work around these imperfections.

Note: From the very beginning of this project, a second set of hands is a great idea. You don't need someone who's done this job before. It's more the fact that you will be working with very long pieces of wood that are awkward, if not impossible, to put up by holding one end.

1 Determine how much molding you need by drawing the floor plan of the room on a piece of paper. You'll be adding the measurements of each wall to that floor plan in a moment.

2 Using a tape measure, measure the length of each wall. Write the measurements on the paper floor plan you created in step 1. Pay special attention to accuracy.

3 Add up all of the wall lengths to figure out how much molding you need. The easiest way to do this is to add up all the feet in each measurement, then add up all the inches and divide by 12; add this second number to the number of feet for the grand total.

STEP 3 Measure all of the walls in the room. Make sure you measure them accurately so you can use these measurements when you cut. Add all the feet and then all the inches. If the inches are greater than 12, divide that number by 12. Add this number to the total number of feet you had previously. To be certain you buy enough, add another 10 percent to this total.

4 Using a pencil and a stud finder, mark off where the studs are on the wall near the ceiling but below where the molding will sit. You'll need to be able to see them, as these are the points at which you'll nail the crown molding onto the wall.

Jane Tip:

FOR STEP 3

Expect to make a few mistakes when cutting your crown molding. To avoid going back to the store for more in the middle of your project, add an extra 10 percent to your total.

Jane Tip:

FOR STEP 5

Make sure you purchase molding that suits the size of your room. If molding is too big, it can visually shrink the room, whereas if it's too small, it will get lost. Remember, however, that you will always be seeing the molding from a distance, and for that reason it will appear smaller than in the store. What seems big in your hand may be perfect once it's up on the wall. Be aware that if you choose a molding larger than $4^3/_4$ inches you will need to install nailing blocks, which are triangular pieces of wood that run the length of the wall and give you something to nail the molding into.

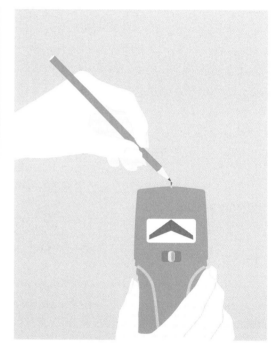

STEP 4 Use a stud finder to find the studs in the walls and mark them with a pencil.

5 Purchasing the molding may sound like an easy thing to do, but with the wide variety of styles, materials, and sizes available, it can be quite time-consuming. You may want to purchase a few 2- to 3-foot samples, take them home, and see how they look.

If you want white or painted crown molding, we suggest getting primed MDF (modified dense fiberboard), as it tends to be less expensive and eliminates having to prime before painting.

Remember to get a few pieces that are as long as your longest walls, if possible, to avoid having to splice two smaller pieces. Splicing is not difficult, but it does take time.

6 Prime and paint the molding *before* you begin cutting. You can certainly paint the pieces after cutting, but even the slightest amount of paint on the edges can throw off your cuts. We learned this the hard way! Unless you're using MDF or another

primerless material, make sure you give all the pieces at least one coat of primer. Apply the paint with an angled sash paintbrush, with strokes going side to side rather than up and down. This will minimize the brush-strokes needed. Let the paint dry, and then apply a second coat, even if it looks great after just one. This guarantees that when you are done, the molding will show off your room as well as possible. When choosing paint, remember that your walls have a flat sheen, so giving your molding a semigloss finish will present them off just enough to help catch the eye.

7 Once your painted pieces are completely dry, it is time to cut. You can use a miter box and back saw combo, or for more efficiency (and fun), you can use a compound miter saw to make your cuts.

Cut the molding bottom side up for accurate cuts. Mark the bottom edge of the molding with a piece of tape so you'll know which way to place it into the miter box. Unfortunately, cutting the board upside down makes it easy to forget which direction you need to cut. Begin by creating two sets of templates, one for an inside corner and one for an outside corner. Label each accordingly (right inside, left inside, right outside, left outside). When you go to cut, you will be able to look down at your drawing from step 1, pick up the template for the cut you need to make, turn it upside down, and then shift your saw to create that angle. This approach has saved us a great deal of frustration.

Once you've marked the length on the wood, place it into your compound miter saw and adjust the angle of the blade and the table it is on. Before making any cuts, compare the angle of the blade and the way it will cut with the template of the cut you want to make. If you are renting a compound miter saw, ask the staff to show you how to make cuts with it before you take it home.

Jane Tip:
FOR STEP 6

If you're using wood or any other natural substance for your molding, be sure to prime both sides of each piece. This will eliminate or at least minimize the warping that many occur by painting just the front.

Jane Tip:
FOR STEP 7

Make sure you are placing the molding on the saw at exactly the same angle each time. One easy way to guarantee this is by attaching a small piece of wood, such as a paint stirrer, to your saw with a hot glue gun to show you where to place each piece. Otherwise the wood will constantly be slipping, and you will end up with different cuts each time. Many miter saws have crown molding attachments that make it easier to install.

STEP 7 Cut sets of templates for when you begin cutting. One should be an outside corner and the other an inside corner. On each, mark the right and left side and add an arrow that points toward the ceiling. These templates can save you a great deal of time and aggravation. Make sure before you make each cut to compare the angle on your template to the one you are about to cut.

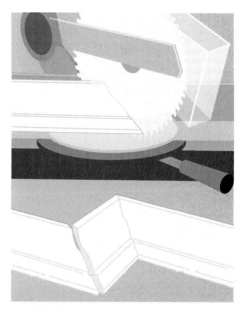

STEP 7 Before actually making your cuts with the saw, compare the angle of the blade to that on your template pieces.

8 When cutting an inside angle, you may want to cut out the excess wood behind the molding in the corner, especially if you are having trouble getting things to butt up to each other. To do this, cut the molding just as you would normally, and then use a coping saw to remove the unpainted part of the wood to match the profile of the molding. The appropriate angle to cut at is 5 degrees. The edge should be just thick enough to touch

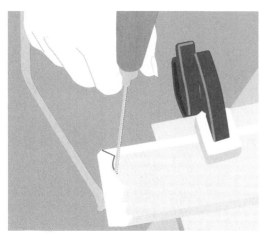

STEP 8 With a coping saw, cut or cope the excess wood that sits behind in the corner on all inside corner cuts.

the piece next to it and look solid but be open enough to not create a problem fitting together. If you find you're close but not close enough, use a rasp or a palm sander to make it even thinner.

9 Attach your crown molding with a finishing nail gun. (You can do this step by hand, but it will take you a great deal

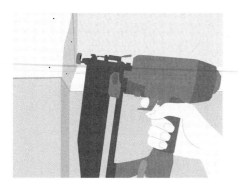

STEP 9 Using a finishing nail gun, attach the crown molding in place. Make sure you shoot nails wherever you made pencil marks.

Jane Tip:

FOR STEP 9
When attaching your molding, attach only the side that is already butting up against another piece. It's important to still have a bit of movement when you go to attach the second piece in each corner. If it is already attached, you will have trouble matching the angles. Once you get them to match, nail them in place.

longer, and you will have many more holes to fill.) Place nails wherever you marked a stud, on both the top and bottom of the molding. Make sure you are wearing both protective eyewear and hearing protection; nail guns can be extremely loud. Hammer in any nails that remain above the surface with a countersetter.

10 Fill in the gaps and the holes with spackle. Let dry, and lightly sand if necessary. Touch up these spots, and any areas that were scuffed during installation, with paint.

11 If at this point you look up and see gaps between the walls, ceiling, and molding, don't panic; we expected this to happen. Remember when we said your walls aren't flat? Here's proof. You didn't do anything wrong. This is where our motto, "Caulk and paint'll make it what it ain't," comes in.

All you need to do is to caulk the edges of the crown molding to fill in any gaps. Apply a bead of painter's caulk with a caulking gun and then go over it with your finger and a damp disposable shop towel (extra-strong paper towel). This will help push the caulk into the open spaces left behind as well as to make the molding look finished. Wear gloves, as this step can get quite messy. Remember, if you painted the molding any color other than white, the caulk will be very obvious. But once it dries, you can simply cover it with paint.

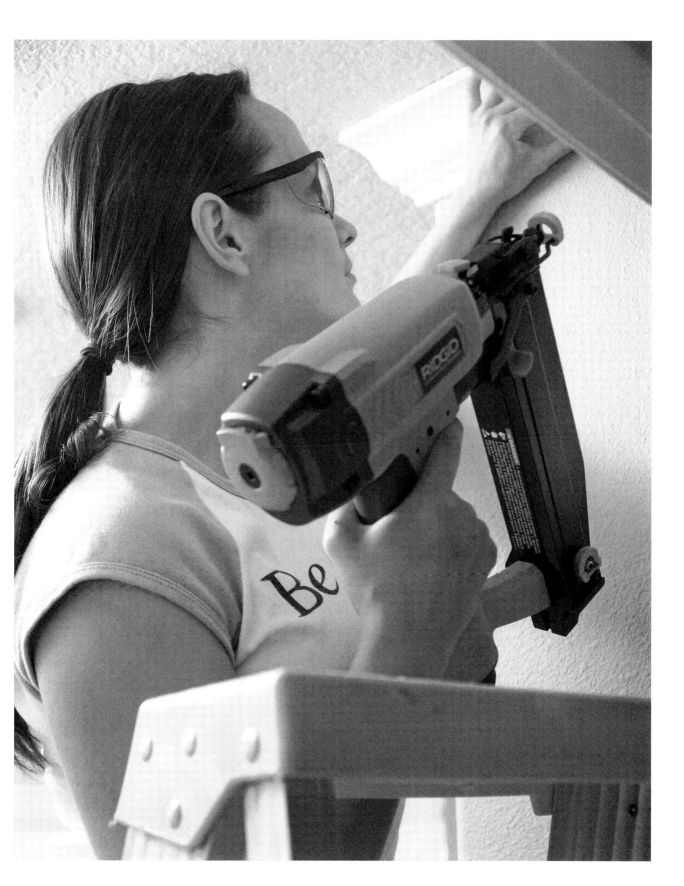

Project: Install Chair Rail Molding

Jane Quotient: ① ❷ ③ ④ ⑤
Time Estimate: 2 to 4 hours plus painting and drying time

Chair railing was conceived as a way to protect the wall surface from chair backs that lean against it. Even though nowadays it's more of a décor choice, it still serves its original purpose.

One of the wonderful things about chair railing is that it seems to bring an essence of class to an otherwise bland dining area. It provides a division on the wall that appeals to the eye. Chair railing is often used as a dividing line, with paint above it and wallpaper or wainscoting on the bottom. In and of itself, chair railing is a classy and distinctive design option.

MATERIALS

Tools
- Tape measure
- Paintbrush
- Level
- Power miter saw or back saw and miter box
- Stud finder
- Drill
- Nail set
- Hammer
- Caulk gun

Supplies
- Chair rail molding
- Primer or varnish
- Pencil
- Safety glasses
- Finishing nails
- Wood putty
- Caulk

Jane Tip:

FOR STEP 3
Consider purchasing a laser level. Many models have the ability to project a line around corners, giving you a straight line all around the room without having to make numerous and repetitious measurements.

1 Measure your walls to determine how much molding to purchase. Always add at least 10 percent extra for mistakes.

2 Prime the molding, both front and back, before installing it. This will help prevent warping. If you plan to paint the molding before installing it, be sure to paint both sides as well.

3 Determine your layout line. This is the height you'll want the chair rail to sit at. To make it a functional chair rail, place it

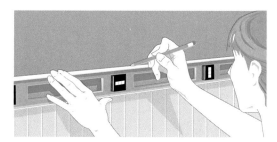

STEP 3 **Once you've determined the height of the chair rail, use a carpenter's level to extend a horizontal line that will indicate the top of the chair rail.**

between 32 and 36 inches from the floor. Consider measuring the back of one of your dining room chairs to be certain the railing will accommodate it. Mark that height on the wall. Take a carpenter's level and extend a horizontal line to indicate the top of the rail.

4 Make your miter cuts at the corners using the power miter saw or the back saw and miter box. Remember to wear safety glasses. If you chose a molding with a simple profile, make 45-degree miter cuts for both inside and outside corners. If the molding is a bit more detailed, you might have to cope the joints for a better fit on the inside corners. Where your chair rail meets door casings and window frames, make a square cut, which is a straight 90-degree angle cut.

5 Use your stud finder to locate the studs in the wall (usually, every 16 inches). Mark the stud locations on the wall and, while holding the chair rail in place, make the marks on the chair rail as well. Drill pilot holes in the chair rail, and then attach it to the wall using the finishing nails and a hammer. Use the nail set to drive the nailhead below the surface.

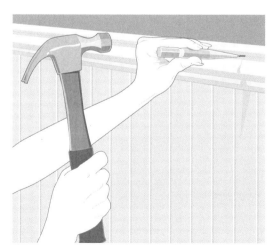

STEP 5 Embed the nailheads into the wood by countersetting them.

Jane Tip:

FOR STEP 4

If your pieces of molding aren't long enough to cover the wall, you can attach two pieces together by making what's known as **splicing.** Cut one end of one piece of the molding at a 45-degree angle on one side of the miter box, and then cut another piece from the other side of the box. You can now overlap the two pieces, which will hide the splice better than had you done a square cut.

Jane Tip:

FOR STEP 5

Using a pneumatic finishing nail gun will cut your work time in half as it not only drives the nail into the wood with one shot but also countersets it simultaneously.

6 Use a little wood putty to cover the nail holes. Once the putty is dry, sand down any rough edges and use touch-up paint to cover the patches. Caulk the edges of the molding to fill in any gaps.

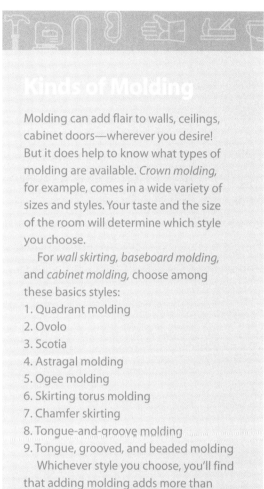

Kinds of Molding

Molding can add flair to walls, ceilings, cabinet doors—wherever you desire! But it does help to know what types of molding are available. *Crown molding,* for example, comes in a wide variety of sizes and styles. Your taste and the size of the room will determine which style you choose.

For *wall skirting, baseboard molding,* and *cabinet molding,* choose among these basics styles:
1. Quadrant molding
2. Ovolo
3. Scotia
4. Astragal molding
5. Ogee molding
6. Skirting torus molding
7. Chamfer skirting
8. Tongue-and-groove molding
9. Tongue, grooved, and beaded molding
   Whichever style you choose, you'll find that adding molding adds more than style—it adds "feeling."

Project: Install Bead-board Wainscoting

Jane Quotient: ① ② ❸ ④ ⑤
Estimated Time: 7 to 10 hours

Wainscoting is that wonderful Victorian-style paneling you find between the chair rail and the floor.

We inherited this cozy architectural element from the Victorian houses of the nineteenth century. Our ancestors commonly used bead-board in less formal areas, and today we carry on the tradition by placing it in our family rooms, sunrooms, and other places we consider casual.

Wainscoting is like the cummerbund of a tuxedo. It adds that perfect degree of formality and class that ties together the entire piece.

In a dining room, where casual and formal often meet, wainscoting is the perfect balancing element for a perfectly harmonized room.

MATERIALS

Tools
- Screwdriver
- Utility knife
- Pry bar
- Tape measure
- Level
- Stud finder
- Stenciling brush
- Circular saw
- Straightedge
- Notched trowel for adhesive
- Nail set
- Hammer
- Jigsaw

Supplies
- Pencil
- Tongue-and-groove bead board
- Varnish or paint
- Protective eyewear
- Paneling adhesive
- #6 finish nails
- Chair rail
- Wood putty or spackle
- Rubber gloves

Jane Tip:

FOR STEP 1
In order not to damage the wall, place a small piece of lumber between the pry bar and wall.

"I just moved into my house. Finally all the improvements I make will be for me!"

Sheila R.
Huntington, West Virginia
Age 42

1 Take off all of the outlet covers. If you have baseboard, take it down as well, first cutting any caulk with a utility knife and then using the pry bar to separate the baseboard from the wall. If you plan to reattach the same baseboard, be extra careful not to damage it—although it can be touched up.

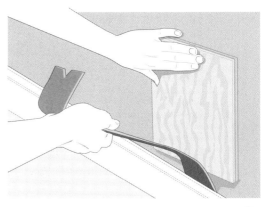

STEP 1 In order to not damage the wall, place a small piece of lumber between the pry bar and the wall.

2 Mark off the line for the top of the wainscoting. Measure from the floor to the height you have chosen for your bead board (usually 32 to 36 inches). Place a pencil mark at this height. Take your level and draw a straight line from the mark. Continue this line until you finish the wall, and then keep it going around the rest of the room.

3 With a stud finder, pinpoint the studs (usually every 16 inches). Draw a short vertical line down from the level line you marked off in step 2. You will use these stud markings later when you nail in the bead board.

4 Before installing the bead board, prime and paint it, both the front and the back. If you plan to paint the new or existing baseboard, prime and paint it now as well— and again, both front and back. Painting both sides of the components helps prevent them from warping later on. Wait for the bead board and the baseboard to dry completely before moving on to the next step.

5 Measure the distance from the top of the baseboard to the level line you drew earlier. Put the wainscoting facedown on your work area (a workbench or two sawhorses will do fine). Cut the bead board to the appropriate height using a circular saw. Use a straightedge to guide the saw. Don't forget your protective eyewear.

6 Attach the beadboard to the wall above the baseboard. Put paneling adhesive on the back of the bead board. (Start by placing the first piece along the stud line. Align the edge of the bead board with the stud. You will nail into it in a moment.) For thorough coverage, apply the adhesive in a continuing S shape in the middle, and then put more adhesive

Jane Tip:

FOR STEP 5
Purchase bead board that is thinner than your baseboard so it does not stick out beyond it. Part of the beauty of wainscoting is the illusion that it is art framed by the chair rail and the baseboard. If the bead board sticks out past them, this illusion is compromised.

Jane Tip:

FOR STEP 7
Use a jigsaw to cut out any allowances for electrical outlets. To create perfect squares, make 4 starter holes with your drill bit (using a drill bit large enough for the jigsaw to enter), one hole for each side of the square. Start in the first hole, cut to the corner, and stop. Go to the next drill hole and cut to that same corner from the opposite direction. This will give you a perfect square every time. Continue this process until you have cut into all four corners. Remember, each hole will be used to cut toward both corners on the side the hole is on.

STEP 6 **For thorough coverage, apply the adhesive in a continuing S shape in the middle.**

around the perimeter of the back. To keep the bead board from shifting while the adhesive dries, use your hammer to drive in 2 #6 finish nails where the stud is located and 2 more #6 nails along the top, securing the beadboard to the wall. The nails along the top will be covered later by the chair rail.

7 After installing the first piece, measure off the next few pieces you will need. Install them on the wall using the same method as above. The edge of the rest of your boards will not always fall along a stud, and that's okay. The interlocking nature of the tongue-and-groove bead board gives enough support while the adhesive dries.

8 Install the chair rail.

9 Using wood putty or spackle, fill in all nail holes on the base board and chair rail. (The nails driven into the bead board should be covered by the chair rail and the interlocking bead board.) Put some spackle between the bead board and the baseboard. We know your measurements were perfect, and you may not feel you need to spackle here, but it really does give the project a nice, professional look. After it dries, touch it up with paint.

Project: Install Baseboard Molding

Jane Quotient: ① ❷ ③ ④ ⑤
Estimated time: 1 to 4 hours

Baseboards give any room they're in a finishing touch. They warm the room, turning an otherwise drab and stark wall into one with personality. They help keep bugs out and charm in.

Installing baseboards is an easy project that takes just a few hours, but the pleasure you get from the result will last for years to come. If your current baseboards are looking drab, consider changing them out. The difference in your dining room will be immeasurable.

MATERIALS

Tools
- Pry bar
- Tape measure
- Paintbrush
- Miter box and back saw or power miter saw
- Hammer or finishing nail gun
- Nail countersetter
- Caulking gun

Supplies:
- Molding
- Pencil
- Primer
- Paint
- Safety glasses
- Finishing nails (brad)
- Spackle
- Sandpaper
- Painter's caulk

Jane Tip:

FOR STEP 1
Most pry bars have a notch or a hole in the middle of one end. Use this to remove any stray nails.

1 If by chance your room doesn't already have baseboards, skip this step. Otherwise, begin by removing the old baseboards with a pry bar. Carefully insert the edge in between the wall and the board, and then pry the boards away from the wall.

A few nails may pull through the board and remain in the wall.

STEP 1 **Pry off your old baseboard by using a pry bar and an excess piece of wood underneath it. The wood will help protect the wall from being scuffed or damaged by the pry bar.**

2 Purchase enough molding to redo the entire room. We suggest that you draw the entire room on a piece of paper. As you measure each wall, write the measurement on the paper next to that wall. Be precise, as these measurements will guide your cuts. Once you've measured the entire room, add the lengths of the walls to get the total. The easiest way to do this is to add all the feet in each measurement, and then add all the inches and divide this number by 12. Add this result to the total number of feet to get the grand total. Then include an extra 10 percent for mistakes.

3 We suggest you buy a molding at least 3½ to 5 inches tall, as most newly constructed homes have 3½-inch baseboards. Remember to buy a few pieces long enough to be used on your longest walls.

STEP 3 Measure all of the walls in the room. Add all the feet and then all the inches. If the inches are greater than 12, divide that number by 12. Add this number to the total number of feet you had previously. To be certain you buy enough molding, add another 10 percent to this total.

4 Once this is completely dry, it is time to cut. Use either a miter box or a compound miter saw to make your cuts. Wear your safety glasses while cutting.

Jane Tip:

FOR STEP 4
Prime and paint the baseboard pieces prior to making any cuts. Consider using a semigloss paint, as this sheen highlights woodwork well. Use one coat of primer and two coats of paint on both sides of each piece to minimize warping.

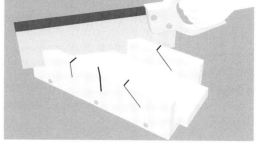

STEP 4 While a miter box calls for a bit more elbow grease than a miter saw, it is a great tool for cutting 45- and 90-degree angles.

Before completing any cuts, determine whether you are working on an inside corner or an outside corner, which dictates the direction you need to cut the 45-degree angle. An easy way to do this is to create two templates, an inside corner and an outside corner, to have next to you as you cut. If you have marked "inside left" on the piece next to you, you will know the angle you need to cut.

If you don't have a single piece long enough to cover a wall, you can splice two pieces by cutting exact opposite 45-degree angles on the attaching ends so they fit together like puzzle pieces.

5 Nail in the boards. The easiest way to attach the boards is with a finishing nail gun. If you prefer doing it by hand, use a hammer and a nail countersetter to set the finishing nails below the surface of the wood.

STEP 5 Be sure to sink the head of the nails below the surface of the wood.

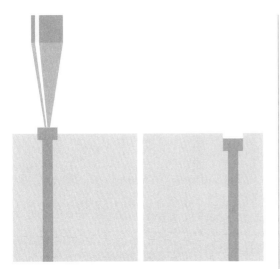

STEP 5 Counterset the brads (finishing nails without heads) with a countersetter and a hammer. If you don't have a countersetter, use a hammer and the sharp tip at the end of a Phillip's head screwdriver to drive in the nail. Just make sure the nail doesn't stick out past the surface of the molding.

"You'll never know what you can or can't do if you never try—and it's almost always easier than you imagined."

Lisa F.
Dalton, Ohio
Age 46

6 Fill in the gaps. Use spackle to fill in the holes left from the nails and any corners that didn't perfectly fit together. Let dry and sand lightly if necessary. Apply a second round of spackle to spots that didn't fill entirely with the first round. Once the spackle is completely dry, touch it up with paint.

7 Caulk the area between the wall and the baseboard to fill in any gaps. It's easiest to do this with a caulking gun and a wet paper towel. Remember, however, that a little caulk goes a long way. This step is a secret the professionals use. If, however, you painted the baseboard any other color than white, caulk is not your best choice. If you stained the wood, ask at your home improvement center what you should use.

Project: Refinish a Wood Floor

Jane Quotient: ① ② ③ ④ ❺
Estimate Time: 5 to 10 hours

Generally speaking, hardwood floors have a romantic nature. There's something about their look, their feel, even that quiet creaking noise they make when walked on, that greatly enhances the charm of any room.

Unfortunately, hardwood floors aren't easy to maintain. Unless well cared for, they slowly deteriorate. Their luster and shine fall prey to the ravages of time. This is especially true in a dining room, where chairs are constantly pushed back and forth, often marring the wood.

In many older homes, people found it easier to place carpeting or some other floor covering over the wood. Although they loved and enjoyed the idea of a hardwood floor, especially in the dining room, refinishing it seemed either too expensive or too overwhelming.

True, refinishing a hardwood floor may seem a daunting task. But this project is not as difficult as you might think, and once it's finished the floor will add life and ambiance to your dining room for years to come.

You can update the wood further by changing the color—darker or lighter—and, best of all, you won't have to redo this project for a very long time. While this is one of the more complicated projects in this book, it's also one that will bring you an unparalleled sense of pride and joy.

MATERIALS

Tools
- Hammer
- Countersetter
- Pry bar
- Drum or vibrating sander and coarse, medium, and fine sandpaper to use with it
- Edge sander and coarse, medium, and fine sandpaper to use with it
- Orbital or palm sander and fine sandpaper to use with it
- Shop-Vac
- Buffer with a fine-grit screen
- Foam applicator pad
- Lamb's-wool applicator
- Foam or natural bristle brush

"I tend to find that when wood floors look their best, the room looks its best."

Lizzie D.
Seattle,
Washington
Age 41

Supplies
- Broom
- Dustpan
- Drop cloths
- Sanding mask or respirator
- Goggles that seal against the face
- Earmuffs
- Hair protection
- Gloves
- Wood putty
- Stain
- Urethane

Note: Most of the equipment can be rented at a local hardware rental shop.

1 Remove everything from the room you plan to work in. Sweep the floor so you can properly inspect it before getting started. Look for loose boards and raised nailheads.

2 Nail down any loose boards and countersink the nails with a hammer and countersetter. If any carpet staples remain, make sure to remove them with pliers or the claw of your hammer. Removing nailheads and leftover staples is important for more than just creating a beautiful new floor; if left behind, they can cause sparks that can easily ignite a fire in the dust collector bag attached to the drum sander. They also can damage the sander itself.

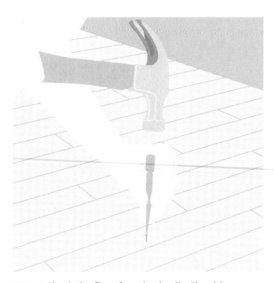

STEP 2 Check the floor for raised nails. Should you find one, counterset or sink it below the floor's surface with a hammer and a countersetter.

3 Further prep the floor by removing what's known as the shoe molding or base shoe molding, which is the strip of wood between the baseboards and the floor. The easiest way to do this is with a pry bar. Avoid damaging the baseboards by putting a shim

Jane Tip:

Maple floors are hard to refinish yourself. If your floors are made of maple, check into having them redone professionally.

Jane Tip:

If your floors are dirty from years of use but not too deeply stained, discolored, or damaged, you may be able to clean and recoat them with a new stain instead of completely refinishing them. If you're unsure, try cleaning them with household detergent and water. Also consider renting a floor buffing machine and cleaning your floor with a mild abrasive pad. Here the idea is to clean the floor, not strip the finish. If the floor looks pretty good after a thorough cleaning, just apply a new finish coat right over the old one.

(a small piece of wood such as a paint stir stick) between the pry bar and the baseboard as you remove the shoe molding. If there is no shoe molding, you can remove your baseboards if you choose to keep them from being damaged by the sander. Be sure to remove any nails left behind.

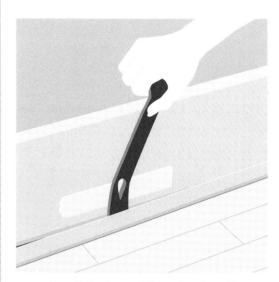

STEP 3 Pry off the shoe molding or baseboard by using a pry bar and a shim underneath it. The wood will help protect the wall from being scuffed or damaged by the pry bar.

4 This step generates a lot of dust. Using disposable drop cloths, create plastic barriers anywhere you don't want dust to go. This includes doorways, vents, and heat registers. If you skip this, you will be unpleasantly surprised at where you'll find sawdust once you are finished.

Protect your lungs, ears, and eyes, too. You can use a sanding mask, but a respirator will offer better protection. Most of us don't think of this as a loud project, but because you'll be working in an enclosed space with a high-volume sander, be sure to use ear protection as well. There is a wide variety of ear protectors out there nowadays—even ones that have a radio embedded in them so you don't have to work in silence.

Safety Check

A portable radio such as an iPod or other personal audio device is *not* proper ear protection. It should seem obvious, but just because you can't hear the machinery over your music doesn't mean you aren't damaging your ears.

You also need goggles. Regular protective eyewear is inadequate because it doesn't seal around your face, and you'll eventually end up with sawdust in your eyes. As we've said before, contacts and sawdust are *not* a fun combination.

Make sure to protect your hands, nails, and hair, as sawdust draws out natural oils and creates dry skin, cracked nails, and split ends. The easiest way to do this is to wear a hat and gloves while working. Each day after you've finished, make sure to moisturize your hair with a deep conditioner and cover your hands and nails with a heavy cream before going to bed. You don't want to end up with a beautiful floor but look like you spent the week working on it.

5 You will more than likely have to rent a drum sander (for heavy jobs, or if the floor is in bad shape) or a vibrating sander (for lighter jobs, or if the floor is basically good and just needs refinishing). When you rent the equipment, don't be shy; make sure the staff shows you exactly how to use it.

To get more at ease with the sander, start with a coarse- to medium-grit sandpaper in an inconspicuous area, like where the couch usually sits. If you make a few mistakes while learning how to use the sander, remember they will be covered anyway.

Start with a medium-grit sandpaper, as you really want to remove only $1/32$ inch from the floor. If a medium grit will level the floor and/or remove the current stains, you won't need anything coarser. If necessary, however, go ahead and use the coarse grit.

Jane Tip:

FOR STEP 4

To protect your hands, purchase a box of gloves that give off aloe when you wear them. You'll end up with softer hands than you had before! If you experience severely dry hands while working with sawdust, consider coating your hands and nails in a heavy cream and then placing a pair of socks over them before going to bed.

Jane Tip:

FOR STEP 6

Always keep the sander in motion. Leaving it run in one place can cause a circular pattern or even a gouge in the floor!

STEP 5 To properly sand your room, start against the wall and work in the same direction that the floor was laid. Turn on the machine and begin walking before you bring the drum down to the floor. This will help to create a more even surface, but you will have to have to sand half the room and then turn around and get the spots you missed the first time.

Start the sander in the middle of the far right wall. Make sure you are always moving with the grain of the wood. Begin with the sander off the floor; slowly begin pushing the sander forward while bringing the drum down to the floor. This tool seems like it can get away from you, which is why most of us are afraid to try this project. But don't worry, you can do this. Take a deep breath and start slowly. Pay attention to what you're doing and stop if you get tired.

As you get to the end of the first row, begin to raise the sanding drum, pulling it off the floor by the time you hit the wall. This is a rather simple technique, but you might want to see how it works by trying it before turning the machine on. If your floor is cupped or warped, you will have to first do your first pass at a 45-degree angle to smooth it out before working with the grain.

6 You've finished one pass; now do the room in reverse. Don't forget to start and end with the drum off the floor. If you're feeling tired, take a break before restarting.

7 Start another forward and reverse pass that is 3 to 4 inches to the left of the first pass so you are overlapping your strokes. Continue to do this for the first half to two-thirds of the floor. Then switch to the other side for the last half to one-third.

8 For hard-to-reach areas such as corners and edges, use an edge sander. Use an 80-grit paper and try to follow the grain the same way you did with the drum sander. You will have to compensate for the differences between the two types of sanders. The best way to do this is to move the sander in an arc-like fashion from side to side, just slightly brushing the already sanded surfaces.

STEP 8 Use the edge sander to sand the edges you couldn't reach with your drum or vibrating sander. Make sure you overlap your strokes with each other and into the sanded area.

9 Now that you've finished the coarse sanding, move on to a medium- or light-grade sandpaper for the next round. If you were lucky enough to start with a medium grit, you saved yourself one-third of the time you'll need to sand. Repeat steps 5 through 8 as needed. Don't forget to make a pass with your edge sander in the areas you couldn't reach with the drum sander.

Jane Tip:

FOR STEP 7

If you have asthma or are susceptible to respiratory problems, consider wearing a respirator when sanding to avoid any irritation to your lungs.

10 Once you've done your pass with the medium-grit sandpaper, check again for raised nails. If you find any, counterset them deep enough to fill in with the same color wood putty. Wood putty works just like a spackle or drywall compound. You apply it using a flexible putty knife, scrape away the excess, and let dry.

Also fill in any cracks or crevices with wood putty. Be careful, however, not to fill in the cracks necessary for the expected swelling and shrinking of your wood floor. Wood floors *do* swell and shrink with the humidity in the room. Typically this happens widthwise, not lengthwise, so you can fill in the cracks at the top and bottom of the boards but not side to side.

11 Go over the floor one last time with a fine-grit sandpaper with the drum sander or vibrating sander. On the edges this time use an orbital or palm sander with the fine-grit sandpaper instead of the heavy-duty edge sander.

Good news. After this pass, you're done sanding!

12 Clean up the dust. Before staining and sealing, be certain there is no dust in the room. If you don't, you risk ending up with an uneven finish. And when we say clean, we mean vacuum *everything*—ceilings, light fixtures, walls, and, last of all, the floors. Work your way from top to bottom. Sawdust is somewhat hard to remove, so be diligent here.

Note: Be careful not to let any moisture get on the wood as it is very susceptible to warping at this stage. If the wood gets wet, you risk having to make another pass with the drum sander. In your cleanup process, don't use any damp mops or paper towels, just a Shop-Vac.

13 Although you've removed the old finish, the floor is still not ready to be stained. What you'll need next is a floor buffer with a fine-grit screen. This is where you'll get your biggest workout. Using it feels like walking a big dog that wants to run and is constantly trying to pull you. *You can do this.* The best place to begin is away from the walls. This way you can move the buffer as you please without being afraid of causing dents or dings. Don't worry; it doesn't take long to get the hang of it.

STEP 13 Using the buffer, go over the entire floor. Start in the middle to allow yourself to get used to the feel of the machine and to avoid damaging the walls.

14 Choose a stain that will showcase your wood floor and make it look its best. You can select either a water-based or an oil-based stain, but the color should fit your taste. If you have any question about what the color will look like once it dries, try this suggestion from a fellow Jane: Test the color in an area that will be covered by furniture or on a sanded piece left over from when the floor was originally laid.

To apply the stain, diligently follow the manufacturer's instructions on the side of the can. We find it easiest to use a foam applicator pad and work in small areas at a time

Jane Tip:

FOR STEP 14
The most common stains for this project are oil-based, but they tend to give off harmful odors that require good ventilation. If you are interested in water-based stains, check at your local hardware store to explore the newest innovations and how they might be right for you.

STEP 14 Apply the stain to the sanded, buffed, and swept floor with an applicator.

(approximately 4 square feet). For most stains, simply wipe it on and then remove the excess with a clean dry towel or rag after a few minutes. Always apply the stain *with* the grain of the wood. Having a second set of hands during this part is often a huge help. One person can be applying stain and the other removing the excess at the same time, eliminating the risk of areas drying and becoming splotchy. Use a pair of foam knee pads during this process to keep down the ache factor.

Let the stain dry as indicated by the manufacturer.

15 Stay off the floor for 12 to 24 hours or as recommended by the stain manufacturer. Footprints can actually be visible if you walk on it while it is drying, so keep the area clear—unless, of course, you *liked* steps 5 through 8!

16 Seal your new floor with a clear finish. Again, you'll have to choose between a water-based and an oil-based finish. The oil will require fewer coats (two or three), but it will dry more slowly (which may be a problem in humid climates) and require extensive ventilation. The water-based urethanes require three to four coats to cover properly, but they are less toxic and

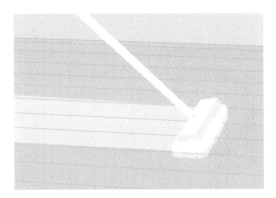

STEP 16 Apply the finish to the floor with either a foam applicator or a mop. Be careful not to overlap too much in order to create the most uniform finish possible.

tend to dry more quickly. Be aware, however, if you used an oil-based stain, then you must use an oil-based sealer. To learn what will work best for your floor and in your climate, ask at your local home improvement center.

It's easiest to apply the finish with a lamb's wool applicator with a long handle for larger sections and with a foam applicator or natural bristle brush along the corners and edges. Try to avoid overlapping, which can create thicker spots and result in unevenness in the

Jane Tip:

FOR STEP 16
New applicators commonly have particles that can easily get trapped in your new finish if the applicators are not properly rinsed out before using. Rinse them with water or paint thinner, depending on the type of finish you are using, to eliminate this possibility.

final result. As with any painting project, watch for dripping.

17 You may notice that your beautiful floor is slightly raised in some areas. Don't worry; you didn't do anything wrong. This is a common reaction of wood to the finish you've just applied. Go over the floor (once it is fully dried) with the buffer again. This will help smooth out any rough spots and make the entire floor even. Just think of how many more calories you are going to burn!

18 Once you've done a pass with the buffer, wipe up any particles that were created with a damp rag to keep them out of your final coat. Apply another coat of urethane varnish to the floor and let it dry completely. Repeat this step if uneven spots remain on your floor.

We know this project was a lot of work. But the next time you have a family dinner and someone says, "Wow, your floors are gorgeous!" think of the sense of pride you'll feel knowing you made that beauty yourself.

Project: Paint Over Old Wallpaper

Jane Quotient: ❶ ② ③ ④ ⑤
Estimate Time: 3 to 5 hours

Wallpaper can be absolutely beautiful. It makes the perfect accent to some of the paneling effects we've reviewed. But the downside to wallpaper is that it ages. You will eventually find that the gleam has gone out of your dining room walls and know that the time has come to remove it.

All that wallpaper may seem like just a bit more than you want to remove. The good news is that you don't have to. You can paint over your old wallpaper. In some cases, even the professionals will choose this option. One ideal scenario for choosing painting over removal is wallpaper that was applied directly to plaster walls over unprimed drywall.

Painting over wallpaper is a great way to save hours of labor and effort while bringing your dining room walls back to life.

MATERIALS

Tools
- Electrical or penlight tester
- Flat head screwdriver
- Putty knife
- 2 paint stirring sticks (optional)
- Paint rollers
- Paint brushes
- Utility knife or razor blade

Supplies:
- Clean sponge
- Plastic bucket
- 2-inch blue painter's tape (enough to wrap around the room at least once)
- Latex or vinyl gloves
- Safety glasses
- Small container of spackle
- 220-grit sandpaper
- Rags
- Drop cloths
- Shellac-based stain-blocking prmier)
- Paint
- Small container of wallpaper adhesive

Jane Tip:
If your wallpaper seams aren't well attached, use a bit of wallpaper paste to put them back in place.

Note: Check to see if the surface is smooth and in good condition. For best results, make sure the wallpaper is securely attached to the wall and that all the seams are close together and firmly attached.

Note: Paint a test patch in an inconspicuous area. We suggest you do this for two reasons:
- To see if the wallpaper will still hold to the wall after the paint is applied.
- To see if you are comfortable with the texture that will show through the paint.

If the wallpaper stays smooth and you like the texture left behind, you're ready to get started. If the wallpaper starts to break away once painted, it may be too old and brittle to hold up the painting. In this case, you'll probably have to remove it.

1 Thoroughly wipe down the walls with a damp sponge. You want to make sure the wallpaper is free of dust and grime. For safety reasons, make sure the wallpaper is dry before going on to step 2.

2 Using your flat head screwdriver, remove all of the switch and outlet covers from the walls that you plan to paint. Once you've done this, cover or mask the outlets and the switches with blue painter's tape.

3 Go over the walls with your hands to feel for any surface imperfections. This will help you to locate dents and dings in the wall that are not visible now—but will be once the wall is painted. Repair dents and scratches with a surfacing compound such as spackle. At this point, put on your gloves and safety glasses. Let the spackle dry and lightly sand (using fine/220-grit sandpaper) any areas that aren't smooth. Once the wall is smooth, remove any residual dust with a damp rag before continuing.

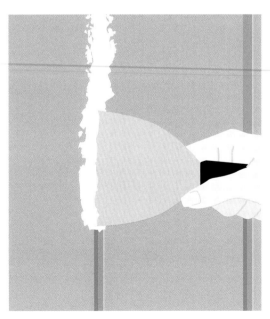

STEP 3 Fill in any discrepancies in the wall using a putty knife and spackle. You may need to apply two coats to get a smooth finish.

Jane Tip:

FOR STEP 4
Disposable paper or cloth plastic-backed drop cloths are usually inexpensive and easy to manipulate, and save you lots of cleanup time. They are available at any home improvement center.

Jane Tip:

FOR STEP 5
From this point on, we suggest wearing latex or vinyl gloves and safety glasses. Getting paint or dust from spackle in your eyes is no picnic!

Jane Tip:

FOR STEP 5
We recommend you have the primer tinted similarly to the background color of the wall paper. This will help to hide both the pattern and possible slight mismatches of the seams. The tinting is free, and it will offer better coverage for your final finish with fewer coats. In the end, it will save you time and money.

4 Finish preparing the walls by taping any areas that lie next to the area to be painted (ceiling, baseboards, window trim, etc.). We recommend you cover those areas with blue painter's tape so as not to pull off the old paint finish below it. Place plastic or cloth drop cloths on the surrounding floors. To keep paint from getting on the floor, attach the drop cloths to the tape on the baseboards and to the floor itself.

5 Stir the primer and, if you're happy with your test patch, apply it to the walls with rollers and brushes. This step will help the paint stick to the wallpaper, so don't skip it.

6 Once the primer is completely dry, start painting. We suggest waiting 24 hours, as the wallpaper will absorb the primer and probably take longer to dry than if you were painting directly onto a wall. When you check the walls the next morning, if any minor blisters or bubbles formed overnight, repair

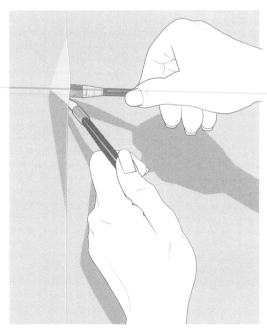

STEP 6 Gently lift up any curling seams or slit bubbles and apply wallpaper adhesive. Then press the wallpaper back down on the wall.

them by slitting them with a utility knife and then glue them to the wall with wallpaper adhesive. Allow the repair to dry and wipe off any excess with a damp sponge.

Jane Tip:

FOR STEP 7

When buying the paint, consider that you may need an extra coat, depending on the design in the wallpaper and the depth of the final color of paint.

7 Once all the areas you treated are dry and look good, you're ready to paint. Make sure to stir the paint before applying it to the wall.

8 Allow 24 hours to dry. Reattach all of the outlet and switch covers. Flip the circuit breakers on.

Project: Remove Old Wallpaper

Jane Quotient: ❶ ② ③ ④ ⑤
Estimated Time: 3 to 5 hours

While painting over wallpaper is a great idea, sometimes you will have no option other than to remove the wallpaper completely.

Although removing wallpaper many not seem like the ideal way to spend a weekend, the dramatic effect on your dining room will be instantaneous.

You'll finally be able to do the things you want to do to showcase your walls. This is the room where you celebrate special events, so removing this reminder of yesteryear will help you celebrate in style.

MATERIALS

Tools
- ▨ Electrical or penlight tester
- ▨ Screwdriver
- ▨ Wallpaper scoring tool
- ▨ Plastic scraper
- ▨ Wallpaper steamer (optional but desirable)

Supplies
- ▨ Clock radio or portable stereo
- ▨ 2-inch blue painter's tape (enough to cover baseboards and windows)
- ▨ Plastic or plastic-backed drop cloths
- ▨ 12-inch brown masking paper tape
- ▨ Protective eyewear
- ▨ Spray bottle or garden sprayer (either will work, but you won't have to refill the garden sprayer as often)
- ▨ Wallpaper remover solution (white vinegar solution or a chemical remover)
- ▨ Latex or vinyl gloves
- ▨ Large clean sponge
- ▨ Plastic bucket

NOTE: Have patience. This may take some time and require a bit of detail, but it's definitely a doable project.

Jane Tip:

Removing wallpaper before painting the walls ensures the best possible results and a smooth finish. If the wallpaper is in good condition, you can repaper or paint right over it (see "Paint Over Old Wallpaper," page 217).

Note: Here are situations in which you *should* remove your old wallpaper prior to painting or rewallpapering:

■ Your walls have more than a single layer of wallpaper on the surface.

■ Your wallpaper is pulling up at the edges.

■ Your wallpaper has bumps left behind from prior wallpaper paste application.

■ Your wallpaper is vinyl or foil, or has plastic film.

■ You are planning to hang *vinyl* wallpaper, which requires a clean, bare surface. If you leave the old wallpaper, the glue under it may get wet and start to mildew.

■ The wallpaper is textured—grasscloth, burlap, or cork.

■ You can hear crinkling sounds when running your hand over the surface of the wall. If you do, the wallpaper has buckled and must be removed.

1 Turn off the circuit breaker(s) for the room you plan to work in. If they are already marked, this should be easy. Check the outlets and switches with an electrical tester to make sure the power is off.

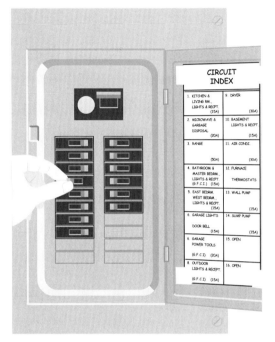

STEP 1 Turn off the circuit breaker for the switches and plugs in the room you are about to start working in.

STEP 2 Insert the tip of the penlight tester into the vertical slots to test the power. If it is still on, the tester will chirp, illuminate, or both.

2 Using a flat head screwdriver, remove all of the switch and outlet covers from the walls from which you'll be removing

Jane Tip:

FOR STEP 1
We recommend using a penlight tester to test for electricity. It's much easier to use than a standard voltage tester and makes us feel more comfortable using it. If you don't have anything to test with, plug a clock radio or a boom box into the outlet in question. Turn the volume up high enough so you can hear when the breaker shuts it off. It will make doing this by yourself much faster and easier.

Jane Tip:

FOR STEP 3
One time-saving item that will help you in this step is a combination 12-inch brown masking paper and blue painter's tape already attached. It may cost a bit more, but in the end the time it saves is worth it.

wallpaper. Cover the outlets and the switches with blue painter's tape. This is important, as it will keep moisture away from the electrical system.

3 This process can be messy. Cover the floor with plastic or plastic-backed drop cloths to keep it dry. Make sure you tape the edges down to keep the drop cloths from moving and exposing the floor while you work. Apply 12-inch brown paper masking and blue painter's tape to adhere them to the baseboards. Let the paper overlap onto the drop cloths for better protection.

4 If you don't have access to a wallpaper steamer, you'll use the technique outlined here, which utilizes a chemical wallpaper remover. Run the wallpaper scoring tool in circles all over the surface. This will allow the solution to properly penetrate the paper when you apply it. You can find a tool like this at almost any hardware store. Pay attention while doing this; apply just enough pressure to perforate the wallpaper without damaging the underlying wall.

STEP 4 Using the scoring tool, apply enough pressure to perforate the wallpaper but not enough to damage the wall. We recommend a circular motion.

5 Put on protective eyewear. Fill a garden sprayer or a spray bottle with wallpaper remover solution and apply it to the entire wall. If you are working on a very large area, use the garden sprayer. Mix the remover with water as warm as you can stand to speed the process.

6 Let the solution sit on the wall for 10 to 20 minutes or longer if indicated by the manufacturer's instructions. Now, wearing your gloves, peel off as much wallpaper as you can with your hands. It should be like peeling a banana. Once you've finished what you can do with your hands, spray the wall a second

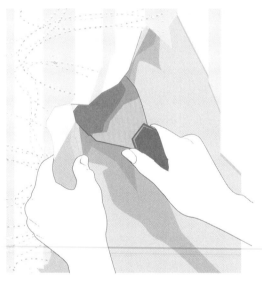

STEP 6 **Once you've pulled off all of the pieces of paper that came loose easily, spray a second coat of remover and let it sit on the wall. Use a plastic scraper to loosen the stubborn spots that are left.**

Jane Tip:

FOR STEP 5

If you are sensitive to chemicals or if you are pregnant, mix 1 cup white vinegar to 1 gallon water instead of using a commercial wallpaper remover. This solution works almost as well and will keep you safe.

Jane Tip:

STEP 6

Avoid using the corner of the plastic scraper to remove the wallpaper. The length of the plastic scraper may take a bit longer, but using the corner can easily make dents in the wall that you will have to fix later.

time over the stubborn spots. Let the areas soak for 10 to 20 minutes before trying to remove the paper. Use a plastic scraper to lightly scrape the surface.

7 Go over the wall several times with a sponge and fresh water to remove the glue residue left behind. Skipping this step will change the bonding ability of the paint and cause it to peel, so don't skip it! We don't expect you'll want to spend any extra time redoing these walls! If the wallboard underneath the wallpaper wasn't primed before it was papered, then as you pull off the wallpaper you might end up with a chalky substance. This means the paper surface of your drywall is coming up too, so STOP IMMEDIATELY! Then,

■ Glue down any loose pieces and seams that have separated.

■ Fill in any uneven areas with a non-shrinking surfacing compound.

■ Sand the patches/repairs, and then apply an oil-based sealer with an enamel undercoat.

■ Paint on top of the wallpaper, or cover it with a wallpaper liner. Do not remove it.

You may also want to call a professional to get further advice specific to your home.

Now that you've got a clean, fresh canvas on your dining room wall, paint a picture that reflects you and everyone you love.

Jane Profile

Inspiration and creation come from loving life.

Leslie "Jane" Yoder

Age: 35

From: Goshen, Indiana

Favorite tool: For me, that's a hard one. I would have to say a Dremel probably. I love my saws and sanders, but I have to land at the Dremel and all the attachments that get the details done.

Projects accomplished: I caulked nearly every seam in my house, installed locks in place of skeleton key locks, painted, put up chair rail, installed insulation, tore down water-damaged/rotted walls, and rebuilt a workbench as well as a craft bench. I built a 4-foot lighthouse out of planks of wood (I learned how to use that miter saw!), refinished a bed for my son, and built tables for my dining room.

Inspiration for starting home improvement: I had just separated from my husband and came across a house I could afford that had room for my son and property to play on. What I didn't know was what terrible shape the place was in. It was December, and I could look directly outside *around* the windows. It became a matter of self-preservation, and that of a mother doing anything she could to take care of her child.

Fears about home improvement: Fears? Plenty! I had never done anything like this before. I was afraid I was going to mess it up, regardless of what the "it" was.

How has home improvement affected your life? I have learned that nothing is beyond me. I can easily and happily grab hold of any project with a feeling of knowing I can and will get it done. I don't need someone else to do it for me. I feel a lot more confident that there's nothing I can't do.

Besides how I feel about myself personally, it has made me more confident and competent in my position at work. I am able to do more tasks that before I would have backed off of and let someone else do. Now I just get up and do it myself!

It has even had an effect on my separation with my husband. I'd always wanted to do things around the house, but my husband would say, "I can do it faster, so move out of the way." I feared my husband was going to look at my finished product and say, "Uh-huh, I knew it." In the end, he looked at me and said, "Good job!" It may not seem like much, but that was huge because he does finish work for a living.

How has doing home improvement affected others in your life? I have friends who are now tackling projects that before they didn't even look at.

My friends ask me for advice or to help them with their home improvement projects. I've helped friends redo things. In fact, we get everybody in on it.

Advice for others just getting started in home improvement: Just do it. It really does come down to that. Do it any way you can, but always keep yourself open to learn a better technique. Look at what needs to be done, and don't try to learn too much about it or you might convince yourself you can't do it. You need to make mistakes along the way. Some of my mistakes ended up being some of the best lessons.

Life was not meant to be just an existence. Live! Inspiration and creation come from loving life. Be bold enough to claim yours, and don't be put aside by anyone or anything that tries to in any way make you back down from the you that you want to be.

Creating a Comfortable
and Inviting Dining Room

Think about dinner parties you've been to, whether with twenty of your best friends or just you and your significant other. What was it about the event that made it so special?

Part of it may have been the company. Part of it may have been the food. But another part that may have played a role was how you felt in the room.

A dining room that is comfortable and inviting almost seems as though it opens its arms to those who enter. It's comfortable to sit in, eat in, and talk in, and it promotes an

environment for conversation, enjoyment, and laughter.

How comfortable do you feel in your dining room? We've all seen movies where a couple sit at opposite ends of a long table in a formal dining hall. Sure, the room is astoundingly beautiful, but it's often cold and dark.

Making your dining room comfortable and inviting is more than just filling it with nice things. It's a way to convey a sense of warmth and heart that all your guests will appreciate and, most important, remember.

Project: Install a New Light Fixture

Jane Quotient: ① **❷** ③ ④ ⑤
Estimated Time: Less than 1 hour

In many a story, you've read how the "soft, warm glow" of the light, whether it was the light of a home, an inn, or a restaurant, was a reassuring sign to the weary traveler that the journey had come to an end.

Lighting is the first way you welcome your. Lighting is probably the number one determining factor of the overall look and feel of any room. In a dining room, lighting is especially crucial. If it is too harsh, it's obtrusive and clinical. If it is too soft or too dark, it can set an improper mood.

Lighting should be welcoming. It should enhance your furnishings, your wall accents, your paint color, your china and silverware, and, ultimately, your food. If your lighting isn't accomplishing these things, it's time to change it out.

MATERIALS

Tools
- Electrical or penlight tester
- Stepladder
- Screwdrivers (probably Phillip head)
- Lineman's pliers

Supplies
- Safety glasses
- Dust mask
- New light fixture
- Wire connectors or wire nuts
- Electrical tape

👓 Safety Check!

Make sure you've turned off the proper breaker—the one attached to the light you plan to change out. Use your electrical or penlight tester to confirm that power is no longer running to the line. If you cannot shut off the power or guarantee that you have, *do not attempt to do this project!* This project is truly very easy, but when it comes to electricity, we're always going to err on the safe side.

> "Lighting is one of those things you never realize the importance of until you get it right."
>
> Phyllis K.
> Madison,
> Wisconsin
> Age 55

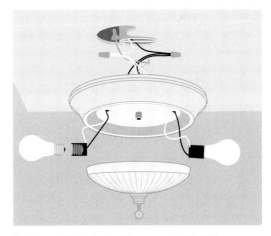

Anatomy of a typical ceiling-mounted light fixture.

Note: Most electrical connections have a black, a white, and a green or exposed copper wire. Each of these has a different purpose:
- black wire = hot wire
- white wire = neutral wire
- exposed green or copper wire = ground wire

The black wire is the one you are most

concerned with. In homes with older wiring, you might find the wires are different colors, all black, or even all white. The wire that causes your electrical tester to light up, beep, chirp, or squawk is the "hot wire." Once you've verified which circuit breaker controls the power for this light, label it on the panel so you'll never have to work it out again.

1 Turn off the power at the breaker. Once you've done this, check to make sure it is truly off by flipping on and off the wall switch to the light you want to change. If the bulb was a working bulb to begin with and nothing happens, you've got the right one. If not, put in a fresh bulb and try it again.

2 Since you'll be working overhead, put on safety glasses and a dust mask. Test the wiring with an electrical tester before removing the old light fixture. Loosen the existing light fixture. This will expose the wire nuts. Wire nuts are the plastic colored caps holding the wires together. Remove them by turning them counterclockwise, as they are essentially screwed onto the wires. Once the cap is off, simply untwist the wires to connect them. Assuming you have the properly colored wires, first separate the hot wire, then the neutral wire, and last the ground wire.

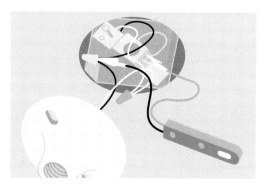

STEP 2 Test the wiring with an electrical tester before removing the old light fixture. If the light on the tester illuminates once you have the leads in place, then power is *still* coming through those wires.

Jane Tip:

FOR STEP 4
The bracket that should be included with your new light is made to hold the weight of the fixture itself. That's why we recommend changing out the old one.

3 Be careful here, especially if the light fixture is heavy. Once you remove the wires, *you* are all that remains between the light fixture and the ground. Use the ladder as leverage to help you maneuver the old light fixture down.

4 Next you'll work with the mounting bracket or strap. There may be one attached to the electrical box from your old light that you can reuse. Quite often the old one will work well—but to be safe, we suggest that you unscrew it and put in the one that came with the new light; the bracket will hold the light onto the electrical box and the ceiling. It is usually rectangular and can be secured with the screws that came with the new light or even the old ones you just removed.

STEP 4 Install the new mounting bracket to the electrical box with a screwdriver and the screws that came with your new light.

5 Get that gorgeous new fixture out of the box and look at the instructions that came with it. Most light fixtures have a particular order in which the pieces are installed, so

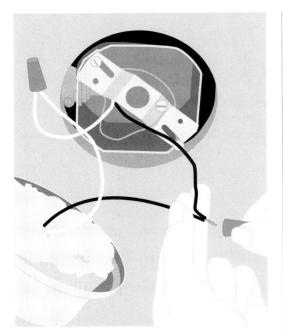

STEP 5 Attach the white wires to each other and the black wires to each other by twisting the ends together and then twisting the wire nut clockwise over the exposed areas until it is on tight.

follow the diagram included with your light to make sure you install your new fixture correctly. To begin, identify the two white or neutral wires (one in the ceiling and one in the new fixture). Again, use your ladder as leverage to help you hold the new light fixture in place. Make sure enough copper is exposed on the neutral wires to make a good connection, but no more than $1/2$ inch should be exposed. Twist the ends of the wires together in a clockwise direction. Place a wire nut on the end of the attached wires and screw it on clockwise. Wrap some electrical tape around the base of the nut to cover any exposed copper wire.

Follow the same procedure with the black (hot) wires.

Finally, connect the ground wire from the ceiling to the one in the fixture. Make sure you secure them with a wire nut. The ground wire nut often is bigger than the other two because the ground is often a thicker wire.

Jane Tip:

FOR STEP 5
Sometimes the ground wire attaches directly to the mounting bracket. It can be helpful to attach the ground wire first. This will often help hold the light fixture so you can complete the installation of the remaining wires with two hands.

6 Now that all the wires are connected, you're ready to hang the new light! Grab the long screws that will hold your new fixture into the ceiling. Every light is made a little differently, so follow the manufacturer's instructions.

👓 **Safety Check!**
Pardon us for a "duh" moment here, but bulbs get very hot! When installing a light fixture, allow a distance of 3 to 6 inches from the bulb to any object. Remember, if a 100-watt bulb is hot enough to cook a brownie in an EZ-Bake Oven, it's certainly hot enough to start a fire!

Note: If you're installing a chandelier, don't worry; it's essentially the same process. Make sure, though, that the mounting box can handle the extra weight, as some chandeliers are ridiculously heavy. If the new fixture is approximately the same weight as the one you just removed, you won't have to worry.

7 You may need a helper at this point if the fixture is heavy. Hold the fixture in position over the screws. Turn it so that the screw heads fit into the keyholes and twist the fixture in place.

Screw the bulbs into the fixture and place the globe on with the corresponding screws.

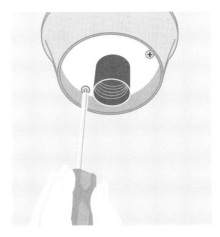

STEP 7 Attach the new light fixture to the electrical box by placing screws in the marked holes and tightening them to the mounting bracket below.

Project: Smooth Old Paneled Walls

Jane Quotient: ① ❷ ③ ④ ⑤
Estimate Time: 2 to 5 hours

If you've ever been in a room that feels like it needs work, you know it's an uncomfortable place to be. As a host, you worry your guests are looking at the flaws and you can't relax. Your guests notice you're acting different and *they* can't relax. It becomes a tennis volley of discontent.

We've already addressed flaws such as aging wallpaper. Another major wall issue common to many dining rooms is what to do with old paneling.

We love wainscoting, as we feel it has a way of adding ambiance to a room unlike any other wall treatment. But unfortunately, over time, wainscoting—or any wall paneling, for that matter—can become scuffed, marred, and, ultimately, unattractive.

One of the more difficult things with older paneling or wainscoting is that if you remove it from the wall, you may damage the drywall or plaster beneath it, and then you'll have a much bigger project on your hands. The good news is that you can take back your walls by filling in the grooves.

Filling in paneling or old wainscoting with spackle is a relatively easy way to make each panel look flush, creating the appearance of flat walls. After a bit of sanding and a little paint, you can love your walls once more, and you can begin to put the focus back on your guests.

MATERIALS

Tools
- Screwdriver
- Putty knife
- Palm sander (optional)
- Paintbrush
- Trowel (optional, but useful)

Supplies
- Rags or sponges
- Dishwasher detergent or degreaser
- Rubber gloves
- Blue painter's tape
- Drop cloths
- Spackle
- Fine- and very fine-grit sandpaper
- Protective eyewear
- Sanding mask
- Primer
- Scrubbing sponge
- Paint

"With a little help from my friends I changed out my whole dining room in just one day."

Lana V.
Las Vegas, Nevada
Age 41

1 Clean the surface of the walls with a sponge or a rag. Use warm water and a small amount of dishwasher detergent or a heavy-duty degreaser like TSP (trisodium phosphate). Make sure you're wearing rubber gloves, as both TSP and dishwasher detergent can be caustic to your skin. Getting rid of the buildup of years of dust and grime, not to mention the spiderwebs, will add years to the longevity of your new paint job.

Wipe down the area with a clean, damp rag to remove any residue. Make sure you thoroughly rinse the walls as any leftover TSP or detergent can prevent the paint from adhering. Don't be afraid to scrub. Believe it or not, this process will help the spackle and the paint stick to the paneling grooves.

2 Now that the walls are clean, find out what your paneling or wainscoting is made of. In the past few decades, some decorators decided to put up a woodlike paneling that simulates the look of more expensive wood; this is adhered to a piece of plywood. A good way to see what is on your walls is to sand off a small patch in an inconspicuous place. If you expose plywood or pressboard, be extra careful not to sand too deep. If you find that you have faux wood (a Formica-like laminate), plan to use at least two coats of primer before painting. If you're lucky enough to have real wood, then one coat of primer should do.

3 Remove all of the electrical outlet faceplates in the area you will be working on, and mask any areas such as wall sconces or light switches you want to protect with blue painter's tape.

4 Mask any areas you don't want painted, and cover the floor with drop cloths.

5 Repair any damage to the wall with spackle or drywall compound and a putty knife. Any nail holes, cracks, dents, and other little problems should be thoroughly filled in. If you have a bright light, such as a

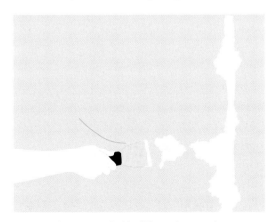

STEP 5 Using a putty knife, fill any damaged areas with spackle.

Jane Tip:

FOR STEP 6
Always wear protective eyewear and a sanding mask when sanding.

Jane Tip:

FOR STEP 7
Some paint companies make a primer specifically for paneling. It's worth paying a few more dollars for it because in the end you will save money on paint costs, as you'll need less of the final color to cover a primed wall. An all-purpose primer can be used on both real wood and woodlike paneling; for Formica-like materials, use a primer specifically made for high-gloss surfaces.

freestanding floor lamp (remove the shade) or flood lamp, bring it into the room and shine it onto the walls. You'll be able to see those hidden wall flaws better.

6 Lightly sand the areas to be painted and spackled with a fine-grit sandpaper. To make this job a quick one, use an electric palm sander. Remember to put on protective eyewear and a sanding mask. For areas that are difficult to get to with the palm sander, use a sanding sponge or even a deck of cards wrapped in sandpaper to get into the grooves of your paneling. Remember, if your paneling is made of a Formica-like material, make sure to sand down the smooth finish; otherwise, the primer will bead up when you apply it.

7 Now you're ready to apply your first coat of primer. You're not priming to paint but rather priming to spackle. The primer you use here will make your spackle adhere much more efficiently.

8 Once your primer is dry, begin the detail work filling in the paneling grooves with spackle. There are several ways to accomplish this; you may end up varying your technique as you proceed through the project.

First, there are two types of spackle: vinyl spackle, which has a muddy, thick consistency, and fast-drying spackle, which is a bit like whipped cream cheese, but lighter.

Although vinyl spackle takes longer to dry and is a bit messier, it can be easier to fill gaps with. You may consider using both types if you find each has benefits and drawbacks.

The majority of the spackle will be applied with a flexible putty knife or a trowel. Fill in the grooves of the paneling from floor to ceiling or as needed, scraping away any excess. Spackle tends to shrink as it dries, so you may need to apply a second coat. Depending on the type of spackle you use, give it anywhere from 4 to 12 hours to dry thoroughly.

9 Gently sand the area and apply a second coat of spackle as needed. Be sure to use a light touch and very fine-grit sandpaper or even the scrubbing side of a sponge, as spackle tends to break down very fast. The second coat of spackle can be applied more generously in problem areas. Again, let dry completely before proceeding.

STEP 9 **Sand down the areas you are about to paint with a palm sander or a sanding block.**

Jane Tip:

FOR STEP 9

Placing a fan in the room will help the spackle dry faster and allow you to finish quicker. But don't be fooled. Just because the spackle is dry on top doesn't mean it's dry throughout. Be patient, and you'll love the results!

Jane Tip:

FOR STEP 11

When you purchase the primer, ask to have it tinted with 50 percent of the color going on the wall. This will allow for better coverage when you apply the wall color and decrease the amount of paint needed.

Jane Tip:

FOR STEP 12

If you're still not happy with the way your wall turned out, instead of adding a flat color, try one of the faux painting techniques we mention in other projects.

10 Once the spackle is completely dry, sand off the excess and smooth the wall. Use a fine-grain sandpaper (220-grit or finer) or a scrub sponge. Wipe away any debris with a clean, damp (not dripping) rag or tack cloth and let dry. Be sure you're happy with the texture and condition of the walls at this stage, as it will be hard to correct any imperfections once you apply the primer. If you find a few problem areas that persist, apply spackle and sand as needed until you're satisfied with the results.

11 Time to prime . . . again! We know you're asking, "Didn't we already prime the walls?" Yes, but that was to help the spackle adhere; now you're prepping the spackle to be painted.

Once the walls are clean and dry, you can apply the second coat of primer.

12 Paint your favorite color on the walls. For best results, let the first coat dry and add a second to ensure a rich, full color.

Project: Put Up a Tin Ceiling

Jane Quotient: ① ② ❸ ④ ⑤
Estimated Time: **18 to 20 hours, depending on the size of your ceiling**

You may never look at or think about your dining room ceiling. It tends to blend in with the rest of the room, adding little, if anything, for effect.

But what if you were to draw attention to your ceiling? Making it a showpiece can bring drama to an otherwise dull surface and inspire conversation among your guests.

One way to do this is by using tin tiles. Traditionally, these are seen in many older homes. Tin tiles come in so many shapes, colors, and sizes that both contemporary and traditional-style homes can use them to create stunning conversation-piece details in a room. You can also enhance a chandelier or any light fixture with special medallion tin tiles that frame the light.

Tin tiles come as small as 6 inches and as large as 24 inches. The larger the room or the higher the ceilings, the larger the tile you should choose. But then again, always choose what you love!

MATERIALS

Tools
- Electrical or penlight tester
- Ladder
- Chalk line
- Stud finder
- Hammer
- Long level (carpenter's level, 4 feet long)
- Drill
- Tape measure

Supplies
- Protective eyewear
- Tin ceiling tiles—12 inches, any design
- 1- x 4-inch furring strips (long pieces of wood)
- Pen and pencil
- 2 1/2-inch screws
- Flathead nails
- Bead-head decorative nails (that match the tile)
- Tin snip
- Protective gloves
- Small wood block

"Having a tin ceiling completely classes up the joint! We love it!"

Marla B.
Kansas City,
Missouri
Age 33

Note: As for many home improvement projects, there are several opinions about how to install tin tiles. Here is one of the common ways to accomplish this task, given that (a) you have a drywalled or plaster ceiling, and (b) it is in good condition. This is a good project in which to involve a friend—or two—not to mention some Advil, as your neck may hurt from looking at the ceiling all day!

1 Turn off the power from your circuit breaker, and then remove all the ceiling fixtures. You should also clear the room of furniture to make it easy to get around—and to keep clean! Check with an electrical tester to make sure the power is off.

2 Since you'll be working overhead, be sure to wear protective eyewear. Because no wall or ceiling is perfectly straight, begin applying tiles from the center of the room out to the edges. First make note of the ceiling's width and length. Then, to determine the center point of your ceiling, hold a chalk line on one corner and stretch it across to the other corner, then snap it to create your line. Do this from each corner to create two diagonal lines in a large *X* on the ceiling. This will give you the center point. If the center point is above where your dining room table will be, this is also a great place to hang a beautiful light fixture or add an accent tin tile around a chandelier.

with a pen, or drive a small nail in to it, leaving most of the nail exposed (you will remove the nails later). Use a long level to check if your ceiling is indeed level. Your house naturally settles over time, which usually causes a slightly slanted ceiling.

4 Mark where the center ceiling joist is. Using the chalk line again, make a line horizontally across the ceiling so that it intersects your *X* at the center point.

5 Attach the first furring strip along the center perpendicular chalk line. Attach it to your ceiling with 2 ½-inch screws or nails.

STEP 2 Using a chalk line, measure diagonally from corner to corner to make an *X* on your ceiling and determine the center point.

3 Behind the drywall or plaster of your ceiling is a series of wood beams known as ceiling joists. You are going to use these to anchor in your furring strips, which are long, thin pieces of wood. These strips are attached directly to your ceiling, perpendicular to the joists. The tiles will be attached to these strips; never attach tiles directly to plaster or drywall.

Using a stud finder, find each ceiling joists. Mark the location and direction of each beam

STEP 5 Installing the first furring strip along the center line, perpendicular to your ceiling joists.

6 Measure 12 inches from the center of the furring strip toward the outer edge of the room and mark it. This is the center of the next furring strip. Attach the strips to the ceiling by driving in flat-head nails or screws at every joist or 16 inches.

Continue to do this on both sides of the center strip until you reach the outer edge. Install each furring strip over top. Be sure not to cover any fixtures you encounter; just make a cutout in the wood and place it around the fixture.

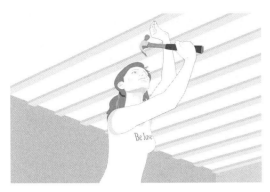

STEP 6 Every 12 inches, install a furring strip. The tin tiles will be attached to the furring strip.

7 Start installing tiles at the center and work your way out to the edge so they end up in a symmetrical pattern. Attach them to the furring strips with the decorative bead-head nails so they won't wreck the look of the tile. If you have a center light fixture, first install all the tiles surrounding the center tile, and then continue to work out to each edge of the wall. At the wall edge, you will most likely need to cut the tile down to fit.

If you have a light fixture, you will need to cut the tin tile to fit around it. The easiest method is to press the tile up against the light fixture box to create an outline in the tin. You can then mark the outline with a pen, and then cut it out using a tin snip. For this part you will want to wear protective gloves— leather is best—as the metal can be sharp.

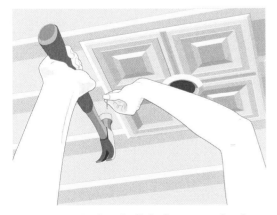

STEP 7 Attach the first tin tile in the center using decorative bead-head nails.

Jane Tip:

FOR STEP 7

If you find any tiles that aren't aligned properly, use a small wood block and a hammer to very gently tap them in place so the seams align.

8 Once you have finished installing the tile, you can choose to create a beautiful edge to your ceiling with either crown molding or decorative tin molding. You can attach this directly to the wall and ceiling; there is no need for furring strips.

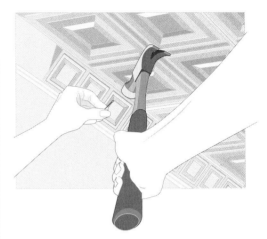

STEP 8 Complete the look of your new ceiling by finishing the edges with tin molding.

9 Depending on the type of tile you purchase, you can choose to paint the tin with a coat of nonyellowing polyurethane to give it a lasting, shiny finish. Be sure to use the type made for metal. As an alternative, you can paint your tiles to match your décor. Before doing so, however, be sure to check with the manufacturer or store where you purchase your tile. Before painting them, clean the tiles with odor-free paint thinner, such as mineral spirits, to remove soil, film, or oil. Don't forget your protective eyewear!

Replace the light fixture and enjoy your gorgeous new ceiling.

A Closing Note (You Made It!)

So you flipped to the end of the book to see what kind of pat on the back or kudos you might get for accomplishing all of the projects in this book, right?

If you have managed to complete or even just start one project in this book, then we are truly proud of you—but more important, you should be proud of yourself. Now that you've seen that you can take the first step, why not try another . . . and then another! If it hasn't already begun, you will be experiencing a level of self-confidence you've never known before.

But even if you haven't started a single project, the fact that you're still with us brings us another opportunity. From our own experience and that of the thousands of others like you, we'd bet that at this point you are:

■ Wondering which room/project you should take on first.

■ Wondering when you will have time to get things started in your home.

■ Hoping you can forget the whole idea—that you could actually change your house into the home you've always dreamed of. You're just hoping you can put this book away in a place you won't find anytime soon.

> "Yay for me! I'm doing it myself!"
>
> Phyllis B.
> Anaheim, California
> Age 37

Regardless of which of the three describes you, you have a chance right here and now to change your life. You can continue to live the life you're living, or you can take a chance and possibly create something amazing. You've been dreaming of that life long enough; it's time to wake up and make those dreams a reality. Take that first step today. Don't wait another minute. Get up from the couch, go to your nearest home improvement center, and buy something for your first project. Then come back home and commit to it.

When we say "commit to it," we know all about those New Year's resolutions, so we don't mean make yourself a promise. It's not that we don't trust you, it's that we know all the reasons you will come up with to convince yourself why you can't get started. So, by *commitment* we mean: Try a sample paint color on your wall; pull off that baseboard molding that's been driving you crazy for years; rip off a piece of that wallpaper that makes you feel like you've been living in your mother's house for the last fifteen years. Take that first step toward starting your first project, because once you make that first hole, tear, or brushstroke, you are that much closer to finishing what you've started.

That first step is the hardest. We know because we've all been there at least once. We've also learned that the second step is easier than the first, and the third is easier than the second. And even if you do hit a rough patch along the way, whatever you do, don't think it's because of your own inabilities that you won't be able to finish it. That's just more of those voices trying to keep you from accomplishing something *you can do.* Remember, if you're having trouble, we're always here to help, and if you can find the courage to ask, you'll find that many other people in your life are by your side as well.

So go ahead and start hammering, sawing, painting, and staining, because with each and every step you'll find a new part of yourself you never knew existed. You might just surprise yourself at how good you are at it and by how much more you like the new you you've found.

That's why we call it Home Empowerment.

P.S. Don't forget to share your stories and projects with us!

Glossary

Adjustable wrench (aka **crescent wrench**). An adjustable wrench that can open and close to fit just about any size nut within its size range. You will want to make sure the one you choose is at least 9 inches long for better leverage.

Allen wrench (aka **key** or **hex wrench**). A wrench for use on fasteners with a hexagonal socket head or depression. Even though it's technically called a wrench, it's closer to a hexagonal screwdriver.

Awl. Resembling a short, stubby ice pick, a sharp pointed tip tool used to start scribe lines or screw holes.

Back saw. A saw that is rectangular in shape with a stiff back and fine teeth, making it one of the more accurate cutting tools. Quite commonly used with a miter box. Typically used to make what's known as "cross-cuts," which are angled cuts.

Backer board. A cement or gypsum-based board commonly used under tile or stone to keep the surface stable and the tile from shifting and cracking.

Bar clamp. A tool with two horizontal, toothed surfaces attached to a bar that when brought together become a clamp.

Box wrench. A tool that has a closed ended, twelve-point socketlike head on either end that surrounds a fastener on all sides, allowing the user to exert the highest torque possible to remove a nut or bolt. Perfect for dealing with rusted or damaged fasteners.

Building codes. Local ordinance standardized building practices created and enforced to guarantee a certain level of safety and quality of construction.

Bullnose tile. A type of tile that is rounded on at least one edge, typically used for trim on a tile job.

C-clamp. A versatile clamp in the shape of a "C," typically made of metal.

Caulk. A compound applied to joints and seams to seal them from potential water and air damage.

Caulking gun. A tool that helps to accurately position caulk neatly and easily into cracks, joints and crevices.

Chalk line. A tool made up of a metal reel that contains a coiled up string and colored chalk that enables the user to "snap" perfectly straight "guide" lines over small to extended areas.

Circuit breaker. A safety switch that "breaks" the flow of electricity to a circuit when there is an overflow or a short. In older homes, fuses that would burn out when an overflow or short would occur were used for this purpose.

Circuit breaker box (aka **service panel**). The panel through which power comes into your home and is divided up and distributed via the circuit breakers. It is where you would turn off all power feeding your home should you need to. The purpose of the Service Panel is to prevent an overload or surge of electricity from entering your home all at once.

Circular saw. A portable, sometimes cordless power saw with a round saw blade, ideal for many straight line cuts and cutting plywood down to manageable sizes. Depending on what type of blade you have mounted, you can cut a variety of materials from wood to metal to masonry.

Combination square. A tool that checks for 45-degree angles with a measuring blade that slides and locks into place to measure much more accurately.

Combination wrench. A wrench with one open end side and one box side.

Compound miter saw. A stationary power saw with a circular blade that allows you to cut at exact angles and overall make more precise cuts. The blade itself can be positioned over the wood to allow the perfect "mitered" (or angled) cut.

Coping. This is the action of cutting a piece of molding along its profile to enable it to butt up against another piece in an "inside corner." You will typically use a coping saw or a rotary tool for this.

Coping saw. A hand saw used to make angled or molded cuts. It has a thin, rigid blade that allows detailed cuts such as curves and circles in thick and thin materials.

Damper. A valve within most ventilation ducts and fireplace flues that can adjust or stop the flow of smoke and/or air.

Drain-waste-vent. The pipes and fittings that carry waste product (both liquid and solid) from a building or a home to a proper waste-management facility such as a sewer or a septic tank. This system also vents out sewer gases through the roof.

Drywall (aka **Sheetrock, wallboard**). A sheeting material usually made up of two pieces of thick paper on either side of pressed gypsum. It is installed after framing and insulation is complete. Drywall is typically what finishes the interior portion of your wall.

Foundation. The base of the structure of any home or building. The foundation is typically made up of rocks, cement, or wood and helps maintain the stability of a structure.

Frame. Sometimes referred to as the "bones" of a home, a "skeleton" that serves as the support structure of any form of dwelling.

Framing square. A ruler marked, L-shaped tool typically used to perfect 90-degree angled cuts.

GFCI (Ground Fault Circuit Interrupter). A type of plug that actually has a circuit built in that will "pop" or switch off should there be a surge of electricity to the appliance or device you have plugged into it. These are now required on plugs next to sinks, showers, bathtubs, or any other water souce. They are extremely valuable in preventing accidental electrocution.

Grit. The size of granules on sandpaper. It is rated on a number system from 40 to 600; the lower the number, the larger and more abrasive the grain. It also can be rated as coarse, medium, fine, and extra-fine.

Ground. An electrical term that relates to the concept of having a way to direct any stray electricity back to the ground/earth through the shortest path possible instead of sending a surge through your wires. Most electrical switches, plugs, and fixtures are made with a ground wire.

Grout. The cement-like substance applied between tiles to finish off the look. It can also be used in a verb form as the actual process of applying the grout to the surface.

Hack saw. A tough and durable hand saw that can be used to cut through certain metals, plastics, and sometimes even glass (with the right blade). The blade is attached by a screw and wing nut on either end to create tension that provides a clean cutting experience.

Hammer drill. A drill that uses a rapid hammer-like action as it drills to penetrate the surface of the material you're working on. This type of drill is ideal for drilling into concrete or masonry or for areas where you just can't create enough force on your own.

Hand tools. Tools that do not require electricity to operate.

Hot wire. The wire in a receptacle that carries the electrical current from the breaker. Usually this wire is sheathed in a black or red plastic casing.

Jane: ("Jane of All Trades"). Any woman willing to take a chance, step outside her comfort zone and accomplish anything she once saw as impossible.

Jane Quotient (JQ). A quick way for you to discern how much experience or skill a project calls for and how much effort is needed. The JQ is a number ranging from 1 to 5. A project with a JQ of 1 is the easiest to accomplish with minimal effort, while a project with a JQ of 5 will definitely be a bit more effort, but still something we know you can do on your own!

Jig saw. A portable saw with a vertical straight blade that allows the user to cut in both straight lines as well as in circles, making almost any shape of cut possible, depending upon the blade you use.

Joist. A horizontal beam in the framing of walls, floors, and ceilings attached on both ends to the wall studs.

Junction box. An enclosed electrical box that enables electrical current to be split to allow for multiple branches of electricity to come off of a single source.

Level (n.). A tool that uses a glass or plastic tube filled with liquid and a single air bubble that can enable its user to determine whether or not surface is level, or flat. A **carpenter's level** is usually between 3 and 4 feet long while a **torpedo level** is usually between 12 and 16 inches long.

Level (adj.). Perfectly horizontal and not leaning one way or another.

Load-bearing wall. A strategically placed wall used to help hold the weight of the floor and/or roof above it.

Locking pliers (aka **vice grips**). Pliers that can be clamped down on the object they are working on.

Layout square (aka **speed square**). A triangular tool that helps you to check for 90-degree angles and beyond. Usually 8 inches or less in size. It also makes an excellent cutting guide when trying to determine irregular angle sizes.

Main water supply shutoff valve. The supply valve that feeds water from the public utility into your home. This allows you to shut off all incoming water supply in case of emergency or to do any extensive plumbing repairs.

MDF (medium-density fiberboard). A product made out of fine wood chips compressed and glued together in such a way that it can take the form of everything from large sheets such as plywood to intricate moldings for crown, baseboard, and chair rail.

Miter box. A U-shaped, open-ended box made of plastic used to make mitered (45-degree) cuts. Usually used in combination with a **back saw.**

Miter joint. A joint that is created by placing two items cut at equivalent angles together.

Needlenose pliers (aka **long-nose pliers**)**.** Pliers that have a long, tapering snout, usually lined with small serrations for a better grip. Ideal for working with wire.

Neutral wire. The wire that carries electrical current from an outlet back to ground. Usually this is the wire sheathed in a white plastic coating.

Palm sander (aka **finishing sander** or **orbital sander**)**.** A portable power sander with a handle that fits in the palm of your hand.

Particleboard. A material made up of glue and wood particles pressed together. While this can serve as a substitute for plywood and is usually less expensive, it may not have the durability your project requires.

Pilot hole. A "starter" hole you create with a drill bit or an **awl** as a drilling or screw guide. Making a pilot hole prior to drilling will often prevent the wood from splitting.

Pipe wrench. An adjustable wrench with one fixed jaw and one moveable jaw used to turn pipes in both easy and hard to reach areas.

Plumb bob. A pendulumlike hand tool that indicates if the surface you are working on is true vertical and not tilted in any way. As a level measures horizontally, a plumb bob measures vertically.

Plumber's putty. A compound often used by plumbers to seal off an area and prevent water leakage. It is often used as a seal under sinks or toilets.

Plumber's tape. A synthetic, nonadhesive tape that is placed on the threads of a pipe before attaching a fixture to ensure that the joint is sealed and won't leak.

Pneumatic tools. Power tools that use compressed air to create force to accomplish a task.

Primer. A substance applied to a surface area prior to a paint application. A primer will usually help seal a new surface and help the paint to adhere to a surface as it creates a "tackiness" that is complementary to the chemical properties of most paints.

Pry bar. A flat crowbarlike tool usually used to "pry" off old wood such as baseboard molding or remove nails. One end is extremely flat, allowing it to double as a wedge.

P-trap. The J-shaped pipe underneath most sinks. Its shape helps to block any toxic sewer gases from coming up through the drain.

Putty knife. A tool consisting of a flat blade used to apply materials, smooth out surfaces, or remove finishes such as paint or wallpaper. Typically, these are available with either flexible or rigid blades. Flexible putty knives are good for applying materials like spackle or putty on flat or slightly round surfaces, while rigid putty knives are ideal for removal of paint or wallpaper.

Receptacle. The individual electrically charged portion of a typical electrical outlet.

Reciprocating saw. A portable power saw that resembles an electric carving knife. It has a small base (or "shoe") and can accept both wide and narrow blades, which allows it to cut surfaces that are flat, curved, vertical, horizontal or even overhead. Usually used more for demolition than for fine detail.

Router. A power tool that uses various "router bits" to cut and shape wood. Routers usually come in three basic forms: fixed base router, plunge router, and a laminate trimmer.

Shim. A thin piece, wedge, or strip of material (wood or otherwise) that is used to fill in an opening or gap between two objects to create a level or plumb surface.

Single pole switch. An electrical switch that turns on and off from only one location.

Slip-joint pliers. Pliers that grab round as well as flat objects and can adjust to many different sizes.

Socket wrench. A wrench that has a depression, or "socket," to place the nut or bolt into, which usually comes as a set with various-size sockets and drive handles. Like a **box wrench,** a socket wrench surrounds the fastener from all sides allowing for more torque.

Spring clamp. A metal clamp that uses the tension of an interior spring to hold something in place. It somewhat resembles a large clothespin.

Staple gun. A powerful, heavy-duty stapler, commonly used in upholstering.

Strike plate. The metal plate attached to a doorjamb where the bolt of a door knob assembly "strikes" prior to closing. Typically it is curved in the direction that the doors opens and closes.

Stud. A general term that refers to a large, very sturdy piece of wood that is part of the vertical "frame" of a wall. Studs typically come in 2 x 4 or 2 x 6 sizes and are spaced at equivalent distances from each other depending on the building code of a given region.

Stud finder. A handheld, battery operated device that indicates where the **studs** are located within your walls.

Subfloor. The layer of flooring, typically plywood, that is attached to the floor joists and on which most flooring is placed.

Three-way switch. A wall switch that can be turned off or on from two different locations.

Tongue-and-groove pliers (aka **groove-joint pliers**). Pliers that can be opened and closed to adapt to many different sizes.

TSP (tri-sodium phosphate). A chemical that when mixed with water can be used to either degrease, clean, or degloss walls before painting.

Utility knife (aka **box cutter**). A hand tool with a retractable and replaceable triangular shaped blade.

Veneer. A thin wood layer placed on top of plywood or particleboard to create the appearance of solid wood.

Volt. The measure of electrical pressure. On power tools, the term "volt" can also indicate the tool's actual power. The higher the voltage, the more powerful the tool.

Voltage tester (aka **electrical tester**). A portable tool used to indicate whether or not there is an electrical charge coming to a given area.

wall anchor (aka **molly bolt** or **toggle bolt**). A metal device used to help attach heavy objects to walls made from wall board, concrete, and masonry. Typically used when a wall stud can not be located.

"Why-to." Before getting started on learning how-to do a project, many of us like to have a better idea on why we should even consider doing the work to begin with. The "why-to" shows you how completing a given project will change your home and how you live in it.

Wire strippers. A plier-like tool that allows you to strip the plastic casing that surrounds most electrical wires.

Wrench. A hand tool with fixed or moveable jaws, used to seize, turn, or twist objects such as nuts and bolts.

Resources

General

BE JANE

The first and largest resource for women's home improvement. Everything you need to answer every home improvement question—how-to's, articles, animated how-to tutorials, Ask Jane, community message boards, and a store to find everything the female do-it-yourselfer needs!
1-877-66-BE-JANE
www.BeJane.com

HUSKY TOOLS
www.HuskyTools.com

MILWAUKEE TOOLS
www.Milwaukeetool.com

RYOBI POWER TOOLS
www.RyobiTools.com

SKIL
www.Skil.com

Electrical Testing Tool Manufacturers

GREENLEE TEXTRON
Manufactures the GT-11 non-contact voltage tester (aka penlight tester), a favorite of ours.
800-435-0786
www.greenlee.textron.com

Home and Safety–Related Organizations

BETTER BUSINESS BUREAU
Check with them first before hiring workers, purchasing products, or scheduling services.
703-276-0100
www.bbb.org

CHIMNEY SAFETY INSTITUTE OF AMERICA
This is a great resource for anything regarding chimney venting and proper usage of your fireplace.
800-536-0118
www.csia.org

CONTRACTORS LICENSE CHECK
We can't emphasize enough the importance of checking to make sure a contractor is actually licensed in your state. (Click on Homeowners, then click on your state's abbreviation. You'll be provided with a phone number for the legal licensing office, which will give the info you need re any licensed contractor. This site enables you to check on the status of a license and in turn offers you more security in choosing the right person.
http://contractors-license.org

ELECTRICAL SAFETY FOUNDATION INT'L
Check out the website below to find out if you are properly protecting yourself when doing electrical work.
703-841-3229
www.electrical-safety.org

NATIONAL ASSOCIATION OF HOME BUILDERS
If you are in the market to build your own home, either by yourself or with the help of a contractor, this resource will help you build the house of your dreams. While they don't offer plans, they do have everything from books to classes to even finding the right builder for your needs.
800-368-5242
www.nahb.org

NATIONAL SAFETY COUNCIL
Most of us aren't aware of the number of injuries that occur in the home every year. This site takes the time to let you know how you can protect yourself and your family from becoming a statistic.
800-621-7619
www.nsc.org

WINDOW COVERING SAFETY COUNCIL
While window coverings can add a beautiful appearance to any window, they can also be a safety hazard for young children. This council teaches you how to keep your window coverings from becoming a hazard to your family.
800-506-4636
www.windowcoverings.org

UNITED STATES CONSUMER PRODUCT SAFETY COMMISSION
This commission is responsible for keeping the public safe from more than 15,000 different types of consumer products. They offer product recalls and safety reviews that run the gamut from children's products to household products, sports and recreation, and specialty items.
800-638-2772
http://www.cpsc.gov/

US DEPARTMENT OF HOUSING AND URBAN DEVELOPMENT (HUD)
This is an arm of the government whose goal is to help people buy homes, support their communities, and gain more access to affordable housing without discrimination.
(202) 708-1112
www.hud.gov

Charitable Home Improvement–Related Organizations

HABITAT FOR HUMANITY
Building homes for underprivileged families all over the world.
(229) 924-6935
www.habitat.org

REBUILDING TOGETHER

Volunteers preserving and revitalizing low-income houses and communities.
1-800-4-REHAB-9
www.rebuildingtogether.org

WOMEN BUILD

Habitat for Humanity International's Women Build department promotes the involvement of women in the construction of Habitat houses.
(229) 924-6935
http://www.habitat.org/wb/default.aspx

Contractor Referral Services

ANGIE'S LIST

http://www.angieslist.com

HANDYMAN NETWORK

www.handymannetwork.com

IMPROVENET

480-346-0000
www.improvenet.com

SERVICE MAGIC

(800) 474-1596
www.servicemagic.com

Personal Resources

SITTER CITY

A parent-babysitter matchmaking site, dedicated to making the search for a babysitter simple, safe, and secure. This is a great resource for when you want to start a project and have no one to watch the kids while you work on your home.
www.SitterCity.com

Home Improvement and Related Retailers

ACE HARDWARE

www.AceHardware.com

THE HOME DEPOT

www.HomeDepot.com

LOWE'S

www.Lowes.com

MENARDS

www.Menards.com

OSH

www.OSH.com

SEARS

www.Sears.com

TRUE VALUE

www.TrueValue.com

Index